LOUISIANA STATE UNIVERSITY STUDIES
Max Goodrich, General Editor

Social Science Series
Walter C. Richardson, Editor

Number Fourteen
Party, Constituency and Congressional Voting

PARTY, CONSTITUENCY
AND
CONGRESSIONAL VOTING

A Study of Legislative Behavior in the
United States House of Representatives

W. Wayne Shannon

Louisiana State University Press

BATON ROUGE

For my mother and father

ACKNOWLEDGMENTS

To Andrew Hacker and Theodore J. Lowi I am
particularly grateful for introducing me
to many of the mysteries of American
legislative behavior that have continued to
fascinate me. To Louisiana State University and
particularly Dean Max Goodrich of the Graduate
School I am grateful for research grants that en-
abled me to complete this study. To Mrs. Crickett
Waldroup of the Louisiana State University Press
I owe a great debt of thanks for rescuing me from
the many infelicities of style that remained after
I had done my own level best to banish them.

CONTENTS

	Acknowledgments	v
	Introduction	ix
I	THE LITERATURE OF CONGRESSIONAL VOTING	3
II	STRANDS OF CONTINUITY	37
III	PARTY DIFFERENCES IN THE EIGHTY-SIXTH AND EIGHTY-SEVENTH CONGRESSES	62
IV	ANALYZING PARTY DIFFERENCES ON MAJOR POLICY ISSUES	81
V	THE SOUTHERN DEMOCRATS AND THE CONSERVATIVE COALITION	95
VI	CONSTITUENCY CHARACTERISTICS AND ELECTION	115
VII	CONSTITUENCY CHARACTERISTICS AND INTRAPARTY VOTING DIFFERENCES	132
VIII	ELECTORAL MARGINS AND VOTING BEHAVIOR	157
IX	CONCLUSIONS	171
	Appendix	185
	Bibliography	195
	Index	199

INTRODUCTION

DESPITE A PRODIGIOUS amount of literature devoted to the study of Congress, the institution remains, in David Truman's apt phrase, a "well-known stranger."[1] There is profound irony in this simple statement of fact in an age when American political scientists have increasingly turned away from the study of supposedly familiar "formal institutions" of government in quest of grand generalizations about "the political system" in the abstract.

The present study treats but a small portion of the professional literature on Congress—that dealing with party, constituency and voting behavior. Since this literature dates back more than half a century, one might assume that the major questions which intrigued its authors would long ago have been answered. The evidence, however, suggests otherwise. As Chapters I and II of this study demonstrate, the literature of congressional voting, taken as a whole, falls far short of providing contemporary students of Congress with an adequate understanding of party and constituency as factors influencing the congressman's behavior.

One major difficulty with the literature of party, constituency, and congressional voting stems directly from its largely ahistorical nature. Various students have conceptualized research problems as if they involved "time-proof" phenomena, yet even cursory scrutiny will reveal that these phenomena vary greatly from period to period. Consequently, carefully derived generalizations—accurately descriptive of Congress in one period, no doubt—have often proved extremely vulnerable to the passage of time. Precisely because congressional phenomena will not

[1]David B. Truman, *The Congressional Party* (New York: John Wiley and Sons, 1959), v–vi.

hold still, it appears doubtful that descriptive and causal generalizations which will remain authoritative can be formulated. At the very least, it must be said that the historical dimensions of congressional voting behavior deserve much more attention than they have received from most American political scientists to date.

It is the purpose of this study to describe the behavior of the congressional parties in the House of Representatives and to investigate the relationship of several constituency factors to party voting during two recent Congresses. The Eighty-sixth (1959–60) and Eighty-seventh (1961–62) Congresses were selected for analysis for a number of reasons. First, it seemed interesting to include one Congress—the Eighty-sixth—whose governing majority faced a President of the opposite party and one—the Eighty-seventh—whose majority party controlled the Presidency. Second, these Congresses are recent enough to be reasonably familiar in most readers' minds. Third, both of these Congresses manifested a great deal of party disloyalty and "conservative coalition voting" on the part of southern Democrats. Given the latter situation, there seemed a particularly great need for a revision of the classic account of southern Democratic congressional behavior by the late V. O. Key, Jr., in *Southern Politics*.[2]

I have relied almost entirely on analysis of House roll calls for insight into congressional behavior. Such an approach, despite a number of shortcomings,[3] seemed the most appropriate available means of studying party and constituency influence in Congress. Through analysis of record votes the behavior of the parties on matters of public importance could be described, and the constituency factors associated with the congressmen's behavior could best be isolated.

It should be understood at the outset that no claim is made here that roll call analysis provides *all* the information necessary to understand legislative behavior in Congress. As everyone who has used the approach realizes, it leaves many important aspects of the legislative process wholly unexamined. The crucially important work of legislative committees, for example, is seldom apparent in record votes. Decisions made by formal party leaders and by members on the floor in non-record votes are left unstudied. The actions of the President and his associates in the executive branch are generally ignored. Numerous additional objections might be raised. The answer to such caveats must be that while ideally it would be desirable to study all of these phenomena, a serious attempt to under-

---

[2] V. O. Key, Jr., *Southern Politics* (New York; Vintage Books, n.d.), 369–82.

[3] See especially Wilder Crane, "A Caveat on Roll-Call Studies of Party Voting," *Midwest Journal of Political Science*, IV (August, 1960), 237–49.

take such an analysis of two Congresses would quickly exhaust the most ambitious of students. It is literally impossible to capture the full reality of a single congressional session. Given this situation, an analytical scheme was chosen which suited one particular set of theoretical needs. Like any other, it has shortcomings. Fortunately, however, it also has a number of virtues—for example, it enables the researcher to highlight similarities and differences between the parties in a systematic manner and relate constituency factors to patterns of party behavior. The exclusive focus on the House of Representatives in this study is likewise dictated by a practical consideration—the desire to facilitate analysis of constituency factors and party behavior. Only in the House, where constituencies are relatively small, can these factors be identified with sufficient precision to permit analysis of their possible influence.

If a new study of party and constituency is to avoid perpetuating the already existing state of confusion, it must benefit from a thorough search through the maze of existing work in quest of continuity in theory, methods, and findings. It is the purpose of the first two chapters to undertake such a search. In Chapter I four major studies are examined. In Chapter II an attempt is made to formulate generalizations from these studies (and from other relevant studies) in order to lay down appropriate theoretical guidelines for the treatment of the Eighty-sixth and Eighty-seventh Congresses that follows.

In surveying the existing studies of congressional voting, it is impossible to escape the conclusion that the intellectual individualism of past researchers in this area is at least as responsible for the confusion and ambiguity that characterize this segment of our professional literature as is the complexity of the subject matter itself. New research has been piled haphazardly upon old, and thus, while factual "findings" abound, their relation to one another remains unclear. All too often, a desire for a "direct approach" or an inclination "to get on with the business of research" has been responsible for the collection of facts which have later proved extremely resistant to interpretation. A careful review of this literature, however, reveals a strand of continuity in attempts by several observers to describe the voting behavior of the congressional parties.

Chapters III through V extend this tradition of inquiry through description of the parties' behavior in the Eighty-sixth and Eighty-seventh Congresses. A second thread of continuity is apparent in the efforts of several writers to relate constituency factors to party and voting behavior. Chapters VI through VIII treat several hypotheses concerning the relation of these factors to party loyalty and opposition in the Eighty-sixth and Eighty-seventh Congresses. Finally, in Chapter IX, conclusions are drawn and certain suggestions are made on strategies of inquiry that future research on party, constituency and congressional voting might most profitably follow.

A final introductory remark should be made at this point on the matter of methodology. As perceptive readers will quickly see, the development or use of new "research tools" or strategies of inquiry is not a primary concern of this study. Clearly, the methods employed here are quite conservative in the context of present developments in American political science. This aspect of the study should be understood in light of two quite different factors. The first is my concern that the study should be readily comprehensible to a wide range of readers with some interest in congressional behavior—not simply to those on the methodological "cutting edge" of American political science. Such a concern is quite straightforward and would seem to require little justification.

The second factor is much less a matter of choice than one of necessity. In several instances, both in terms of data and methods, less desirable alternatives have been chosen over better ones on grounds of necessity. For example, aggregative data have been employed in investigating constituency influences, while survey data on constituents' attitudes could have done the job more nicely. The latter data were simply not at hand and could not be collected without huge expenditures of time and funds, neither of which was available. Similarly, the revolution that has taken place since the inception of this study in computer software, i.e., programs, for social scientists would have greatly facilitated the analysis of the available data had its recent developments been available at that time. Such tasks as the scaling of roll call votes and relating voting behavior to constituency characteristics could have been executed not only more easily but more adequately with computer programs for scaling and multiple regression analysis that are now rather commonly available.[4] This second aspect of the study's methodological simplicity is an unfortunate product of necessity. Whether or not the absence of more complex and sophisticated methods greatly influences the results of the following analysis is a question that will have to be answered by each individual reader in light of his own tastes, knowledge, and experience.

---

[4] I have in mind especially the remarkable set of standard programs developed for the use of the Institute for Social Research at the University of Michigan. These programs, which have been widely used by political scientists under the auspices of the Inter-University Consortium for Political Research, are an excellent example of the benefits of the revolution referred to above.

Party, Constituency and Congressional Voting

Chapter I

THE LITERATURE OF
CONGRESSIONAL VOTING

ANY NEW STUDY of party, constituency, and congressional voting must ask what has been learned from existing studies in this area. What is known about the relation of party and constituency to voting behavior? Do the congressional parties differ significantly? How often? On what kinds of issues? Can constituency factors help to explain deviation from party voting? If so, which factors seem to be the most important ones? Is it possible to formulate generalizations on these matters that will transcend particular historical periods? Certainly, these are questions to which the abundant literature of congressional voting should provide answers.

At least four major works and a host of minor ones have been undertaken in this area since the turn of the century. The pioneering effort to investigate the influence of party on legislative voting must be credited to A. Lawrence Lowell, whose now-classic monograph *The Influence of Party Upon Legislation in England and America* was published in 1901. In an empirical spirit rare among American political scientists of his time, Lowell examined patterns of voting in the British House of Commons, the U.S. Congress, and several state legislatures during a number of sessions to determine the extent to which voting in these legislative bodies followed party lines. Arbitrarily establishing a category of "party votes" (those on which 90 percent or more of the members of one party opposed 90 percent or more of the members of the other), Lowell examined roll call votes in the selected sessions to see what proportion of the total would meet this rigorous test. His findings are now well known among American political scientists. In the case of Congress Lowell concluded:

The amount of party voting varies very much from one Congress, and even from one session, to another, and does not follow closely any fixed law of evolution. . . . Whereas during the middle of the century the amount of party voting . . . was at least as great in Congress as in Parliament . . . on the average party lines at the present day are decidedly less strictly drawn than in the House of Commons. . . . In Congress the amount of party voting depends largely upon the accident of some question on which the parties are sharply divided happening to come up for decision.[1]

The record of "party voting" for the five Congresses examined is summarized in Table 1. Although the average for the House and Senate in these sessions in nearly 30 percent, this figure obscures a very wide range of party behavior. Lowell concluded that the amount of party voting in

TABLE 1

"PARTY VOTING" IN FIVE CONGRESSES
EXAMINED BY LOWELL, 1845–1901†

| | | Percent "Party Votes" | |
Year	President	House	Senate
1845–47	Polk	10.7	16.0
1863–65	Lincoln	30.2	5.8
1887–89	Cleveland	13.6	46.9
1897–99	McKinley	50.9	39.6
1899–1901	McKinley	49.3	34.3
Average "Party Vote" per Session		30.9	28.5

†The material presented here has been compiled from data included in A. Lawrence Lowell, The Influence of Party Upon Legislation in England and America in Annual Report of the American Historical Association for 1901. (2 vols.; Washington, 1902), I, 538–44. Unanimous roll calls and those on which more than 90 percent of both parties voted alike are excluded. Inclusion of the latter roll calls would slightly lower each percentage above.

Congress fluctuated considerably from session to session during these years, and that the reasons for such striking variations were not readily apparent. In the case of the House of Commons he saw a distinct trend toward party unity from the middle of the century to the 1890's. This he attributed without further explanation to the influence of the Second

1A. Lawrence Lowell, The Influence of Party Upon Legislation in England and America," in Annual Report of the American Historical Association for 1901 (2 vols.; Washington, 1902), I, 336–37.

and Third Reform Acts, but he was able to make no such generalization about party voting in the United States. He was satisfied to note simply that "the influence of party upon legislation is on the whole much greater in England than in the United States." Interestingly enough, Lowell chose not to draw inferences from the study with regard to the consequences of these differences in party behavior for the political process in the two countries. In fact, his remarks at the end of the study have a curiously contemporary ring. "It is no part of the object of this paper," he wrote, "to describe . . . [the consequences of party unity or lack thereof] still less to attempt to weigh them in the balance or suggest remedies for them. The first effort of the student of government today must be to discover the facts, in the faith that any light thrown upon political conditions cannot fail to help toward a wise solution of the problems they involve." [2]

In light of its pioneering nature, and the fact that its empirical and quantitative approach was at the time almost unique, Lowell's monograph must be regarded as a major landmark in the study of party and legislative voting. When viewed from a contemporary perspective, however, it clearly raises many more questions than it answers. First, Lowell chose not to subject to further analysis the great majority of roll calls which failed to evidence party votes. Most subsequent observers of the legislative process would undoubtedly agree that Lowell's 90 percent versus 90 percent criterion is too difficult for American parties to meet; a great deal more might have been learned had other standards been employed. Second, Lowell completely ignored the obvious question stemming from his observation that the amount of party voting "depends largely upon the accident of some question on which the parties are sharply divided happening to come up for decision." On what kinds of issues, then, did the parties differ? On what kinds of questions was cohesive party opposition most common? Least common? Finally, Lowell considered the congressional parties only as aggregates and did not attempt to identify the causes of deviation from party voting in the case of individuals or groups of congressmen; he made no attempt, for example, to introduce constituency factors to see if they might account for such deviations. Thus, while he was able to establish with rigorous quantitative methods the truth of what contemporaries such as Woodrow Wilson observed about the contrast of party behavior in Parliament and in Congress, he left many of the most important questions that he raised unanswered.

It seems clear, however, that Lowell, who was one of the most sophis-

2*Ibid.*, 333, 350.

ticated students of party in his time, regarded constituency as a major causal factor which might explain deviation from party voting in the case of American legislators. At least he hinted at this in *The Government of England* where he wrote: ". . . in the American state legislatures [where] party lines are not often strictly drawn, a member will vote according to his own opinions or those *of his constituents* [italics mine], with little regard to the effect his vote may have upon the prospects of the party in other places." [3] The point to be made here is that Lowell did not attempt to introduce controls for such constituency factors in *The Influence of Party Upon Legislation*. His accomplishment was to demonstrate only that the congressional parties were seldom cohesively opposed to one another. Having shown that, he offered merely the general explanatory remark that "thorough party government" is probably impossible to obtain in the United States. The institutions of England, he thought, were conducive to party government, while those of the United States were obstacles in the way of its development.[4]

It is curious in retrospect that after Lowell so impressively demonstrated the potential of quantitative methods in the study of party in the legislative process no major study of congressional voting was undertaken for another fifty years. In the 1920's Stuart A. Rice did develop several simple statistical devices to describe quantitatively the behavior of groups in legislative bodies. Unfortunately, however, no major use was made of these techniques in the study of Congress until much later.[5] Rice applied these concepts to a session of the New York assembly in 1921 and found that the cohesion of the party groups at that time was rather high, but his findings are of little use for the purposes of this study.[6] Rice also applied these devices to the United States Senate, but sought only to demonstrate their potential use—not to carry out a substantive study.

Twenty-three years after Rice suggested the promise of quantitative methods in the study of legislative behavior, Julius Turner published his book-length monograph *Party and Constituency: Pressures on Congress*, the most thorough study of congressional voting since Lowell's *The In-*

[3]Lowell, *The Government of England* (2 vols.; New York: Macmillan, 1908), II, 532, quoted in Austin Ranney, *The Doctrine of Responsible Party Government* (Urbana: University of Illinois Press, 1962), 60.

[4]Lowell, *The Influence of Party Upon Legislation*, 343–44. With regard to the United States, Lowell considered the "separation of powers" system especially important. The U.S. Constitution, he thought, was conceived in an anti-party spirit.

[5]See Stuart A. Rice, *Quantitative Methods in Politics* (New York: Alfred A. Knopf, 1928), 207–28 *passim*.

[6]*Ibid.*, 213.

fluence of Party Upon Legislation.[7] Turner's study appeared at the height
of the revived interest in the question of "party responsibility" that per-
vaded the American political science profession after World War II. It
immediately attracted a great deal of attention and has since been regarded as a major source of support for those who have attempted to
demonstrate that American legislative parties are "responsible" (or, at
least, more "responsible" than their critics suggest).[8] In Turner's words,
his study is an attempt to measure as accurately as possible "the relative
effectiveness of pressures on Congress from certain sources, and to find
the objectives toward which these pressures are directed."[9] The "sources
of pressure" with which the study is specifically concerned are party and
constituency. His intention was to test traditional assumptions about
these factors by subjecting them to systematic quantitative analysis,
whereby their association with roll call votes might be measured. There
is no need to speculate blindly about these factors, he argued, since "material is available through which we can compare the congressman's record with our knowledge of his party and constituency, and record in
numbers and percentages the degree to which attributes of party or constituency correspond with the congressman's behavior."[10]

Party and Constituency, by virtue of its ambitious scope and the unusually great attention its conclusions have attracted, ranks high in importance among studies of voting behavior in Congress. Even today it remains perhaps the most serious attempt to deal with both party and
constituency as influences on congressional voting. In terms of methods
and findings, it deserves careful analysis.

Before turning to the major features of *Party and Constituency* a

[7]Julius Turner, *Party and Constituency: Pressures of Congress* (Baltimore: Johns
Hopkins Press, 1951).

[8]For a full explanation on this term one must turn to the writings of several critics
of the American party system. The literature of American party criticism (and apol-
ogetics) is voluminous. For classics of criticism in the "more responsible parties" tradition, see E. E. Schattschneider, *Party Government* (New York: Farrar and Rinehart,
1942); James MacGregor Burns, *Congress on Trial* (New York: Harper, 1949); *The
Deadlock of Democracy* (Englewood Cliffs, N.J., Prentice-Hall, 1963), and the Report
of the Committee on Political Parties of The American Political Science Association,
published as *Toward a More Responsible Two-Party System,* a supplement to the
American Political Science Review, XLIV (September, 1950). For the anti-reform
position, see Clinton Rossiter, *Parties and Politics in America* (Ithaca, N.Y., Cornell
University Press, 1960), Ernest S. Griffith, *Congress: Its Contemporary Role* (New
York: New York University Press, 1951), and Herbert Agar, *The Price of Union* (Boston: Houghton Mifflin, 1950). On this controversy generally, see Ranney, *The Doctrine of Responsible Party Government.*

[9]Turner, *Party and Constituency,* 11.

[10]*Ibid.,* 13.

word must be said about the concept of "pressure," for it raises some potentially serious problems. Party and constituency are here conceptualized simply as forms of "political pressure." Without explanation or qualification, the use of pressure in this context is likely to strike many readers as overly mechanistic. It seems to suggest that the congressman is inert and is simply moved in one direction or another by the strength of the forces that play on him. Such an assumption will appear to most contemporary observers of the legislative process to entail a vast oversimplification of the congressman's actual role. Unfortunately, Turner devoted little time in his preliminary remarks to an explanation of the "forces," party and constituency, which are, after all, rather complex. More important, perhaps, he failed to consider even briefly the problem of *how* these forces affect the congressman. Do such words as "pressure" and "force" imply that the congressman has direct contact with party leaders and constituents? Must constituents and party leaders actually make demands on the congressman? Turner did little to clarify such questions; he proceeded to carry out his study without attempting to specify the exact meaning of such terms as "force," "party," and "constituency." A clue is provided in the statement that the forces "may be applied through conventional types of coercion or through the appeal of loyalties or ideologies." [11] It may be assumed that Turner intended the party and constituency variables to cover a variety of phenomena, both interpersonal and psychological. The party variable, in other words, encompasses such diverse forces as a personal appeal by the speaker or whip, a strictly internal feeling of loyalty to the party as a group, or agreement with the ideological position of one's party colleagues. Constituency, likewise, may be understood to include such forces as actual demands from constituents, a vague sense of loyalty to the "folks back home," or a conscious calculation on the congressman's part that he must vote in a certain manner to protect himself from an enterprising opponent who might use his legislative record against him. "Pressure," conceived in this manner, must of necessity be broadly and loosely defined, and it is important to understand that the methodology of quantitative roll call analysis does not permit investigation of the specific means or processes by which it is brought to bear (if it actually is) on the congressman. In fact, one may be entitled to wonder if "pressure" is the right concept at all.

   Given these qualifications, Turner's general approach should raise no serious objections. He attempted to examine patterns of congressional voting in relation to two broad, hypothesized causal variables, party and

11*Ibid.*, 11.

constituency. Party is defined for purposes of the investigation by the congressman's formal affiliation, and constituency characteristics are indicated by such objective factors as metropolitanism-ruralism, foreign-native origin of the population, and geographical section.[12] The assumptions of Turner's methodology in general are those which usually apply where an attempt is made in the social sciences to employ statistical techniques to investigate the relationship between social or political phenomena and supposed causal factors. Turner stated these assumptions as follows:

If two large groups of individual units are selected, and if these units have all important attributes in common except one, and that factor is common to all members of one group and no members of the other, and if the two groups differ in behavior, we conclude that the one factor not in common to both groups is responsible, or closely related to the factor responsible, for the difference in behavior of the two groups. . . . The sample must be large enough so that we may be reasonably sure that the result is not the reflection of mere chance. A careful effort must be made to remove, or make allowance for, factors common to one group and not to the other in addition to the one factor believed to cause the observed difference in behavior. . . . The statistician must usually depend on the large size of his sample and the laws of probability to overcome the effect of uncontrolled variables.[13]

Enough has been said for the moment of Turner's methods. However, it will become apparent that his substantive findings are in some cases affected by the methods employed. It will therefore be necessary to continue to emphasize methodological matters as this discussion proceeds.

Unquestionably, the portion of Turner's work most familiar to students of the congressional parties today is Chapter II, which is addressed to Lowell's question—what is the influence of party upon legislation?

---

[12]At this point the specialist may wonder how Turner classified congressional districts according to the foreign-native factor. Of course, the information was taken from the U.S. Census, but one may question how the classifications were made where congressional districts cut across county lines. Prior to the publication of the *Congressional District Data Book, Districts of the 88th Congress* (Washington, D.C., Government Printing Office, 1963), census data of the type employed were available only for counties and lesser units—not for congressional districts. Though Turner devotes no space to this problem, it may be that his classification scheme is questionable. The only reliable way to classify congressional districts that cut across county lines (most in large cities do) would be to piece together information from census tracts. Turner admits that he has not done so. He explains only that where information was not available, he "estimated" it. In some cases he omitted districts from the analysis. It is not possible to judge from his description how he overcame this difficulty. See Turner, *Party and Constituency*, 102.

[13]*Ibid.*, 13.

Here we find Turner's central conclusion that a party is a "significant determinant" of most congressional legislation. Unfortunately, many who have used this finding have failed to make clear just how it was arrived at and thus exactly what it means. It is highly dubious that the data presented in the chapter in question support the argument that the parties are "more responsible" than their critics charge. In fact, upon close analysis, it is difficult to avoid the conclusion that Turner himself drew unwarranted inferences from his data when he brought them to bear on the highly emotional "party responsibility" controversy. At the very least, the matter reveals some not entirely obvious difficulties of conducting "value-neutral," empirical research. Since one of Turner's major purposes in *Party and Constituency* was to cast light on the controversy between the would-be reformers of American parties and their intellectual opponents, the possibility arises that his negative position on the matter of party reform conditioned his findings.[14] As Chapter II is examined, it will be useful to keep this possibility in mind.

Following Lowell, Turner first demonstrated that if the accepted standard of party performance in the legislature is to be the party vote, evidence taken from selected sessions of the British House of Commons and the U.S. House in the twentieth century reveals comparatively little party influence in Congress. The results of this analysis may be seen in Table 2. As the table clearly reveals, the level of party voting in Commons for the sessions in question was consistent and high, averaging 94.9 percent for the four sessions. Party voting in the U.S. House, on the other hand, was neither consistent nor frequent. The smallest number of party votes, 7.1 percent, were taken in the 1928 session; the largest, 31 percent, in the 1930–31 session. The average for the ten sessions amounted to less than one-fifth of all the roll calls taken. It is interesting to note, in fact, that the average amount of party voting in the House was considerably lower in these twentieth century sessions than in the nineteenth century sessions studied by Lowell.[15] It is apparent from the table that Lowell's generalization that party voting fluctuates rather wildly from session to session in Congress applies as well to these sessions as to the nineteenth century sessions examined above.

By comparison with French parties under the Third Republic, Ameri-

14Turner discussed the controversy over party reform at the beginning of Chapter II, citing what he considered an unwarranted assumption of both party critics and apologists—that "under the present system the parties do not unite behind distinctly differentiated programs." *Ibid.*, 22. See also his article "Responsible Parties: A Dissent from the Floor," *American Political Science Review*, XLV (March, 1951), *passim.*

15See above, p. 4.

can congressional parties appear in an equally unfavorable light. Turner employed Rice's index of cohesion to demonstrate that "American parties were less cohesive than those stable and organized French parties which were directly represented in the Chamber, but more cohesive than

TABLE 2

COMPARATIVE "PARTY VOTING": PARTY VOTES
CAST IN BRITAIN AND THE U.S.,
SELECTED SESSIONS†

	Britain, Commons		United States, House
Year	Percent "Party Votes"	Year	Percent "Party Votes"
1924–25	94.4	1921	28.6
		1928	7.1
1926	94.8	1930–31	31.0
		1933	22.5
1927	96.4	1937	11.8
		1944	10.7
1928	93.6	1945	17.5
		1946	10.5
		1947	15.1
		1948	16.4
Average	94.8	Average	17.1

†Source: Julius Turner, *Party and Constituency: Pressures on Congress* (Baltimore: Johns Hopkins Press, 1951), p. 24.

some of the *groupes* formed after the election for parliamentary purposes." [16] While the average index of cohesion of the French Communists, Socialists, and Radical Socialists, for example, was found to exceed 90 in 1930, the average cohesion for the Democrats and Republicans, respectively, in the U.S. House during six sessions from 1921 to 1944 was 62.2 and 67.9. [17]

If party voting and cohesion are the standards by which the American congressional parties are to be judged, then, they compare rather un-

[16]Turner, *Party and Constituency*, 26–27. The "index of cohesion" is a simple device developed by Stuart A. Rice to measure party unity on roll call votes. It is calculated by dividing the votes cast by the majority of the party by the total of party members voting, multiplying by 100 to derive the percentage of the total in the majority, and converting the resulting percentage from a 50–100 scale to a 0–100 scale by subtracting 50 from the percentage figure and multiplying the result by two. Calculation of the index is explained by Turner on page 26.

[17]*Ibid.*, 27. The above calculations are based on a table presented by Turner.

favorably with British parliamentary parties and major French parliamentary parties under the Third Republic during the sessions for which
data are available. Does this necessarily mean that party is not a significant factor in legislative voting in the American Congress? No, Turner
emphatically answered; such a conclusion is unwarranted. The use of
proper methods will reveal that party *is* a significant factor. The argument is best put in his own words: "Quantitative analysis of roll call
votes shows, contrary to majority opinion, that significant differences
exist between our major parties. While it is true that American discipline falls short of that achieved in some European democracies, and is
less effective than party discipline in the McKinley era in the United
States, evidence of great party influence can still be found. Party pressure seems to be more effective than any other pressure on congressional
voting, and is discernible on nearly nine-tenths of the roll calls examined." [18]

On what basis did Turner arrive at this conclusion? What is meant by
"significant differences"? To beg such questions is not to quibble over
unimportant technicalities; it will be seen that Turner's method is criti-
cally important to his argument at this step of the analysis. Consequently,
his methodological assumptions deserve the most careful scrutiny. It is
best to allow him to speak for himself again as he explains how it is
possible to decide whether party is a significant determinant of Legislative voting.

A usual method employed by statisticians to determine whether the behavior of
two groups is significantly dissimilar is to determine the probability that the
observed behavior could occur if the two groups had been selected by chance.
If, from a glass bowl containing the names and votes on a roll call of 250 congressmen, we should select at random 125 men and call them Democrats, and
125 whom we would call Republicans, what chance would there be that the
voting behavior of these synthetic parties would differ to the extent found in
the actual roll call vote? The chances that they would disagree in proportions
as great as 5 to 120 and 120 to 5 are extremely slim. The chances are much
greater that the proportions of "yea" votes in the two synthetic parties would
be similar. A customary statistical level for separating significant group behavior
from the doubtful or insignificant is one chance in one hundred; that is, those
roll calls may be judged significant in terms of party on which the chances were
less than one in a hundred that the parties would differ to that extent if their
membership was selected by chance. The method used to determine the probability that the observed division would occur is the chi-square test.[19]

[18]*Ibid.,* 23.
[19]*Ibid.,* 30.

The question here, then, is whether "significant differences exist between our major parties." [20] It should be noted that the crucial word "significant" is employed here in its special statistical sense.[21] An unarticulated assumption, of course, is that statistical significance, i.e., deviation from randomness to a certain degree, is an appropriate measure of party performance. This is in fact, however, a highly dubious assumption.

Turner's conclusions are really quite simple—but also quite deceptive if close attention is not given to the steps by means of which they are reached. If one relies, he demonstrates, on Lowell's party vote test or on Rice's index of cohesion for standards of party performance in the legislature, the American parties compare rather poorly with the British and French parties. However, it should not be concluded that there is *no* relationship between party and legislative voting in Congress. If another test is employed, the argument runs, it may be shown that there is a relationship between party and voting in Congress on almost 90 percent of the roll calls taken during the sessions studied. In other words, Turner proposes, though he does not actually put the matter in these terms, the substitution of a test of statistical significance (the chi-square in this case) for such other possible measurements as the party vote and the index of cohesion. In this way, he argues, a relationship between party and legislative voting that is obscured by the use of these other standards becomes apparent.

It is doubtful, however, that statistical significance is an appropriate standard for measuring party performance in the legislature. Whenever Turner employs this standard to maintain that there are significant differences between the parties on a particular roll call, his statement must be understood as meaning: *On this particular roll call there is not more than one chance in one hundred that the observed voting behavior of the parties could have occurred, if their membership had been selected by chance.*[22] Strictly speaking, the chi-square test indicates no more than this; it is only a test of statistical significance, which may be used in this context to measure the difference between observed behavior of the parties and what would be the expected behavior if members were selected by chance from a list of all congressmen.

If all of this is properly understood (and it seems unlikely that those

20*Ibid.*, 23.

21For a discussion of statistical significance, see any elementary statistics text. The concept is discussed in simple language in Claire Selltiz, Marie Jahoda, Morton Deutsch, and Stuart W. Cook, *Research Methods in Social Relations* (New York: Henry Holt, 1959), 415–16.

22Italics mine.

who have made so much of Turner's conclusions have understood his
methodology) , it is not very startling that Turner says "party was a significant factor" on almost 90 percent of the roll calls he studied. After
all, hardly anyone would expect legislative parties to perform in a completely random manner. It is not surprising, therefore, that they do not.
It may, in fact, depending on one's standards of judgment, be neither
important nor meaningful to say that they do not, if this is all one says.
Here, an important point must be raised that is not always recognized.
What various commentators have meant by "significant" influence of party in the legislative process is largely a matter of normative judgment.
Lowell, of course, was implicitly saying that party unity must be very
high for party behavior to be considered significant. The "party responsibility" critics have argued that legislative parties should at least be unified enough to enact a coherent party program and facilitate public understanding of the political process. Party, in other words, must perform
in such a manner to be a significant factor in the eyes of these observers.
It is unlikely that the "majority opinion" which Turner cited—that no
significant differences exist between our parties—was in 1950 (or at any
time, for that matter) based on a statistical deviation-from-randomness
concept of the type that underlies Turner's conclusion that party is a
highly significant factor in congressional voting. For this reason it should
be clear to the careful observer of the dispute over party responsibility
that Turner's methodological assumptions need not necessarily be accepted by the responsibility school.

Thus Turner did not, as he seems to think he did, prove the party
responsibility critics wrong with *Party and Constituency.* It may be argued that he merely selected a test that American parties could easily
pass, so to speak, whereas Lowell had chosen one they could seldom
pass.[23] Turner's conclusions are not invalid, then, as long as the reader
understands that they are based on the concept of statistical significance.
Unfortunately for his ideological case, however, few observers of the
legislative process have had statistical significance in mind in discussing
the merits of party performance in Congress. Even the loosest and most
heterogeneous of our major parties, historically speaking, would hardly
be expected to perform as if its legislative representatives had been picked

---

[23]It may be objected that the chi-square does not ordinarily constitute a test (in
the sense of norm or standard) . But in fact it does as Turner employs it. He is in
effect saying, if party is statistically associated with legislative voting, then the parties are significantly different. The seemingly value-free statistical test becomes, in a
rather subtle manner, a normative device.

at random. Not even the most ardent of the "responsibility" critics would argue that the post-1932 Democrats and Republicans have voted in Congress as if at random. This portion of Turner's work—unfortunately the portion which has attracted the most attention—is thus open to very damaging criticisms.

Turner employed two additional standards by which the parties might be judged. The most cursory examination will reveal that these, like the statistical significance test, are ones that even the least cohesive legislative parties may be expected to satisfy with little difficulty. First, he argued, very few congressmen vote more often with the other party than with their own when majorities of the two parties oppose one another. Of 4,658 major party members in the House during the sessions studied, only 181 or 4 percent voted more often with the opposition.[24] Again, the conclusion appears less than startling. Few would expect that many American representatives—even those disposed to disagreement with major segments of their party's policy positions—would vote with the opposition more often than with their own party. Second, the "party vote" test shows that the parties cast party votes more often than any "synthetic" group which might be assembled on the basis of regional or constituency factors. For example, Turner writes: ". . . 90 per cent of the Republicans have opposed 90 per cent of the Democrats on a much larger proportion of issues than the proportion of issues on which 90 per cent of the congressmen representing any other measured dichotomy in American politics have disagreed. Groups based on metropolitan-rural or foreign-native division, in fact, were never in the four sessions 90 per cent united in opposition to each other. The only synthetic groups which cast *party votes* were the North and the South." [25] Again, the test seems to be a reasonably easy one for the parties to pass. It would be surprising indeed to find that sectional groups or congressmen from similar constituencies were aligned against one another to the extent that they cast more party votes than the parties themselves.

In concluding the analysis of Chapter II of Turner's *Party and Constituency* it is difficult to avoid the judgment that his standards for the measurement of party influence on legislative voting are so undemanding that their use predetermined the conclusion that party is a highly significant factor in the legislative process. Even such an "objective and sensitive test" as the chi-square, as used by Turner, takes on a normative

[24]Turner, *Party and Constituency*, 31.
[25]*Ibid.*, 33.

connotation which sets a low level of expectation for party performance and necessitates the conclusion that the influence of party is pervasive.[26] Thus the crucial importance of methodology is apparent. Once the premises implicit in the method are accepted, Turner's conclusions about the congressional parties are bound to follow.

An additional difficulty is posed by Turner's tendency to overgeneralize from his findings—to claim to have demonstrated the validity of propositions that are in fact beyond his ability to support or invalidate with the data at hand. This tendency is perfectly illustrated by the following quotation from the beginning of Chapter III of *Party and Constituency:* "The preceding chapter has shown that party pressure in the modern American Congress, while less effective than in other countries, was nevertheless important on most roll calls, and was more effective than the pressure of other American groups. *Party discipline in Congress, in other words, was sufficiently strong so that voters could distinguish between the behavior of the two parties.*" [27] As this discussion has shown, Turner's argument in Chapter II rests mainly on the use of the chi-square test and demonstrates only that there is some association, statistically speaking, between party and voting on nearly 90 percent of the roll calls examined. From this evidence Turner proceeded to generalize "empirically" that "party discipline . . . *was sufficiently strong so that voters could distinguish between the behavior of the two parties.*" [28] Anyone who has followed closely the argument in his second chapter must conclude that there is no factual basis whatever for such a generalization. Not only is it extremely dubious that all or most votes on which party is a statistically significant factor may be understood in terms of party by the electorate, but also there is simply no evidence in Turner's study to warrant such a conclusion. To answer this kind of question, it would be necessary to resort to another type of study—one that could effectively probe the perceptions of voters. However much Turner may have wished to demonstrate that congressional voting behavior permits the electorate to understand the legislative process in terms of party, he clearly had no right

[26]Nowhere does Turner seem to recognize that the chi-square test, as used here, is more than an objective device. As a test of statistical relationship, it is objective. That probability should be the test of party performance, however, is a statement of Turner's values. He makes a subtle leap from "is" to "ought" without seeming to recognize it. In other words, what a legislative party "should" be like is a normative question which requires a statement of values on the part of an observer as well as an empirical demonstration that present party practice either facilitates or prevents their attainment. The question can never be settled by facts alone, however objective the technique by which they are gathered.

[27]Turner, *Party and Constituency*, 35. Italics mine.

[28]Italics mine.

to conclude that he had established the validity of this proposition in Chapter II of *Party and Constituency*.

In Chapter III Turner raised another important question which Lowell ignored—that of the similarity and dissimilarity of the parties' positions in various areas of policy. Though the chapter is not without its problems, principally posed by the difficulties of assigning roll calls objectively to such policy areas as "states' rights," "bureaucracy," "regulation of business," etc., Turner did demonstrate that sharp party differences during the sessions studied were to be found much more often in some policy areas than in others. The method employed here is based on Rice's "index of likeness," which provides a means of stating the similarity of the two parties on any given roll call on a 0–100 scale.[29] Some of his results are summarized in Table 3, which is taken from *Party and Constituency*. In the four sessions studied (1921, 1931, 1937, and 1944), as the table indicates, there were fairly clear party differences on such issues as the tariff, patronage, and social and labor issues. On the other hand, the positions of the parties were much more similar on such issues as civil rights, foreign affairs, veterans' claims, and prohibition. Though it is very doubtful that another student, attempting to replicate Turner's study, would assign these same roll calls to the same categories, the table does indicate something of the high points of agreement and disagreement between the parties. There are several policy areas in which the parties were in considerable disagreement, and several in which their positions are difficult to differentiate. Table 3 would seem to throw quite a bit of doubt on Turner's claim, mentioned earlier, that "voters could distinguish between the behavior of the two parties." In a number of these areas it would seem to be very difficult for voters to perceive differences in the parties' positions.

In Chapters IV, V, VI, and VII Turner focused his attention on the influence of constituency factors on congressional voting. Having shown that there were "significant" differences in the voting behavior of the two parties, which he attributed to "the pressure of party leaders, organization, and ideology," he turned to "comparable sources in the constituencies" in the hope that the efficacy of the latter might be compared with that of party.[30] The particular constituency characteristics investigated are metropolitanism-ruralism, foreign-native population, and sec-

---

[29]Turner, *Party and Constituency*, 36–37. The "index of likeness" permits comparison of two parties' voting behavior. It is calculated by subtracting the percentage of yea votes cast by one group from the percentage of such votes cast by the other and subtracting the resulting figure from 100.

[30]*Ibid.*, 72.

tional location. By controlling the party variable and adopting the methods of analysis described earlier, based on the chi-square and Rice's in-

TABLE 3

AVERAGE INDEX OF LIKENESS
OF PARTIES ON VARIOUS ISSUES†

Kind of Issue	All Roll Calls		Substantive Roll Calls‡	
	Number	Average Index	Number	Average Index
Tariff	11	13.7	5	21.4
Patronage	24	22.9	15	26.9
Government Action	9	36.1	9	36.1
Bureaucracy	20	30.2	13	38.2
Public Works, specific	8	38.9	7	39.4
Social & Labor	18	40.8	13	43.7
Farm	27	42.7	20	44.6
States' Rights	20	50.0	10	50.5
Executive & Congress	32	39.4	21	51.0
Public Works, general	5	74.8	3	59.0
Government Regulation	30	58.3	16	64.1
Armament	20	60.7	13	65.4
Negro	6	68.7	3	66.0
Immigration	9	65.4	6	66.5
Foreign Affairs	17	51.0	9	68.4
Business Claims	11	56.3	8	68.4
Veterans & Claims	9	60.6	4	71.5
Women's Rights	3	74.7	3	74.7
District of Columbia	5	76.2	2	78.0
Indians	4	83.7	4	83.7
Civil Service	7	85.3	7	85.3
Prohibition	3	92.0	1	99.0

†Source: Julius Turner, *Party and Constituency: Pressures on Congress* (Baltimore: Johns Hopkins Press, 1951), p. 38.
‡Includes amendments, amendments to conference reports, final votes, and conference reports only.

dices, he attempted to investigate the significance of these constituency variables.

Using the chi-square method, the index of likeness, and the index of party loyalty,[31] Turner ably pointed out the potency of metropolitanism-

[31]The "index of party loyalty" is simply the percentage of times a party member votes with the majority of his party when majorities of both parties oppose one another.

ruralism. The chi-square test revealed that metropolitan groups within the Democratic and Republican parties differed significantly[32] on 33.6 and 18.6 percent of the roll calls in the four sessions studied.[33] As the index of party loyalty demonstrated, however, the direction of the association between the urban-rural factor and voting behavior varied a good deal from session to session. In the 1937 and 1944 sessions metropolitan Democrats were much more loyal to the party than were their rural colleagues. In the 1921 and 1931 sessions the direction of this relationship was exactly reversed; rural Democrats were more loyal than their urban counterparts. Republicans by and large were less divided along urban-rural lines than the Democrats in all of the sessions examined.[34] There was in general a consistent tendency in all sessions, Turner noted, for "an insurgent Republican . . . to vote like a regular Democrat and an insurgent Democrat . . . to vote like a regular Republican," which seems closely related to the urban-rural factor.[35] Democrats with constituencies similar in terms of urban-rural makeup to those of the regular Republicans at any time were more likely to vote like the latter than like their colleagues, and vice versa. Turner concluded that "members from similar districts (and therefore inferentially subject to similar pressures) tend to vote for the same legislation, regardless of party ties." [36] It is possible, of course, that some other variable, closely related to urbanism-ruralism, was responsible for the apparent relationship. In order to guard against this possibility Turner controlled both the party and foreign-native factors by concentrating on the southern Democrats, all of whom were in the native constituency category. A distribution of the southern Democrats according to the "index of party loyalty" suggested that, while the urban-rural factor lost some of its potency when the foreign-native factor was controlled, in three of the four sessions under examination urban-rural differences remained apparent.[37]

The foreign-native factor, according to Turner, appeared to be related to significant differences in voting behavior much more often among Democrats than among Republicans. The chi-square test revealed that significant differences existed between Democrats representing foreign and those representing native constituencies on almost three-eighths of

---

[32]Again, the word is used in the statistical sense as described above. "Significant" means only that the resulting distribution could have resulted from chance in no more than one in a hundred cases.

[33]Turner, *Party and Constituency*, 75.

[34]*Ibid.*, 81–87.

[35]*Ibid.*, 87.

[36]*Ibid.*

[37]*Ibid.*, 88–90.

the roll calls examined. Such differences existed between comparable groups of Republicans on only approximately one-seventh of the roll calls. The index of party loyalty indicated clear differences between Democrats from foreign constituencies and those from native constituencies in all of the sessions examined. The index revealed no such differences between comparable groups of Republicans.[38] As in the case of the urban-rural factor, the evidence suggested that "the pressures of foreign and native constituencies forced congressmen of different parties to tend to vote alike." [39] Also, as in the case of the urban-rural factor, the location of Democratic insurgency shifted radically from the two earlier sessions to the two later sessions. As the nature of the Democratic party changed after 1932, the representatives of the foreign constituencies who had been insurgent in the earlier sessions became the most loyal members of the party. After 1932, the higher the percentage of foreign population in the constituency, the higher was the loyalty of the Democratic representative; the lower the percentage of foreign population, the greater the tendency to vote with the Republican regulars. While the differences in the case of the Republicans were not as outstanding, this tendency was exactly reversed.[40]

In light of the traditional emphasis placed by American political historians on sectionalism as a factor in our party alignments and, especially, the persistence of North-South cleavage in our politics, most observers would expect the influence of section to be clearly apparent in congressional voting. To test this general hypothesis, Turner divided the Democrats into groups based on North-South location of the constituencies[41] and the Republicans into several rather arbitrary groups based on geographical location.[42] Significant sectional differences among the Democrats, as one might expect, were frequent, occurring in 40 percent of the roll calls examined.[43] Turner concluded, however, that of the three types of constituency factors examined, the sectional factor accounted for fewer Democratic differences than the foreign-native, though it accounted for somewhat more than the metropolitan-rural. The following frequency distribution of indices of likeness indicates that the differences accounted for by the three factors are not striking.

Employing the "index of party loyalty," Turner revealed some very in-

---

38*Ibid.*, 102–104, 107–109.
39*Ibid.*, 110.
40*Ibid.*, 104–107, 110.
41The South is defined as the eleven Confederate states and Oklahoma. *Ibid.*, 131.
42The process of classification is described in detail in *ibid.*, 146–47.
43Turner, *Party and Constituency*, 131.

teresting dimensions of the sectional differences among the Democrats. Though southern Democrats were more loyal to the party than were their northern colleagues in the 1921 and 1931 sessions, a striking reversal of this situation is apparent in the two later sessions. While, for example, almost two times as many southern as northern Democrats fell into the highest range of loyalty (95.1–100) in the 1930–31 session, almost ten times as many northern Democrats as southern fell into the same range

TABLE 4

INDICES OF LIKENESS OF NORTH-SOUTH,
METROPOLITAN-RURAL, AND FOREIGN-
NATIVE DEMOCRATS IN FOUR
SESSIONS, 1921–44†

Range of "Index of Likeness"	Number of Roll Calls		
	North–South	Met.–Rural	For.–Native
0– 55	30	22	43
56– 70	25	24	17
71– 85	33	38	43
86–100	138	142	123
Total	226	226	226

†Source: Julius Turner, *Party and Constituency: Pressures on Congress* (Baltimore: Johns Hopkins Press, 1951) , p. 132.

in 1944. [44] After 1937 there was a much greater tendency for southern Democrats to vote with the Republicans to create what has since come to be known as the "conservative coalition." Whereas only 2 percent of the southern Democrats were to be found in the range of party loyalty below 75 in the 1930–31 session, 61.1 percent fell into this range in the 1944 session.[45]

Among the Republicans, the sectional factor seemed somewhat more powerful than the other two constituency factors examined, but the patterns of sectional influence were more complex than those apparent among the Democrats. When frequency distributions of Republicans falling into different ranges of the index of party loyalty were constructed, the largest percentages of insurgents in the 1921 and 1931 sessions were located in the Border and West Central states. In 1937 the center of

[44]*Ibid.*, 134–37.
[45]*Ibid.*, 137

insurgency shifted to the Pacific and West Central states. In 1944 the center was located in the Pacific states and the Northeast.[46] The period studied, Turner noted, appeared to be one of sectional transition. "In the most recent sectional alignment across party lines, the Republican Interior and Democratic South oppose the Republican Coast and the Democratic North." [47]

At the conclusion of his study, Turner ably demonstrated the combined effects of party and constituency by focusing on voting behavior in the 1944 session. Of those Democrats whose constituencies were characterized by all of the variables associated with Democratic loyalty, three-fourths fell into the range of highest loyalty to the party—90.1 to 100. [48] On the other hand, those Republicans whose constituencies were characterized by all of the variables associated with Republican loyalty were concentrated heavily at the other end of the distribution in terms of their loyalty to the Democratic majority; three-fifths fell into the range of least loyalty, 0 to 10. [49] In other words, where party and constituency factors coincided, the result was impressive party loyalty. Southern, rural, native Democrats and coastal, metropolitan, foreign Republicans provided cases in which all of the constituency factors associated with party loyalty were set against the party factor. The result is that these congressmen fell into relatively low ranges of party loyalty. Only five of ninety-one rural southern Democrats were above 90; forty-seven, or more than half, were below 70.1. Only four of forty-six Republicans, all of whose constituency factors are set against party, were above 90.1; half were found to be in the ranges below 80.1. [50]

Despite the damaging criticisms which may be leveled at certain aspects of Julius Turner's work, taken as a whole *Party and Constituency* is an impressive analytical feat. Once Chapter II is seen in the proper perspective and the limits of Turner's data are clearly understood, the conclusion is inescapable that the study represents a great step forward in the investigation of party and constituency influence on congressional voting. The most cursory comparison of *Party and Constituency* with Lowell's *The Influence of Party* reveals the comparative sophistication of Turner's work. Lowell's exclusive concern with party as a determinant of legislative voting is replaced with a broader conceptual scheme which

46*Ibid.*, 146–52.
47*Ibid.*, 163.
48*Ibid.*, 166–68.
49*Ibid.*
50*Ibid.*, 168–73.

permits investigation of both party and constituency factors. At the same time, additional devices such as Rice's "index of cohesion" and "index of likeness," the "index of party loyalty," and the chi-square test of significance are employed to overcome Lowell's restrictive dependence on the party vote. Lowell's treatment of roll calls as an aggregate of votes undifferentiated in terms of issue-area is overcome to some extent by Turner's attempt to classify them into rough policy areas and to compare the parties' stands on various issues. While Turner was at times less than careful in generalizing from his findings, his contribution cannot be denied. He demonstrated beyond question that party is statistically associated with voting on an overwhelming percentage of House roll calls, and that deviant constituency characteristics may be employed to explain many of the commonly observed lapses from party voting in Congress. Perhaps most important of all, by reviving and demonstrating the utility of quantitative methods Turner heightened the interest of his colleagues in this area and paved the way for additional studies in the tradition of *Party and Constituency.*

The late V. O. Key, Jr., a man not ordinarily given to superlatives, referred enthusiastically to the next study to be examined here—Duncan MacRae's *Dimensions of Congressional Voting*[51]—as the most technically proficient study of congressional voting behavior undertaken to date.[52] There is no need to dispute Key's judgment. By comparison, for example, MacRae's measurements of both voting behavior and constituency characteristics are much more refined than those employed by Turner. Rather than rely on such measuring devices as Rice's indices and the party vote and on subjective judgment in assigning roll calls to issue-areas, MacRae utilized cumulative (Guttman) scaling both to classify roll calls and to place congressmen on the policy dimensions that the scales revealed.[53] This technique is much more sophisticated than the alternative classification schemes employed by Turner, the *New Republic,* and the AFL–CIO's Committee on Political Education, among

[51]Duncan MacRae, Jr., *Dimensions of Congressional Voting* (Berkeley: University of California Press, 1958) .

[52]V. O. Key, Jr., *Public Opinion and American Democracy* (New York: Alfred A. Knopf, 1961) , 489.

[53]Those who are not familiar with the logic and methods of Guttman scaling may wish to turn to Appendix I, which discusses these matters. It is doubtful that the reader who is totally unfamiliar with scaling will be able to appreciate MacRae's work without understanding the logic of this approach. Guttman scaling is discussed frequently in the remainder of this study. It will be understood better in the case of most readers if Appendix I is perused at this time.

others.[54] In order to compare the voting behavior of congressmen with the characteristics of their constituencies, MacRae utilized census materials on occupations to compile data on the socio-economic makeup of congressional districts.[55] The study also differs from *Party and Constituency* in its focus on constituency factors rather than on party. Mac-Rae utilized the scales not so much to address the question of differences in the parties' policy positions as to investigate the association of constituency factors with the scale patterns.

In order for the findings of MacRae's study to be fully understood, some explanation of his use of scale analysis is required. One may well ask: What are the advantages of this relatively laborious technique in roll call analysis? Why go to all this trouble? Conventional terms such as "liberalism" and "conservatism," MacRae would answer, are fraught with grave difficulties as descriptive concepts in the study of legislative voting. If conservatism, for example, is to have any precise meaning as a general description of congressional voting, conservatives ought to manifest the same kind of voting behavior in all issue-areas, but in fact conservatives in economic matters may not be conservative in an area such as race relations or civil rights. The classification is not precise enough for purposes of scientific investigation. Moreover, judgments of sameness and dissimilarity in issue-area in the context of roll call analysis often involve more than meets the eye. It is often supposed that civil liberties issues (for example, free speech and free association issues which arise in attempts of the government to control domestic communism) are quite distinct from issues involving governmental regulation of the economy or the redistribution of wealth. Yet the groups who support liberal policies in each of these areas may be virtually identical.[56]

[54]Turner's attempt to classify roll calls subjectively into issue-areas has been discussed above. Turner's aim, of course, was to break down roll calls into like sets, but the difficulties of such an approach are obvious. Investigator A has his idea of what constitutes a set of roll calls of like content, but so does B. It is not unlikely that they will disagree. This problem is ignored altogether by the *New Republic*, COPE, and a number of other agencies whose purposes are to rank congressmen (generally so that they may be rewarded or punished at the polls) according to liberalism or conservatism, depending on the ideological bearings of the rating agency. Many observers of Congress today feel that this approach is not suitable for serious scholarly purposes. See Appendix I, *passim*.

[55]MacRae's assistants pieced together information on percentage of farmers and farm managers and percentage of professional and managerial personnel among males employed from the 1950 Census. The data had to be combined from county and census tract units. Today, of course, the *Congressional District Data Book* provides this information.

[56]MacRae, *Dimensions*, 203–14. As we shall see, MacRae's Democratic Fair Deal Scale includes roll call items in both the socio-economic and civil liberties areas,

If reasonably precise descriptions of congressional voting behavior are to be obtained, it is necessary somehow to surmount this difficulty, which was noted in the discussion of one portion of Turner's *Party and Constituency*.[57] Some method which avoids the pitfalls of subjective judgment must be devised to classify roll call votes. "A method is needed for classifying together those political contests [roll call votes in this context] that share common elements or variables, and separating them from other contests."[58] If the relationship between roll call votes and constituency factors is to be understood, a means must be devised to permit analysis of "a single clearly defined variable rather than a mixture of several variables."[59]

The means MacRae chose for measuring the dependent variable is Guttman scaling, which serves both to identify dimensions underlying voting behavior and to place congressmen on these dimensions. In opinion or attitude research, for example, such scales are often employed to indicate "unidimensionality"[60] (that all questions relate to a common universe of attributes—places on a single attitude continuum) and to place respondents ordinally along such a continuum. In the same manner, scales in studies of legislative voting may be employed both to indicate that roll calls which form a scale are parts of a single dimension and to place congressmen ordinally on that dimension.

Dimensions of congressional voting, then, constitute "common continua on which members of a legislative body place themselves and are placed by relevant audiences."[61] Such dimensions in the context of legislative voting are not merely attitudinal but in all probability result from a complex mixture of factors—interest groups, administration pressures, party, constituency, and sub-cultures, as well as the congressman's ideological preferences. Moreover, these dimensions are conceived as shifting from time to time; the dimensions of one era will not necessarily coincide with those of another.[62]

Studies employing scaling methods completed previous to *Dimensions of Congressional Voting* had revealed that congressional roll calls might

---

indicating that for the House Democrats in the Eighty-first Congress, at least, the civil liberties liberals were to be found among the most liberal Democrats on welfare state issues.

[57]See above, p. 17.

[58]MacRae, *Dimensions*, 203.

[59]*Ibid.*

[60]For a discussion of this concept see Samuel A. Stouffer and others, *Measurement and Prediction*, Vol. IV of *Studies in Social Psychology in World War II* (Princeton: Princeton University Press, 1950), *passim.*

[61]MacRae, *Dimensions*, 203.

[62]*Ibid.*, 211.

be separated into a number of distinct issue-areas including domestic labor and welfare, and foreign policy. N. L. Gage and Ben Shimberg had indicated that the *New Republic*'s selected roll calls in the Seventy-ninth and Eightieth Congresses were not in fact unidimensional—that foreign policy roll calls could not be successfully scaled with those on domestic economic issues.[63] George Belknap's study of the Senate in the Eightieth Congress had revealed four major scales and demonstrated again the distinctness of domestic economic and foreign policy issues.[64] Thus MacRae settled with some confidence on Guttman scaling as the most satisfactory means of classifying roll calls and voting patterns in his own study, which focused on the Eighty-first Congress.

The scaling procedure employed in *Dimensions of Congressional Voting* is actually quite complex and need not be described in detail here.[65] The author's own procedure in this study, which is described in Appendix I, is much more simple, but accordingly, less sophisticated. It should be understood here only that MacRae's procedures would be impractical, if not impossible, to employ in a study unaided by paid assistants.[66] As Appendix I demonstrates, however, scaling may still be profitably employed by a single investigator whose aims are more modest than MacRae's. At any rate, if the logic of scale analysis is understood, there is no need to trace here the actual steps in the procedure followed by MacRae and his assistants.

Several scales were constructed for the House Democrats and Republicans separately.[67] The most detailed of these—the Democratic Fair Deal Scale—included roll calls on such seemingly diverse matters as housing,

[63]N. L. Gage and Ben Shimberg, "Measuring Senatorial Progressivism," *Journal of Abnormal and Social Psychology*, XLIV (January, 1949), 112–17.

[64]George M. Belknap, "A Study of Senatorial Voting by Scale Analysis" (unpublished Ph.D. dissertation, University of Chicago, 1951).

[65]The procedure is described in some detail in Appendix A of MacRae, *Dimensions*, 315–33.

[66]MacRae obviously delegated much of the computational work of his study to assistants. Nine assistants are mentioned in the preface to *Dimensions*. The matter is of importance only in documenting this author's point that MacRae's methods are probably beyond feasibility for a study carried out by one unaided investigator.

[67]MacRae's interests led him to the decision to scale the Democrats and Republicans separately. The scales utilized in the following study of the Eighty-sixth and Eighty-seventh Congresses were constructed for members of both parties. MacRae's point that separate scales permit the use of roll calls that will not scale for both parties is well taken. If one wishes to point up the differences in the parties' positions, however, it seems best to place the members of both parties on common scales. See MacRae, *Dimensions*, 222 and Appendix I of the present study.

rent control, labor unions, the House Committee on Un-American Activities, and internal security.[68] Contrary to expectations, the domestic socioeconomic issues and the civil liberties issues were found to constitute a single dimension. Foreign affairs roll calls, on the other hand, were found to be unscalable with those on domestic issues.[69] The domestic issues included in the Fair Deal Scale, with the exception of the civil liberties roll calls, formed two separate scales for the Republicans.[70] Separate Foreign Aid, Race Relations, and Agriculture Scales were constructed for each of the parties.[71]

Having constructed these scales, MacRae employed correlational techniques to examine the possibility of relationships between them. He concluded that for each of the parties all scales were positively associated with one another to some degree, indicating a factor common to all—perhaps a "combination of urbanism, domestic liberalism, and internationalism, as opposed to rural, conservative isolationism." [72] In other words, even though the roll calls for each of the parties were not so ordered as to satisfy the criteria of scaling, they were substantially associated with one another statistically.

Up to this point MacRae had demonstrated only the possibility of constructing scales from House roll calls in the Eighty-first Congress—a possibility previously explored successfully by other investigators working with roll call data for other Congresses.[73] The real innovative importance of his work lies in the uses to which the scales were put to investigate relationships between voting patterns and constituency characteristics. Though this analysis is quite sophisticated from a methodological point of view, its results are not as clear as might be expected.

Cross tabulation of scale scores and the constituency characteristics revealed some interesting, if somewhat confusing, relationships.[74] Among the Democrats farm representatives proved more conservative than their urban colleagues on the Fair Deal Scale.[75] Southern Democrats, however,

[68]MacRae, *Dimensions,* 223–28.

[69]*Ibid.,* 224.

[70]*Ibid.,* 229–32.

[71]*Ibid.,* 233–43. In the following summary, discussion of the agriculture scale has been omitted.

[72]*Ibid.,* 250. The method of correlation is the Kendall rank correlation coefficient (tau) .

[73]See above, pp. 25–26.

[74]Scale scores were distributed according to percent farm and percent professional and managerial workers. Then, for each class of percentages the median scale score was computed.

[75]MacRae, *Dimensions,* 261.

clustered at the anti-Fair Deal end of the scale regardless of the urban-rural nature of their constituencies.[76] When urban Democrats were considered alone, however, though there were considerable differences in their constituencies in the percentage of professional and managerial employees, the representatives of higher status constituencies manifested only a very weak tendency toward greater conservatism on the Fair Deal Scale.[77] Farm Republicans, as in the case of the Democrats, were more conservative on the Republican Fair Deal Scale than were their urban counterparts.[78] And again, when urban Republicans were considered alone, there was no clear relationship between scale scores and the professional-managerial population factor.[79] The Democratic Race Relations Scale resulted, as would be expected, in an almost perfect division of northern and southern Democrats. Rural Democrats were less liberal than urban Democrats in the area of race relations, but, again, in the urban areas no relationship appeared between scale scores and the occupational variable.[80] Among the Republicans no marked differences appeared between the urban and rural congressmen on the Race Relations Scale. In the urban areas, however, a slight tendency appeared toward association of liberal scores on race relations and lower status constituencies.[81] In the area of foreign aid no clear relationships appeared between scale positions and constituency factors for the Democrats.[82] Though rural Republicans were in general somewhat less favorable toward the foreign aid program than urban Republicans, in the cities no relationship appeared between scale scores and occupations.[83]

In addition to the socio-economic variables discussed above, MacRae employed one political constituency variable—marginality of election—in order to investigate the hypothesis that congressmen who won their seats by narrow margins may be somewhat more affected by constituency pressures than those with safer margins of election.[84] An earlier study by MacRae of voting in the Massachusetts legislature presented some evidence that legislators elected marginally were more responsive to such pres-

[76]Ibid.
[77]Ibid., 263
[78]Ibid., 265.
[79]Ibid., 266.
[80]Ibid., 267–70.
[81]Ibid., 271.
[82]Ibid., 276–78.
[83]Ibid., 277.
[84]Congressmen were divided into three groups—those whose electoral margins were below 5, between 5 and 10, and over 10 percent of the two party vote.

sures.[85] Analysis of the effect of marginal constituencies on members of the Eighty-first Congress, however, yielded no clear answer to the question. For reasons which MacRae did not explain the Republicans seemed to become more sensitive to constituency factors as marginality increased, but the Democrats did not.[86]

One of the most interesting findings of MacRae's attempt to relate voting patterns to constituency characteristics is the apparent influence of sectionalism, which, since 1932 and especially since World War II, has seemed to many observers to give way to socio-economic factors as a determinant of political tendencies. The analysis is somewhat clouded by the problem of defining sections, and it may well be argued that Mac-Rae's division of Republicans into sectional groupings is disturbingly arbitrary.[87] Certainly it is difficult to argue today that there are obvious geographical sections of the United States (apart from the South—and even here problems arise) which manifest readily identifiable political subcultures. Yet if MacRae's groupings are accepted for the purpose of analysis, there is no denying that sectional variations are apparent in his data. On the Democratic Fair Deal Scale, for example, for any given percentage of farm population, western representatives appeared at the liberal end of the scale with northern, border, and southern representatives following in that order.[88] Less surprising is the finding that for any given percentage of farm population, northern Democrats were most liberal on the Race Relations Scale, followed by border and then southern Democrats.[89] Sectional variations also appeared among the Democrats on foreign aid measures. Rocky Mountain and Pacific Democrats were consistently more favorably disposed toward foreign aid than their northern, border, and southern colleagues in that order.[90] Coastal Republicans rated higher scores in this area than those from the interior.[91]

It will have been apparent to the reader who appreciates the difficulties inherent in this kind of research that *Dimensions of Congressional Voting* is a very impressive study—conceptually, methodologically, and sub-

[85]Duncan MacRae, Jr., "The Relation Between Roll Call Votes and Constituencies in the Massachusetts House of Representatives," *American Political Science Review*, XLVI (December, 1952), 1046–55.

[86]MacRae, *Dimensions*, 284–89.

[87]MacRae's scheme for dividing the parties into sectional groupings is described in *ibid.*, 261, 277.

[88]*Ibid.*, 261–62.

[89]*Ibid.*, 267–70.

[90]*Ibid.*, 276–77.

[91]*Ibid.*, 277–78.

stantively. If the findings on the relationship of scale scores and constituency characteristics are somewhat cryptic, the fault is not in MacRae's approach. It is not because of the analytical scheme that at times the data are stubbornly resistant to interpretation. Again, there can be little doubt that the approach is the most sophisticated of any student of these problems who has published his work.

Another study, David B. Truman's *The Congressional Party*, must be considered along with the works of Lowell, Turner, and MacRae as a major attempt to investigate party voting in Congress.[92] In many ways Truman's *The Congressional Party* is a more inclusive study than those considered to this point. By Truman's own admission, he is only incidentally concerned with "the relative importance of party affiliation among the influences affecting the behavior of senators and representatives."[93] His purpose is more ambitious—to ask "what can be learned of the nature and contemporary features of the Congress through an examination of the parties and their leaders as they reveal themselves in legislative behavior and particularly in voting on the floor of the two chambers."[94] There is no need to judge the success of this larger purpose here; only those portions of *The Congressional Party* will be considered which employ roll call analysis to analyze the relationship of party and/or constituency to congressional voting. There are two questions of interest here: What are the advantages and limitations of the methods Truman employs? What do the findings of his study contribute to our understanding of congressional voting behavior and its relation to party and constituency?

In answering the first question it is difficult to avoid the judgment that the portions of *The Congressional Party* addressed to roll call analysis compare rather unfavorably with MacRae's book. This is especially apparent because both Truman and MacRae decided to study the Eighty-first Congress and thus their respective approaches may be readily compared. There are two difficulties with Truman's approach. First, for reasons which are not quite apparent, he employed the Rice-Beyle method of cluster-bloc analysis—a much less appropriate device than cumulative scaling for arriving at close measurement of policy dimensions in congressional voting.[95] Second, while he might easily have done so, he seems to have made no sustained, systematic effort to compare voting patterns

---

[92]Truman, *The Congressional Party*.

[93]*Ibid.*, vi.

[94]*Ibid.*, vii.

[95]This technique was developed by Stuart Rice and modified by Herman C. Beyle. It is described in Truman, *The Congressional Party*, 45–50, 320–30.

with constituency characteristics. The latter point may be partially met
with the objection that Truman's concerns were somewhat different from
those of Turner and MacRae. However, at several points in his analysis
Truman did make judgments about the relationships between voting behavior and constituency factors; he was simply less systematic than Turner and MacRae in doing so.[96]

One wonders whether at the beginning of his study Truman was aware
of the applications of scale analysis to the study of congressional voting.
If he was, it is difficult to understand his preference for a technique
which is both extremely cumbersome and at the same time relatively insensitive as a tool for examining party behavior through roll call votes.[97]
The rationale of the Rice-Beyle technique is rather simple, though it is
extremely difficult and laborious to apply to a legislative body of any size.
Its elements, in Truman's words, are "tabulating the frequency of voting
agreement between all possible pairs of members of a legislative body
and identifying by inspection those clusters or blocs of at least a designated minimum size, but including less than the whole number of legislators, among all of whom, pair by pair, the rate of agreement is equal to
or greater than some designated minimum figure." [98]

In the Truman study the task of tabulating paired agreements was accomplished with the aid of electronic computing equipment. Roll calls
were punched on IBM cards, and as the cards were passed through a
computer, the voting behavior of every congressman was compared with
that of every other congressman of the same party.[99] (It thus became apparent that legislator A agreed with legislator B on a certain number of
the roll calls; that A agreed with B and C; A agreed with B, C, and D,
etc.) The time-saving computer routine, however, was not entirely without its disadvantages. Limitations imposed by the available computing facilities dictated that no more than seventy-four roll calls could be passed

[96]This point is discussed below and documented. See p. 35.

[97]Truman in the appendix to *The Congressional Party* does discuss the alternative approach of scale analysis very briefly. He concludes, as is certainly the
case, that both techniques have their particular disadvantages. He glosses over the
similarity of the two approaches somewhat too easily, however, with the statement
that "votes that will not scale almost certainly will not produce sizable blocs with
any degree of cohesion." See page 330. This statement is by no means true at its
face value. It is argued here that the difficulty with the Rice-Beyle approach as a
measuring device of tendencies in the congressional parties lies precisely in its use
of a series of roll calls which might not fall along a single "dimension" in Mac-
Rae's sense.

[98]*Ibid.*, 320.

[99]*Ibid.*, 323. This routine obviously eliminates the possibility of identifying
bipartisan blocs.

through the computer for analysis at one time.[100] Consequently, Truman was forced to design the research procedure to meet this requirement. Though the immediate difficulties were overcome by arranging the roll calls into technically manageable sets according to party behavior measured by the "index of cohesion" beginning with those of lowest cohesion and working upward, there is no justification for this procedure other than the technical limitations of the computing facilities. Since these sets constitute the raw material out of which voting blocs were identified, it would seem particularly unfortunate that an element of so purely accidental a nature affected the design of the study at this crucial stage.

A second disquieting feature of Truman's use of the Rice-Beyle technique is the low "designated minimum" of agreements common to a group of legislators which is required to call that group a bloc. While this was a difficulty for Rice, who used rates varying from 80 percent to 60 percent, it would seem to be a more serious problem for Truman, who lowered the minimum to 50 percent in the case of the Senate. It is not simply the arbitrary nature of the cut-off points that is disturbing; the 50 percent minimum is so low that it is not clear that the legislators designated by it are in any real sense a bloc.

That the legislators constitute a bloc in any meaningful way is even more questionable when it is understood that a bloc of clustered pairs need not have agreed on the same specific roll calls; they need only have agreed with one another on at least a designated minimum number of the total. (For example, congressman A may agree with congressman B on roll calls 1, 2, 3, 4, and 5 out of 10. If congressman A, then, agrees with C on 1, 3, 5, 7, and 9, and B agrees with C on 2, 4, 6, 8, and 10, under the 50 percent minimum the three will be designated as a bloc.) It should be apparent that such a method sacrifices one of the major advantages of scale analysis—the ability to reveal distinct policy dimensions. Where a precise measurement of voting behavior is desired as a dependent variable to be related to supposed causal variables (such as constituency), the Rice-Beyle technique would seem to be a much less useful device than cumulative scaling.

With these difficulties in mind, the substantive findings of Truman's study may now be examined. In the Senate two fairly consistent groups of Democrats appeared on low cohesion roll calls in both sessions—one lib-

[100]Truman does not explain precisely why the computing facilities at hand would accommodate no more than seventy-four roll calls at a time. The most probable reason would seem to be a limitation imposed by the memory capacity of the equipment. See *ibid.*, 322.

eral and more internationalist, the other conservative and less internationalist—according to Truman's description of the roll calls underlying
the designated minimum agreements. Very largely, the conservative
group consisted of southerners.[101] On the high cohesion roll calls essentially the same pattern appeared, although the dissenting southerners
were too unstable to be considered a bloc; "they were, in fact, not a bloc,
but a splinter of modest and variable proportions." [102] Senate Republicans on low cohesion roll calls "split into sharply distinctive blocs composed of essentially the same members in both sessions." As with the
Democrats, sectionalism was apparently an underlying factor in the split,
though in this case it appeared to stem from an East-West cleavage, especially on foreign policy issues.[103] As with the Democrats, the Republican bloc structure remained largely the same on both the low and high
cohesion sets.[104]

In the House, Democrats divided into two stable blocs on the low cohesion roll calls. Again the split appeared to be basically sectional with
southerners and border-staters defecting from the position of the majority.[105] For example, Truman said, "the cleavages within the Democratic
party in the House showed marked parallels to those in the Senate. The
familiar North-South division was again the dominant characteristic, and
it is evident, even more than in the Senate, that deviation from the majority and coalition with the Republican opposition were peculiarly
characteristic of Southern representatives but by no means of all Democrats from the South." [106] House Democratic bloc structure on high
cohesion roll calls revealed these same cleavages. Dissent was again
apparently based mainly on southern defection from the remainder of the
congressional party.[107] House Republicans, in contrast, on lower cohesion roll calls evidenced considerable fractionalization; several small
blocs appeared, whose underlying causes were not readily apparent.[108]
On the high cohesion House roll calls there was no fractionalization
as one large bloc of thirty-one members appeared.[109]

Even if misgivings with regard to the Rice-Beyle technique as employed here are suppressed, Truman's findings are not without difficul-

[101]*Ibid.*, 50–63.
[102]*Ibid.*, 63–72.
[103]*Ibid.*, 72–82.
[104]*Ibid.*, 82–90.
[105]*Ibid.*, 150–67.
[106]*Ibid.*, 167.
[107]*Ibid.*, 167–72.
[108]*Ibid.*, 172–86.
[109]*Ibid.*, 186–90.

ties of interpretation. Only his conclusion that the parties diverged clearly on matters of substantive policy is both straightforward and in line
with the conclusions of Turner and MacRae. However, this conclusion
stems from analysis of selected "administration support votes," not from
the Rice-Beyle data.[110] It should also be noted that Truman's findings are
generally lacking in precision, since by combining presidential requests
in several issue-areas, he sacrificed sensitivity with regard to the question:
On what kinds of issues do the parties' positions diverge? Certainly this
question should be at the center of an inquiry of this sort. Unfortunately,
it is neither adequately put nor answered.

The results of Truman's cluster-bloc analysis, while interesting, raise a
good many questions which are not adequately answered in *The Congressional Party*. Why, for example, do the various blocs appear? To what
extent can they be accounted for by constituency characteristics? If these
questions can be approached only with considerable difficulty, the difficulty would seem to stem at least partially from the nature of the analytical scheme, which fails both to isolate distinct ideological or policy dimensions and to relate voting patterns on such dimensions to hypothetical
causal factors in a systematic manner. As has been seen, the legislators
included in the various blocs need not have agreed on the same roll
calls; rather, each must agree with every other on a designated minimum
of the total. It is consequently very difficult to analyze the ideological dimensions underlying bloc behavior, for roll calls that would fall into separate dimensions in scale analysis are merged. Domestic economic issues,
foreign policy issues, and race relations issues, for example, may comprise a set of roll calls used to identify blocs. A sensitive measurement of
ideological dimensions is sacrificed, and it is possible only with great
difficulty (and then only unsystematically) to compare well-defined voting patterns with constituency characteristics.

It has been indicated that Truman found the cleavages in the congressional parties to be primarily sectional—North-South among the Democrats and East-West among the Republicans. This is a most interesting
finding, particularly since it runs counter to the literature of American
party processes, which stresses the decline or erosion of sectionalism and
the rise of a class-based politics since the "Roosevelt revolution," and especially since 1945. [111] Though similar sectional influences were appar-

---

[110]"Administration support" measures were identified as those involving presidential vetoes, reorganization plans, confirmation of appointments, ratification of
treaties, and requests made by the President in messages or communications. See
ibid., 327.

[111]See for example V. O. Key, Jr., *Politics, Parties, and Pressure Groups* (5th

ent in both Turner's and MacRae's studies, the procedures on which this generalization is based in *The Congressional Party* are hardly sufficient to convince the reader that other cleavages have not been overlooked.

While Truman was not primarily interested in questions involving the causal force of party and constituency in congressional voting, he did, nevertheless, treat this question at several points in his analysis. While, at times, he was systematic in attempting to relate constituency factors to bloc behavior, no consistent scheme for identifying possible relationships was employed throughout the study. For example, in the case of the southern House Democrats, Truman compared bloc membership with such constituency characteristics as urban-rural makeup, size of urban places, electoral competition, and percentage of nonwhite population, and reasonably concluded that there were no obvious and consistent constituency characteristics which seemed to relate to party loyalty or a lack thereof.[112] The analysis is not always this thorough. As has been seen, Truman found considerable fractionalization in the House Republican Party on low cohesion roll calls. There is some evidence that this bloc structure is partially sectional in nature, but Truman made no attempt to employ constituency factors to discover possible relationships with the various blocs. He noted that "no obvious demographic or political factor was identified that consistently distinguished the components of the Republican 'right' from one another," and that their constituencies did not appear to differ with regard to urban-rural makeup. There is, however, no systematic attempt at this point to relate the Republican blocs to constituency differences. Throughout the study, one has an uneasy feeling that Truman prematurely concluded that constituency differences will not explain the observed bloc formations. In the case of the House of Representatives a more thorough analysis might have been based on such characteristics as median incomes, occupations, percentage of nonwhite population, and political competition. In fact, such factors might not have proved relevant to the observed bloc formations, but again they might have. Without more systematic investigation it would seem unwise to conclude that constituency factors will not account for the observed behavior.

If I have been somewhat critical of certain aspects of David Truman's *The Congressional Party,* it should be remembered that I have made no

---

ed.; New York: Thomas Y. Crowell, 1964) , pp. 245–53, *passim,* and W. Dean Burnham, "The Changing Shape of the American Political Universe," *American Political Science Review,* **LIX** (March, 1965) , 7–28.

[112]Truman, *The Congressional Party,* 164–67.

attempt here to assess the quality of the study as a whole. Moreover, certain of its findings—especially those relating to the sectional nature of cleavages within the congressional parties—are quite interesting. The point that my discussion has sought to establish is only that careful consideration of party and constituency influence on congressional voting is rendered very difficult by Truman's approach.

Chapter II

STRANDS OF CONTINUITY

THE REVIEW in the first chapter of four major congressional voting studies has illustrated the bewildering diversity of the literature of party, constituency, and voting behavior. A summary of this material leaves no doubt that while many points of departure have been taken, and a variety of research schemes employed, reliable generalizations are difficult to uncover. This situation may result at least as much from the manner in which these studies have been conducted as from the admitted complexity of the subject matter itself. The difficulty one encounters in attempting to grasp these studies as a whole stems largely from the fact that they are addressed to slightly different types of questions and employ methods that are often quite dissimilar. The results of the various studies, consequently, are extremely resistant to comparison. In part, this situation cannot be helped, since two of the four writers whose work has been examined—MacRae and Truman—studied the same Congress and neither could take advantage of the other's approach in formulating his own. However, there is no denying that the theoretical and methodological disparity of these studies owes something to the failure of the more recent researchers, such as MacRae and Truman, to take stock of existing work. A look at the minor studies in this area reveals the same difficulty; new projects continue to be undertaken with little concern as to whether or not they add to an existing body of literature on party and constituency.

If political scientists working in the area of legislative behavior are to overcome such difficulties, they must devote more effort to developing both theories and research strategies which will yield comparable results. Reasonably similar theoretical problems will have to be treated with reasonably similar kinds of methods. Since the existing studies are accomplished facts, they cannot be redone with these ends in mind. But some effort must sooner or later be devoted to reordering and integrating the existing studies so as to provide a common basis for further inquiry.

What kinds of findings, then, emerge from a half century of research on congressional voting? In order to answer this question it is necessary to rearrange the material already discussed, supplementing it wherever possible with findings from other sources. It then becomes apparent that despite the diversity noted, the existing studies of congressional voting suggest strands of continuity in theory, methods, and findings. The assumption of this chapter is that these strands of continuity should be drawn out, made explicit, and incorporated in future research.

For purposes of analysis, the extensive literature of party, constituency, and congressional voting has been divided into two related but distinct categories—one centering primarily on description of the congressional parties and the other on the identification of factors related to voting behavior. Problems in the first category involve such specific questions as: Do the congressional parties differ significantly? if so, to what extent? on what kinds of policy issues? Problems in the second category center on a somewhat different question: What factors influence the congressman's vote? Since description and inferences about causation are closely related exercises in the social sciences, these two categories overlap substantially, but for analytical purposes it is helpful to keep them separate. When this scheme is followed it becomes clear that some fairly definite propositions about the behavior of the congressional parties and about factors related to congressional voting behavior do in fact exist.

The first question that might be asked involves the nature of the congressional parties. How unified are they and how often do they oppose one another? The simplest approach to this question—that of tabulating Lowell's party votes—provides one kind of answer. For fifteen sessions of the House studied by Lowell and Turner the average percentage of party votes per session from 1845 to 1948 was 21.7.[1] If cohesive opposition of the congressional parties is measured by the party vote, it can be said with certainty that such opposition in the last hundred years has been apparent in only a small minority of the roll calls taken. That party opposition and cohesion are only very imperfectly measured by the party vote, however, should now be obvious. The device is extremely crude, and, strictly speaking therefore, we are entitled to say no more than that the congressional parties have seldom opposed one another to the extent of

[1]Data for these sessions are reported in Tables 1 and 2. See above, 00-00.

90 percent versus 90 percent. Ideally, it would be desirable to know much more about party opposition and cohesion for this period, but unfortunately such information is not available in usable form. In Table 5,

TABLE 5

PERCENTAGE OF HOUSE ROLL CALL VOTES
FALLING INTO VARIOUS CATEGORIES OF PARTY OPPOSITION:
HOUSE OF REPRESENTATIVES IN
FIVE CONGRESSES EXAMINED BY LOWELL[†]

| | Congress (Year) | | | | | |
	29th (1845–47) Percent	38th (1863–65) Percent	50th (1887–89) Percent	55th (1897–99) Percent	56th (1899–1901) Percent	Average Percent Per Session
Party Vote v. Party Vote	10.7	30.2	13.6	50.9	49.3	30.9
Party Vote by One Party v. a Non-Party Majority of the Other	42.2	33.8	37.7	29.1	24.3	33.4
Non-Party Vote v. Non-Party Vote	38.2	28.1	29.7	13.9	18.6	25.7
Total Roll Calls on Which Parties Voted Majority v. Majority	91.1	92.1	81.0	93.9	92.2	90.1

†This material is taken from A. Lawrence Lowell, *The Influence of Party Upon Legislation in England and America* in *Annual Report of the American Historical Association for 1901* (2 vols.; Washington, 1902), 538–41.

however, which is based on Lowell's calculations, there is some indication that reliance on the party vote may have caused students of American parties to underestimate partisan opposition in Congress, at least in the nineteenth century sessions.[2] When party votes are added to those roll

2Because Turner does not present this kind of data, no comparison is possible with the later Congresses he examined.

calls on which one party "party voted" against a majority (but less than 90 percent of the other) these two categories comprise 64.3 percent, or almost two-thirds, of the total votes recorded. Moreover, the parties opposed one another by simple majorities or more on 90.1 percent of all roll calls.[3] Thus, while the parties most often failed to maintain as much cohesion in opposition as Lowell's criterion requires (90 percent versus 90 percent), it is clear that they opposed one another in some manner on an overwhelming percentage of roll calls. Since Lowell chose not to emphasize this fact in his analysis, it has been largely overlooked. A more precise account of party opposition might be obtained by extensive reworking of raw data which Lowell included for three of the five Congresses he examined, but such an exercise lies beyond the bounds of this study.[4]

A second approach to description of party differences is based on Stu-

TABLE 6

AVERAGE INDEX OF COHESION FOR DEMOCRATS AND
REPUBLICANS IN SIX HOUSE SESSIONS
EXAMINED BY TURNER[†]

Year	Democrat		Republican	
	I of C	Percent	I of C	Percent
1921	69.4	84.7	74.4	87.2
1928	61.3	80.7	57.8	78.9
1930–31	69.6	84.8	62.3	81.2
1933	63.1	81.6	71.7	85.9
1937	53.9	76.9	70.2	85.1
1944	56.0	78.0	70.8	85.4
Average	62.2	81.1	67.9	84.0

[†]The material presented here is from Julius Turner, *Party and Constituency: Pressures on Congress* (Baltimore: Johns Hopkins Press, 1951), 27.

art Rice's index of cohesion. This information is drawn from fewer sessions and is not comparable to that based on party votes since the index measures party cohesion independently of opposition.[5] With what infor-

[3]Unanimous roll calls and those on which 90 percent or more of both parties voted alike were excluded by Lowell.

[4]Lowell published raw data in the form of roll call descriptions and numbers of party members voting for and against for the Thirty-eighth, Fiftieth, and Fifty-sixth Congresses.

[5]The "index of cohesion" has been discussed in Chapter I. See above, p. 11, (fn. 16).

mation is available, however, it is possible to piece together something of a rough general picture of party behavior. Table 6 presents average index of cohesion data for six sessions of the House examined by Julius Turner. For all roll calls in the six sessions examined the average indices of cohesion for Democrats and Republicans are, respectively, 62.2 and 67.9. (The comparable percentage figures are 81.1 and 84.) Although these figures are all from twentieth century sessions, if interpreted cautiously they provide a complement to the earlier party vote data. At first glance they make the parties appear much more cohesive than do the earlier figures. In light of traditional arm-chair generalizations about the disunity of our congressional parties, it is surprising that on the average 81.1 percent of House Democrats and 84 percent of Republicans voted with the majority of their party colleagues during these sessions. However, there is a rather obvious drawback inherent in the use of the index of cohesion in this manner without a further control that unfortunately is not available. These figures indicate nothing whatever about party opposition. While it would have been feasible for Turner to measure the cohesion of the parties on roll calls in which a majority of one opposed a majority of the other, he did not use this approach. Consequently, much of the cohesiveness measured in this manner may result (and there is no way of knowing without redoing the research) from roll calls on which the parties agreed with one another. Many such roll calls may have been entirely noncontroversial. In terms of party *differences,* it is not altogether clear what these index of cohesion figures mean.

On the question of party opposition, then, there is very little hard statistical information. Of the four major studies that were examined in Chapter I, only those of Lowell and Turner are primarily concerned with party differences. When the few findings of their studies are exploited, the available sources are exhausted.[6] Aside from what is known from more conventional historical sources such as biographies, memoirs, and non-quantitative studies of various periods and administrations, there is little more that can be said about party opposition and cohesion over the long haul of American history. The only generalization which emerges

[6]V. O. Key, Jr., in *Southern Politics,* presents some information similar to that offered by Turner, based on the index of cohesion. Again, Key's data are not absolutely comparable, since he excluded roll calls on which "dissenters amounted to less than 10 percent of the prevailing vote and those on party organization." To compound the difficulty, two of the four sessions that Key examined overlap with those examined by Turner, and the roll calls for all of the sessions he examined were merged. Key found the average index of cohesion of House Democrats to be 58.5 and that of Republicans to be 66 for roll calls examined in the 1933, 1937, 1941, and 1945 sessions. See Key, *Southern Politics,* 369–70.

from the information at hand is that party voting as defined by Lowell does not frequently appear in the sessions studied.

Even this simple generalization, however, is fraught with difficulties. How, for example, can one account for the substantial variations which are apparent in party voting from Congress to Congress? Table 7, which summarizes Tables 1 and 2, illustrates the striking ups and downs of party voting since 1845. While the range of party voting from Congress to Congress seems to have narrowed considerably since 1937, it is amazingly wide for some of the earlier Congresses. How can such a startling increase in party voting as took place between 1889 and 1897 and such a falling-off as took place between 1921 and 1928 be explained? Moreover, how can the ups and downs apparent between sessions of a single Congress be understood? These latter variations are submerged in the data which

TABLE 7

PARTY VOTING:
AN HISTORICAL PERSPECTIVE ON PARTY BEHAVIOR
IN THE U.S. HOUSE OF REPRESENTATIVES†

Year	President	Percent of Party Votes
1845–47	Polk	10.7
1863–65	Lincoln	30.2
1887–89	Cleveland	13.6
1897–99	McKinley	50.9
1899–1901	McKinley	49.3
1921	Harding	28.6
1928	Coolidge	7.1
1930–31	Hoover	31.0
1933	Roosevelt	22.5
1937	Roosevelt	11.8
1944	Roosevelt	10.7
1945	Roosevelt-Truman	17.5
1946	Truman	10.5
1947	Truman	15.1
1948	Truman	16.4
Average, all		21.7

†The sources of this information are Tables 1 and 2 in Chapter I.

have already been presented, but in approximately half of the Congresses examined by Lowell party voting was about twice as frequent in one session of a Congress as in the other. In the Fifty-Fifth Congress, for example, party voting dropped from 85.7 percent in the first session to 20 percent in the second.[7] There is little on these variations in the literature of congressional voting, and since Lowell no investigator has sought to explain them. Some clue to variations from Congress to Congress may be found in an attempt to relate the behavior of the legislative parties to electoral alignments in the national party system as a whole. It is interesting with regard to this possible theoretical perspective to note, as Figure 1 reveals, that the peaks of party voting historically appear to follow what the late V. O. Key, Jr., called "critical elections"—the elections of 1860, 1896, and 1928, 1932.[8] A peak also appears after the massive "reinstating election" of 1920.[9] The lowest troughs, on the other hand, are to be found in the 1840's, when both the Democrats and Whigs were about to be realigned on the sectional question, and in 1928, just before the unification of the Smith-Roosevelt forces, which produced the New Deal coalition. Though further inquiry along these lines is beyond the bounds of the present study, it is important to note that party voting in the House manifests a historical dimension too often ignored.[10] The range of party opposition and cohesion from Congress to Congress is too great to be glossed over with the single generalization that "our parties seldom differ." Since the purpose of this chapter is to state what is known about party, constituency, and congressional voting, it is important to stress the historical dimension. Until more is known about these ups and downs, it would seem premature to attempt to advance generalizations.

To this point differences between the congressional parties have been described by examining their opposition and cohesion without regard to the substance of policy. A second question may now be raised—that of the policy content of party opposition. For most critics of American parties (and apologists too, for that matter) this has been a central concern. What, then, are the policy differences apparent in party voting in the House in the studies that have been conducted?[11] Immediately upon

[7]Lowell, *The Influence of Party Upon Legislation,* 336.

[8]See V. O. Key, Jr., "A Theory of Critical Elections," *Journal of Politics,* XVII (February, 1955), 3–18.

[9]Philip E. Converse and others, "Stability and Change in 1960: A Reinstating Election," *American Political Science Review,* LV (June, 1961), 269–80.

[10]This line of thought, of course, does little to explain variations in party behavior from session to session of single Congresses. Perhaps close study of notorious cases would identify additional factors.

[11]The word "policy" is preferred to the more common "ideology," which seems to the author an uncommonly troublesome word. The debate over the ideological or non-ideological nature of American parties often founders on the problem of what is meant by ideology. Does ideology necessarily involve a rigid *Weltan-*

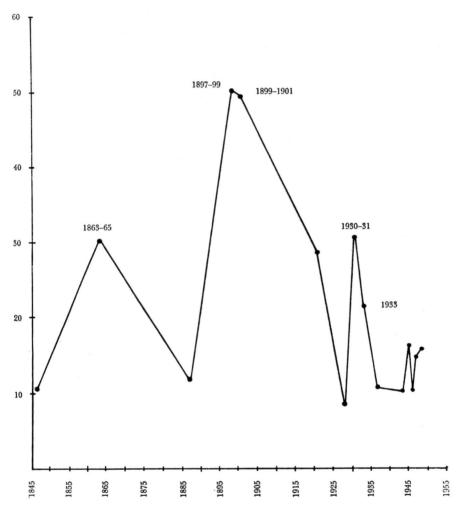

Fig. 1—Percentage of party votes in fifteen sessions of the House of Representatives: 1845–1948

framing this question, familiar difficulties are encountered, and the four studies examined offer much less help than might be expected. Lowell left the matter entirely open, noting only that "the amount of party voting depends largely upon the accident of some question on which the

---

schaaung? Does it connote thought determined to some extent by one's structural position in society? Is ideology somehow non-rational? There is no need to meet these problems here, if they can be avoided.

parties are sharply divided happening to come up for decision." [12] And although Turner dealt with the problem explicitly, MacRae ignored it altogether and Truman was only incidentally concerned with it. Fortunately, some additional help may be found in minor studies of congressional voting and in fragments of larger works not mentioned in Chapter I.

What does this literature reveal about the policy content of party voting in Congress? Are the parties different? On what kinds of questions? Again, the historical dimensions of party behavior become apparent. The data available on this matter cover a period of slightly more than a century. Can anything be said with confidence about the policy dimensions of party voting in the House over this entire period? First, although there is nothing for the earlier periods to compare in precision of measurement with the policy scales developed by MacRae in *Dimensions of Congressional Voting*, it is obvious that the policy dimensions of party voting in Congress have been altered considerably over time. Second, such general concepts as "liberalism" and "conservatism," as they are employed in current descriptions of congressional voting, are of little use over the entire period, since they are usually defined in terms of issues raised in the twentieth century.[13] Third, at any single point in time (and this would seem to hold true for the entire period for which data are available) the parties have been sharply opposed on some policy issues and scarcely opposed on others. These highly partisan issues change so greatly from time to time that generalization becomes extremely hazardous, if not impossible. However, a brief examination of the available information on the policy differences of the congressional parties is worthwhile.

The entire body of evidence available for nineteenth century sessions consists of semi-raw data included in Lowell's *The Influence of Party Upon Legislation in England and America*. While ideally these data ought to be rearranged on some basis other than the party vote, the in-

---

[12]See above, p. 5.

[13]"Liberalism" and "conservatism" as concepts used to describe the policy dimensions of roll call voting are often no more precise than the same concepts in political theory. As these concepts are employed today, however, they are largely defined in terms of issues that have been in the forefront of national politics since 1932—issues rooted in controversies over the welfare state at home and internationalism or multilateralism abroad. Race relations issues and civil liberties issues are often included. Most commentators seem to agree that liberalism consists of attitudes favorable to welfare, internationalism, racial equality, and freedom of political expression. The terms liberalism and conservatism are so tied to these kinds of issues that they can be applied only with great difficulty to earlier political periods.

adequacy of which has been constantly stressed, it is possible to employ the information as presented to derive some idea of party differences on policy in this period. By examining the substance of party votes, conceived as peaks of cohesive party opposition, it is possible to roughly identify the issues on which the parties were most sharply distinguished.[14] Not surprisingly, in all three Congresses for which Lowell published data the parties were nearly unanimous on matters pertaining to control of the House. Party votes were common on questions of internal organization— those directly affecting patronage, contested elections, etc. Beyond these obvious sources of cohesion the parties opposed one another on very different kinds of policy questions in the three sessions. In the Thirty-eighth Congress, which met from 1863 to 1865, the parties differed mainly on matters pertaining to the Negro, the conduct of the Civil War, the status of the Confederate states, and intentions regarding their return to the Union. Republicans, of course, consistently supported policies in favor of southern Negroes, vigorous war programs, punishment of the rebels, etc. All but a handful of party votes in two sessions of this Congress occurred on such matters. The Fiftieth Congress, which met from 1887 to 1889, stands out among the Congresses examined by Lowell for its virtual absence of party voting (save for questions related to control of the House). Except for the Mills Tariff Bill, on which two votes are recorded, no issue of major importance seems to have occasioned a party vote. In this case the party vote is too insensitive to reveal policy differences. The Fifty-sixth Congress (1899–1901), on the other hand, saw so many party votes that it is difficult to generalize about their policy content. Republicans evidenced 90 percent unity on most matters of importance, and party votes occurred on such major issues as anti-trust policy, the value of currency, war revenues, and tariffs. In this Congress Republicans supported policies in favor of weak anti-trust regulation, hard currency values, high war revenues (and thus taxes), and high tariffs. On the sectional question the Democrats maintained their southern sympathies on a party vote authorizing the Census Bureau to inquire into abridgment of the suffrage in the southern states.

Information on the policy dimensions of roll call voting in twentieth century Congresses may be taken from several sources. Despite the heterogeneous nature of this information and the means used to gather it, it is useful to piece together a rough portrait of party behavior. Some help is available from Julius Turner, who addressed this question more

---

[14]It will be remembered that Lowell made no analysis of the policy content of party voting. The analysis here is based on raw data included at the end of *The Influence of Party Upon Legislation*, 433–77.

straightforwardly than any of the other investigators mentioned in Chapter I. Turner, it will be remembered, classified roll calls for four sessions of the House (1921, 1930–31, 1937 and 1944) into policy categories and employed Rice's index of likeness to investigate the interparty differences.[15] If an index of likeness of 50 or less is taken as a rough, arbitrary standard for sharp party difference, the parties were sharply opposed only on questions pertaining to the tariff, government action (intervention), bureaucracy, specific public works projects, social and labor matters, and farm policy.[16] Tariff issues were raised in two sessions, 1921 and 1937, and in both cases Democrats favored low duties and Republicans, high duties.[17] Issues that Turner classified under "Government Action" were voted on in 1930–31, 1937, and 1944; in each case the Democrats favored increased governmental activity.[18] Questions concerning the size of the federal bureaucracy arose in 1921, 1937, and 1944. Here, when each session is viewed separately, it becomes apparent that party differences were more related to control of the executive branch than to permanent policy preferences. Republicans consistently favored expansion in the 1921 session, while they sharply opposed Democratic expansionism in the later sessions of 1937 and 1944. [19] Since public works roll calls were infrequent during the 1921 and 1930–31 sessions, it is difficult to generalize about the parties' positions in this period. In the two later sessions, however, party opposition was sharp with Democrats favoring works projects.[20] In the area of labor and social issues differences between the parties clearly became more pronounced in the later sessions. Although in 1921 little difference was apparent in the issues raised, during the later New Deal sessions opposition became quite sharp, with Democrats taking the side of labor and social reform in every case.[21] Farm issues were raised in every session, and in each case Turner found the Democrats more favorable to the interests of farmers.[22]

As has been noted, both Duncan MacRae's *Dimensions of Congressional Voting* and David Truman's *The Congressional Party* are focused on a single Congress, the Eighty-first, which met in 1949–50. While it

[15]The "index of likeness" has been explained in Chapter I, 17.

[16]It should be noted again that assignment of roll calls in this manner to policy areas is risky business. The chances of agreement on such assignment by several investigators would seem very low. Again, we are forced to make do with the information we have.

[17]Turner, *Party and Constituency*, 68–69.

[18]*Ibid.*, 67–68.

[19]*Ibid.*, 45–47.

[20]*Ibid.*, 51–53.

[21]*Ibid.*, 58–61.

[22]*Ibid.*, 64–66.

would be convenient to employ these studies to reveal something of the
policy dimensions of party behavior in the Harry S. Truman era, neither is designed primarily to highlight inter-party policy difference. Since
MacRae constructed separate policy scales for each of the parties, it is
virtually impossible to compare the parties' positions on the dimensions
revealed by the scales.[23] Ironically, therefore, while his study is notable
for its great precision in the measurement of policy dimensions underlying voting, its design prevents comparison of the parties with respect
to these dimensions. Likewise, whatever virtues the Rice-Beyle-Truman
cluster-bloc scheme may have, ability to reveal anything precise about interparty differences on matters of policy is not among them. The cluster-
bloc scheme actually serves to obscure the policy dimensions of congressional voting.[24] Consequently, those parts of *The Congressional Party*
based on this approach are virtually useless for describing interparty policy differences. To deal with this matter, however, Truman constructed
an "Administration support index" for both the Senate and the House.
His index was composed of roll call votes on such matters as vetoes, presidential reorganization plans, and questions on which the President revealed an "express preference" in a message to Congress, a communication with an individual legislator, a speech, a press conference, or a
meeting with a group of legislators.[25] Frequency distributions of scores
on these indices for both the Senate and the House revealed that "the
centers of gravity of the two parties were not only distinguishable but
consistently different." [26] While a good deal of deviation was apparent
in both parties, their modal positions in the distribution based on the index were clearly distinct. This conclusion, however, fails to specify anything exact about the policy content of the issues composing the index.
In short, this is too crude a means of measuring the policy differences
between the legislative parties since it fails to separate questions on domestic economic and social issues, foreign policy, civil rights, etc. David
Truman's analysis of party differences indicates only that the Democrats
tended to support the administration more than the Republicans. Knowing something already about the nature of the policies supported by
President Truman's administration, an observer might infer that Democrats were more liberal or reformist or internationalist than Republicans,
but the analytical scheme itself does not adequately reveal these differences.

23See above, p. 26.
24See above, pp. 31–36.
25Truman, *The Congressional Party* 327.
26*Ibid.*, 283.

Clinton Rossiter, in his *Parties and Politics in America,* attempts to demonstrate the "real differences between the two parties" by examining roll call votes in the House and Senate from 1933 to 1959. [27] Specifically disclaiming "scientific accuracy," he simply selected the roll calls which seemed to be most important in reflecting liberalism and conservatism or internationalism and isolationism during these years—in other words, what he thought to be the most important policy decisions made by Congress.[28] Rather than employ criteria such as the party vote, the index of cohesion or the index of likeness, Rossiter merely arrayed the raw data of these roll calls, listing the number of members in each party who voted pro and con on each issue. Interpreting this information, he concluded that "the Democrats and the Republicans are . . . at least a city block apart on issues like taxation, welfare, farm subsidies, regulation of business, regulation of labor, the tariff, and 'foreign entanglements.'" [29] Rossiter's resort to metaphor may appear at best a mixed blessing to those confused by the disparate standards used in the various studies of congressional parties. If, for the sake of expediency, one accepts his selection of roll calls for this period, it is still necessary to know something about the length of "city blocks." A few quick calculations may help to throw some light on this matter. By rearranging these data for the House of Representatives in terms of party votes and Rice's indices of cohesion and likeness, some comparability may be gained. The importance of the standard selected immediately becomes obvious. In a total of forty measures on which roll calls were taken, there is not a single party vote. Even if the standard is relaxed to 75 percent of one party versus 75 percent of the other, only eight of the forty votes satisfy this criterion. Moreover, on eighteen, or nearly half, of the forty votes, majorities of both parties voted on the same side of the question. Index of likeness and cohesion data, however, throw a somewhat different light on the matter. As Table 8 reveals, on the domestic roll calls the parties averaged in the 50's in the index of likeness for both the periods of Democratic and Republican control of the White House. On foreign affairs roll calls the index varied from 56.3 in the Roosevelt-Truman period to 82.5 in the Eisenhower era, indicating a significant convergence in the parties' positions on internationalism. The index of cohesion figures indicate that while both parties averaged over 50 (75 percent unity) on domestic issues, each of the parties was considerably more cohesive when in control of the White House. It should especially be noted that the President's party main-

27Clinton Rossiter, *Parties and Politics,* 127–34.
28*Ibid.,* 128
29*Ibid.,* 133–34.

tained an average index of cohesion of over 63 (over 80 percent unity) in each case. In the area of foreign affairs, on the other hand, the parties' records clearly diverge. While Democrats were impressively unified in the

TABLE 8

AVERAGE INDEX OF COHESION AND
LIKENESS FOR DEMOCRATS AND REPUBLICANS
ON SELECTED HOUSE ROLL CALLS 1933–59†

| | Average Index of Cohesion | | Average |
	Democrats	Republicans	Index of Likeness
Domestic Liberal—			
Conservative Issues, 1933–52	63.8	53.2	53.9
Foreign Affairs, 1933–52	74.9	36.8	56.3
Domestic Liberal—			
Conservative Issues, 1952–59	51.1	63.0	50.8
Foreign Affairs, 1952–59	46.1	22.5	82.5

†Source: Clinton Rossiter, *Parties and Politics in America* (New York: Signet Books, 1964), 129–33.

Roosevelt-Truman period, their cohesion dropped off markedly during the Eisenhower years. In neither period were the Republicans able to maintain much unity. By the 1950's their index of cohesion had declined to 22.5, revealing that on the average approximately 40 percent of their members dissented from the position of the majority. Hopefully, this rearrangement of Rossiter's material has rendered it somewhat more comparable to the material previously considered. It can be said that Democrats by and large have taken the liberal side of both domestic and foreign issues since 1933, with some decline in unity since 1952. Republicans took the conservative side of these issues in the Roosevelt-Truman period, but a majority supported liberal internationalist foreign policies in the Eisenhower years, making it rather difficult to distinguish clear party positions in this area. Though this party opposition did not result in party voting in Lowell's sense, the likeness and cohesion data suggest that the parties maintained clearly divergent positions at least on domestic economic and social issues. On foreign policy, however, only the Democrats were united to this extent during the Roosevelt years. Rossiter's "city block" separating the parties on these issues is certainly not very long. In fact, it seems almost to have vanished in the 1950's.

The parties' positions on foreign policy during this same period are

documented by several studies devoted specifically to Congress and foreign policy-making. In *Congress and Foreign Policy*,[30] Robert A. Dahl
concluded, on the basis of selected foreign policy roll calls from 1933 to
1948, that "despite the frequently reiterated assertion that American
parties are little more than political versions of Tweedledum and Tweedledee . . . a striking difference" was apparent in their voting behavior.
At least before 1943, Republicans were isolationist, while Democrats
supported internationalist efforts. Republicans tended to oppose foreign
involvement, tariff reduction, participation in international organizations,
and foreign aid and loans, while Democrats tended to support these
measures.[31] One cannot argue with these tendencies which are plainly
apparent in the data, but again there is the matter of degree.

To what extent were the parties opposed on these issues? Since Dahl
presented his data in the form of percentages of both parties in favor
of various issues, it is a simple matter to construct index of likeness figures for these votes.[32] The figures, as did Rossiter's, reveal that the differences in party behavior on foreign policy are not always as sharp as
the author's verbal conclusion might indicate. Differences are most apparent in the case of the tariff, international organization from 1933 to
1940, and neutrality and isolation from 1933 to 1941, on which the indices of likeness were respectively 49, 48, and 43. Differences on military
policy and foreign aid loans and grants might easily be called less than
striking, since the index figures for these policy areas were respectively
88 and 77.

The ambiguity of party policy with respect to military affairs is supported by George Grassmuck who, in his *Sectional Biases in Congress
on Foreign Policy*, examined roll calls in this area from 1926 to 1941 and
found that neither party took a consistent stand either for, or against,
military expansion.[33] H. Bradford Westerfield, in *Foreign Policy and
Party Politics*, examined roll calls on foreign aid from 1943 to 1950 and
found that both parties were divided sectionally on this aspect of foreign
policy.[34] Eastern Republicans and southern Democrats were most noticeably dissident from the majority position of their parties, the former ap-

---

[30]Robert A. Dahl, *Congress and Foreign Policy* (New York: W. W. Norton,
1964) .

[31]*Ibid.*, 188–91.

[32]*Ibid.*, 189.

[33]George Grassmuck, *Sectional Biases in Congress on Foreign Policy* (Baltimore:
John Hopkins University Press, 1951) , 54.

[34]H. Bradford Westerfield, *Foreign Policy and Party Politics* (New Haven: Yale
University Press, 1955) , 32–46.

parently more internationalist and the latter less so than were their colleagues.[35]

Some additional clues to party differences in recent years on both
domestic and foreign policy may be found in various indices such as the
"presidential support" and "larger federal role" scores compiled by the
Congressional Quarterly and in the key liberal-labor votes compiled by
the AFL-CIO's Committee on Political Education. Though these indices
are somewhat less precise than other possible measurements in that
they cut across distinct policy dimensions of congressional voting, they
are useful if their limitations are borne in mind.[36] Lewis A. Froman has
employed *Congressional Quarterly* measurements in *Congressmen and
Their Constituencies* to establish that during the first session of the
Eighty-seventh Congress the parties' positions were clearly distinguishable.[37] As Table 9 reveals, according to these measurements the parties
were most divergent on the larger federal role issues, somewhat less so

TABLE 9

SCORES OF NORTHERN DEMOCRATS, SOUTHERN DEMOCRATS, AND
NORTHERN REPUBLICANS ON THREE SERIES OF
HOUSE ROLL CALL VOTES†

| Region and Party | Average Scores | | | |
	Kennedy Domestic Support Percent	Kennedy Foreign Support Percent	Larger Federal Role Percent	Total
Northern Democrats	83.8	83.9	92.7	(163)
Southern Democrats	56.9	57.2	56.4	(101)
Northern Republicans	34.4	53.3	17.3	(168)

†This table is quoted almost verbatim from Lewis A. Froman, *Congressmen and
Their Constituencies* (Chicago: Rand McNally and Co., 1963), p. 91. Forman compiled this data from the *Congressional Quarterly Weekly Report*, Nos. 42, 45, 1961.

on Kennedy Domestic Support issues, and still less on Kennedy Foreign
Support. Again, it is apparent that the parties' positions on foreign poli-

35*Ibid.*

36We have made this point above in our discussion of MacRae's use of Guttman
scale analysis. The AFL-CIO COPE scores are particularly lacking in precision
since domestic and foreign issues are combined in varying proportions from year
to year. At least, however, they offer a ranking of congressmen on liberal issues
as they are perceived by a major interest group.

37Lewis A. Froman, *Congressmen and Their Constituencies* (Chicago: Rand Mc-
Nally, 1963), 90–91.

cy have converged in recent years, as more Republicans have become internationalist and more southern Democrats less so. William J. Keefe and Morris S. Ogul have employed information published by the AFL-CIO's COPE to establish that in the years between 1947 and 1960 Democrats have scored distinctly more favorably than have Republicans on key liberal-labor legislation. On forty-two key roll calls of interest to the AFL-CIO from 1947 to 1960 Democrats scored 70.7 percent and Republicans 26 percent.[38]

Although MacRae's *Dimensions of Congressional Voting* and Truman's *The Congressional Party* resist comparison with the studies just examined (the end of which is to investigate the opposition of the congressional parties in specific policy areas), both describe in part the congressional parties. And insofar as these studies are descriptive of the congressional parties, they fall into a common category. Both are interested in revealing the structure of the parties *taken separately*. Truman's cluster-bloc scheme is intended to identify intra-party voting blocs, while MacRae's Guttman scaling analysis is meant to identify scale types inside each party which are somewhat analogous to these blocs. Both studies demonstrate that the parties were subject to considerable internal cleavage in the Eighty-first Congress. Both schemes reveal something about party cohesion and internal policy division at the same time. Each, though they are quite different, reveals in its own way that among both Democrats and Republicans there were men of extremely diverse policy orientations. Both indicate that the predominantly liberal, internationalist Democrats had their conservative unilateralists and that the more conservative Republicans had their liberal dissidents.

What, then, do these studies reveal about the congressional parties? Do the parties differ significantly? If so, to what extent and on what kinds of issues? The following factual conclusions may be drawn:

1. Party voting has occurred on approximately one-fifth of the roll calls taken during the fifteen sessions studied. (The average somewhat obscures the fact that party voting has been less frequent in twentieth century sessions.)

2. One party "party voted" against a majority of the other party on about two-thirds of the roll calls taken during the sessions studied by Lowell.

3. In the more recent sessions studied by Julius Turner both Democrats and Republicans maintained average indices of cohesion above 60 (more than 80 percent unity).

[38]William J. Keefe and Morris S. Ogul, *The American Legislative Process* (Englewood Cliffs, N. J., Prentice-Hall, 1964), 276–78.

4. Great fluctuations are apparent in cohesive party opposition from Congress to Congress and from session to session of single Congresses.

5. There is some evidence that variations in cohesive opposition of the parties in the House are related to national party realignments. The highest levels seem to have been reached immediately following critical elections. The lowest levels seem to have preceded such elections.

6. The policy dimensions of party opposition have changed considerably from period to period.

7. Liberalism and conservatism, as these concepts are employed in current studies, do not serve well to characterize the policy dimensions of party opposition in past eras.

8. Though policy conflict has varied greatly from time to time, never have the parties been sharply opposed on all issues that came before the House. The Democrats and Republicans were most cohesively opposed in the late 1890's.

9. In the 1860's the parties differed most sharply on matters related to the Civil War, the secessionist states, and the Negro. In the 1890's the most highly partisan issues involved the tariff, currency values, and anti-trust policy. Since 1932, the sharpest differences have appeared on domestic economic issues and foreign policy, though differences in the latter area have decreased since 1952. [39]

Though all of these generalizations have been borne out in the studies examined, there remains some doubt that they will answer the questions that have been posed since Lowell's time about "the differences between our parties." If one point stands out in the descriptive literature on the congressional parties, it is the tendency of individual observers to produce the most diverse sorts of conclusions from fairly similar data. For example, while Lowell concluded that the American congressional parties seldom opposed one another cohesively, a contemporary observer, Clinton Rossiter, concluded, also on the basis of reasonably similar data that the parties in recent years have been "at least a city block apart" on major issues. Such diverse perspectives should give us pause. How are

[39]It should be noted that the literature on differences between the parties in Congress in various historical periods has been dramatically expanded very recently by the appearances of several substantial studies. Unfortunately, these have come too late to be considered here. The reader's attention is directed especially to James S. Young, *The Washington Community, 1800–1828* (New York: Columbia University Press, 1966); Thomas B. Alexander, *Sectional Stress and Party Strength: A Study of Roll-Call Voting Patterns in the U.S. House of Representatives, 1836–1860* (Nashville: Vanderbilt University Press, 1967); Joel H. Silbey, *The Shrine of Party: Congressional Voting Behavior, 1841–1852* (Pittsburgh: University of Pittsburgh Press, 1967); and David B. Mayhew, *Party Loyalty Among Congressmen: The Difference Between Democrats and Republicans, 1947–1962* (Cambridge: Harvard University Press, 1966).

they to be explained? In part, certainly, they may be accounted for by the methodological decisions made by each author (e.g., whether or not to depend on the party vote as an indication of party differences). More important, however, would seem to be the fact that such decisions are closely related to the ideas of particular observers about what constitutes a proper, or perhaps acceptable, role for the congressional parties. In a sense, what is likely to be seen when looking at the behavior of the parties varies greatly, depending on what one wants to see or, at least, is willing to settle for. Such questions as "whether the parties are really no more than Tweedledum and Tweedledee," then, cannot be settled by the "facts" about the behavior of the parties. Not only facts but also value judgments are required if such questions are to be answered. Once this point is grasped, a great source of confusion is removed. Differing conclusions about the congressional parties have been rooted not so much in conflicting facts about their behavior as in differing conceptions of how the parties *ought* to perform. For example, when Democrats oppose Republicans 70 percent to 57 percent, a judgment must be made. Is this the manner in which our parties ought to behave? Ought we to expect more? Such a judgment surely cannot be objective. It will depend largely on the desires of individual observers. Facts alone cannot establish what the parties *ought* to do.

A close look at the second designated category of problems—those pertaining to factors influencing the congressman's voting behavior—reveals considerable theoretical and methodological continuity. While no two investigators have treated these variables in precisely the same manner, many agree that party and constituency are the most important influences on voting behavior. Again, while no two writers have treated constituency in quite the same way, they commonly regard socio-economic make-up, sectional location, and electoral marginality as important determinants of voting behavior.

Julius Turner is the only political scientist who has sought to employ the logic of statistical inference to *compare* the influence of party and constituency on congressional voting. It will be remembered that he employed the chi-square to investigate the significance of party and roll call voting and concluded that party pressure "is discernible on nearly nine-tenths of the roll calls examined." This conclusion, however, is subject to the rather strict limitations of the chi-square. Strictly speaking, Turner was justified in concluding only that on most House roll calls members of the same party voted together to a greater extent than they would have if they had been voting at random. As has already been noted, this is not an altogether satisfactory conclusion. Use of the chi-square did reveal that party was a significant factor on far more roll calls than was any one of the three constituency variables investigated. The major difficulty with a test of statistical significance in this context, however, is its inability to state anything about the strength of the relationships that are apparent. The chi-square as a test of significance can be used to ascertain only that on x number of roll calls party and/or constituency were significantly related to voting behavior. It cannot be used to investigate the comparative strength of these factors on various roll calls. Turner's conclusions, therefore, must be limited to the observation that party was significantly related to voting choice on more roll calls than was constituency. No other political scientist has used this method of comparing party and constituency influence, and its strict limitations would argue against its continued use in roll call analysis.

The remainder of the material with which the discussion deals is somewhat different from Turner's analysis in Chapter II of *Party and Constituency*, in that both party behavior and policy choices of congressmen are conceptualized as dependent variables to be explained by constituency factors of one kind or another. Since the analytical schemes in these studies are reasonably similar, their results are rather easily compared. The portions of *Party and Constituency* in which constituency factors are used to explain deviation from party loyalty fall into this category. By using frequency distributions of the index of loyalty for party members with different constituency attributes, Turner neatly demonstrated that constituency characteristics greatly help to account for loyalty and disloyalty in both parties. Here his analysis can be accepted without qualification. As far as it goes, it is quite sound. In the 1937 and 1944 sessions sectional location, rural population, and native stock were shown to be closely related to Democratic disloyalty. In the 1921 and 1931 sessions, however, these same factors were positively related to Democratic loyalty. Here again, historical variations must be taken into account. Coastal location, city population, and foreign stock were closely related to Republican disloyalty.[40]

Duncan MacRae's analysis of the influence of constituency is similar to Turner's in broad outline, though both the dependent and independent variables (voting behavior and constituency composition) are conceptualized somewhat differently. As measurements of voting behavior, Guttman type scales were used in place of the index of party loyalty, and occupational characteristics, section, and electoral marginality were used to differentiate constituencies. Again, a brief summary of material

40 Turner, *Party and Constituency*, 72–163, *passim*.

covered in Chapter I is required. The occupational factor, first, was related to the scales in a manner less obvious than might be expected.
Though a high percentage of constituents engaged in farming appeared
to dispose both Democrats and Republicans to conservatism on domestic
issues, higher concentrations of professional and managerial workers in
the cities seemed to make for very little difference in voting behavior.[41]
On race relations matters high concentrations of farmers were apparently related to more conservative voting behavior for Democrats, but no
such relationship existed for the Republicans.[42] In the urban areas there
was a slight relationship between race liberalism and lower occupational
status for Republicans, but not for Democrats.[43] On foreign aid issues
farm population was associated with a somewhat more conservative position for Republicans, but not for Democrats.[44] In the urban areas no relationships were apparent between the foreign policy scales and occupational characteristics.[45] Sectionalism appeared important in some policy
areas, but not in others. On the domestic, social, and economic issues, for
example, southern Democrats clustered at the conservative end of the
scale regardless of the rural-urban nature of their constituencies.[46] And,
or course, southern Democrats were grouped at the conservative end of
the race relations scale.[47] On foreign policy sectional variations were
apparent for both of the parties. Western Democrats were most liberal in
this area followed by northerners, border staters, and southerners.[48] Republicans from both of the coastal areas were found to be more liberal
than those from the interior.[49]

Although David Truman's analysis of constituency and voting behavior in *The Congressional Party* is more casual than those of Turner and
MacRae, it deserves a brief mention here. Attention has already been
called to the main features of Truman's analysis, especially with regard to
the absence of a thorough exploration of the relationship of bloc membership and constituency composition. It is important only to note, therefore, that Truman saw sectional differences as the most important correlates of bloc structure in both the congressional parties.[50]

Lewis A. Froman, in *Congressmen and Their Constituencies,* conduct-

[41]MacRae, *Dimensions,* 260–67.
[42]*Ibid.,* 267–70.
[43]*Ibid.,* 270–71. .
[44]*Ibid.,* 277.
[45]*Ibid.,* 276–77.
[46]*Ibid.,* 261.
[47]*Ibid.,* 267–69.
[48]*Ibid.,* 276.
[49]*Ibid.,* 277–78.
[50]Truman, *Congressional Party,* 42–93, 145–92, *passim.*

ed a similar type of analysis to test the relationship of socio-economic constituency characteristics to roll call voting. By holding the party variable constant, Froman claims to have found relationships between four constituency factors—percentages of owner occupied property, nonwhite population, urban population, and population density—and the *Congressional Quarterly's* Kennedy Support Score during the first session of the Eighty-seventh Congress.[51]

On additional study of the relationship between constituency characteristics and voting behavior may be mentioned, though it is somewhat different from those already considered. Warren Miller and Donald Stokes, in an ingenious investigation that will be discussed further below, examined the relationship between constituency attitudes (survey data) and roll call votes (scaled according to the Guttman procedure) and found fairly strong relationships in the policy areas of domestic economic issues and civil rights, but no relationship at all in the area of foreign policy.[52]

Several attempts have been made to investigate the relationship of electoral competition and roll call voting. Not surprisingly, the findings of these studies are difficult to compare, since individual investigators have had slightly different purposes and have employed somewhat different research schemes. Actually, a close inspection of this literature reveals that two distinct hypotheses have been investigated. The first is that a relationship exists between electoral competition itself and the policy stance of the congressman. The second is slightly different—that as electoral marginality increases, the legislator becomes more sensitive to *other* constituency influences. The first idea has been explored by Samuel P. Huntington, who found that congressmen from competitive districts took more extreme policy positions (Democrats more liberal and Republicans more conservative) than those from areas more dominated by one party.[53] Close attention to Huntington's article reveals that he was not so much interested in exploring the effect of marginality taken as an independent

[51]Froman's measure of association is the phi coefficient. Since phi is only applicable to fourfold distributions of two dichotomous variables, it is not at all clear how he applied it to measure association between two variables that are not dichotomous (the *CQ* "Kennedy Support Scores" and the constituency characteristics). Since he does not explain his analysis at this point, it is impossible to judge its validity. It should also be noted that the correlations are rather low. The highest is .26. See Froman, *Congressmen and Constituencies*, 92–93.

[52]Warren E. Miller and Donald E. Stokes, "Constituency Influence in Congress," *American Political Science Review*, LVII (March, 1963), 45–56. The correlation coefficients in these three areas were, respectively, 0.3, 0.6 and –0.09. p. 49.

[53]Samuel P. Huntington, "A Revised Theory of American Party Politics," *American Political Science Review*, XLIV (September, 1950), 669–77.

variable as in countering E. E. Schattschneider's somewhat ambiguous suggestion that where the American parties are "most evenly balanced numerically . . . they are most alike in programmatic terms." [54] The second hypothesis has been suggested by Duncan MacRae, who found that in the Massachusetts House of Representatives, "representatives whose previous election margins were close tend to reflect constituency characteristics in their votes more closely than do those with wider margins." [55] The status of both these hypotheses, after some additional research, remains in considerable doubt.

Lewis A. Froman explored the relationship between degree of electoral competition and both party loyalty and liberalism-conservatism for Republicans and northern Democrats.[56] While Froman cited MacRae's Massachusetts study as a source of his hypotheses, his work is not a replication of MacRae's since no attempt was made to control other constituency factors to examine their influence as marginality increased. Froman presented a simple table showing the relationship between electoral competition and voting behavior with other factors uncontrolled. He concluded that while party loyalty did not decline markedly as marginality increased, policy stance became more moderate.[57] The first conclusion can be accepted, but the second cannot. The data in Table 10, which Froman presented, simply do not support this conclusion. In each case the differences in policy stance are quite small as competition is varied, and in several cases changes are in the wrong direction. Interestingly, these data may be used (though Froman does not employ them for this purpose) to test Huntington's idea that congressmen from more competitive constituencies are more "extreme" in their policy positions than are those from safer constituencies. This hypothesis is, ironically, just the opposite of the one Froman tested. In fact, these data will not support either hypothesis convincingly. As marginality is not shown to be positively related to policy moderation, neither is it shown to be related to extremism. Thus, Huntington's earlier findings are cast into doubt by an analysis not intended to subject them to scrutiny. To make the matter more confusing, Duncan MacRae's attempt to extend his earlier investigation of the Massachusetts House to the U.S. House yielded a rather cryptic result. As marginality increased, Republicans became more responsive to constituency characteristics, but Democrats did not.[58] Thus, neither hy-

[54]*Ibid.*, 669.
[55]MacRae, "The Relation Between Roll Call Votes and Constituencies", 1055
[56]Froman, *Congressmen and Constituencies*, 110–17.
[57]*Ibid.*, 115–16.
[58]MacRae, *Dimensions*, 284–89.

pothesis has been convincingly borne out for the U.S. House of Representatives.

TABLE 10

ELECTORAL MARGINS AND POLICY CHOICE: HOUSE;
FIRST SESSION, EIGHTY-SEVENTH CONGRESS[†]

Degree of Party Competition		Kennedy Domestic Support	Larger Federal Role	Conservative Coalition
Republicans				
1	↑	29.8	10.6	79.3
2		34.0	16.5	74.0
3		35.8	20.6	71.1
4	Safer	34.1	17.4	78.3
Democratic				
	Safer			
5		86.2	93.4	14.4
6		81.8	93.6	12.2
7		84.3	94.3	8.6
8	↓	85.0	95.0	9.7

†Source: Lewis A. Froman, *Congressmen and Their Constituencies* (Chicago: Rand McNally and Co.; 1963) , 114.

The following generalizations, consequently, may be extracted from the studies included in the second category:

1. Party is statistically related to voting behavior on more roll call votes than are three constituency factors—metropolitanism-ruralism, foreign-native population, and sectional location.

2. The socio-economic characteristics of constituencies are related to the party loyalty and/or policy choice of the congressman. Although all of our information on this matter is limited to sessions of the House after 1921, historical variations are evident. There is evidence that the correlates of party loyalty and disloyalty are altered greatly by party realignments. Julius Turner discovered that all three of the constituency factors associated with Democratic loyalty in the 1921 and 1931 sessions became associated with disloyalty in the 1937 and 1944 sessions.

3. After 1932 socio-economic constituency characteristics have been related to party loyalty and/or policy choice in the following manner:

a. Metropolitanism, foreign and nonwhite population, and population density have been positively associated with Democratic loyalty.

b. Rural and native population and high percentage of owner-occupied housing have been negatively related to Democratic loyalty.

c. Rural and native population have been positively related to Republican loyalty.

d. Urban and foreign population have been negatively related to Republican loyalty.

e. For Democrats farm constituencies are related to domestic conservatism.

f. On racial issues, farm population is positively related to conservatism for Democrats, but not for Republicans.

g. On foreign affairs issues, farm population is positively related to conservatism for Republicans, but not for Democrats.

h. In urban areas low socio-economic status is positively related to racial liberalism for Republicans, but not for Democrats.

4. Sectional factors since 1932 have been related to party loyalty and/ or policy choice in the following manner:

a. Southern location is associated with Democratic disloyalty.

b. Southern Democrats tend to be more conservative than their colleagues in all policy areas.

c. Coastal Republicans tend to be more disloyal than those from other sections.

d. Coastal Republicans have been distinctly more internationalist than those from the interior.

Though these generalizations have emerged from one or more of the studies examined, their tentative nature should be strongly emphasized. Often they are rather cryptic. It will be noted that no attempt has been made to formulate generalizations about the relationship of electoral competition and voting. The reason is simply that the information available is at best inconclusive and at worst openly contradictory. Clarification must await further testing of the hypotheses mentioned. Consequently, there remains today a need for continued inquiry into the relationship of the factors that have been examined to congressional voting.

Chapter III

PARTY DIFFERENCES
IN THE EIGHTY-SIXTH
AND EIGHTY-SEVENTH CONGRESSES

A NUMBER of quite different approaches may be taken to describe the behavior of the congressional parties. Each, it has been seen, is likely to have its own unique advantages and shortcomings. Of the several techniques available for the purpose, none is sufficiently versatile to convey everything that the investigator would like to know. It would seem appropriate here, then, to rely on several which are particularly effective in answering specific questions about the parties. Two approaches—Turner's use of the statistic, chi-square, and David Truman's Rice-Beyle cluster bloc scheme—have been rejected. Both of these, for all of their laboriousness in application, would seem for reasons previously elaborated to possess little merit as tools for description of party behavior. I have employed a number of reasonably simple devices such as the party vote, a slightly altered version of the party vote that may be called the modified party vote, the index of cohesion, the index of likeness, and the index of party loyalty to answer several questions about party opposition and cohesion. Since there may be some tendency today to resort to novel, high-powered devices in the study of legislative behavior, the continued applicability of these relatively straightforward techniques is strongly emphasized. To describe the policy differences of the parties in the Eighty-sixth and Eighty-seventh Congresses, I have employed the simple strategy of dividing roll calls taken during these congresses into three categories—modified party votes, majority opposition votes, and party agreement votes—to examine the policy content of recorded votes on which the parties were more or less in opposition. To obtain a somewhat more accurate focus on the policy dimensions of party behavior in

62

recent years, I have utilized certain roll calls of major importance (in the form of Guttman scales) to highlight the differences between the parties. As the analysis proceeds, it will become clear that one obvious source of party disunity in recent years has been the tendency of southern Democrats to break away from their northern colleagues on a number of important policy questions. So great has the dissidence of southern Democrats become in these years that a major revision of V. O. Key's treatment of their behavior in earlier sessions is now in order.[1]

An understanding of the political environment of the period is helpful in analyzing party behavior in the Eighty-sixth and Eighty-seventh Congresses. No attempt has been made here, however, to account in depth for presidential actions or legislative activities beyond those manifest in roll call voting.[2]

In one sense, at least, the Eighty-sixth Congress met under unusual conditions. A Republican President faced for his third two-year period a Congress controlled by the opposition party. While such sharing by the two major parties of our national institutions has not been uncommon throughout American history, President Eisenhower was the first Chief Executive of either party to be faced with three consecutive Congresses controlled by the opposition. The general political environment was such from 1959 to 1961 that the institutional disharmony between President and Congress so often typical of American politics was unusually great. The congressional Democrats, fresh from a confidence-inspiring landslide victory in the elections of 1958, were anxious to seize initiative from the White House and establish their own record before the presidential election of 1960. The President, a "lame duck" due to the 22nd Amendment, nevertheless exerted a maximum effort (considering his distaste for presidential leadership of Congress) to curb the Democratic spenders, or "budget busters," as he called them, who appeared so anxious to expand old federal programs and initiate new ones. Throughout the session he reiterated his firm intention to use the veto power if necessary to prevent spending from getting out of hand.

[1]See Key, *Southern Politics*, 369–82.

[2]As already noted in the Introduction the author is well aware that this aproach to legislative politics captures only a small part of the activity in the House of Representatives during this period. There is no implication here that other phenomena are somehow less important than roll call voting. Our argument is that analysis of roll call votes is merely one valid approach to the study of party and constituency influences in Congress. An exclusive analytical focus on roll calls does facilitate treatment of a broader range of behavior in one respect. This mode of analysis allows the observer to treat several sessions of Congress. An attempt to capture the total reality of even a single session would quickly exhaust even the most ambitious investigator.

As the first session of the Eighty-sixth Congress wore on, it became clear both to those who wished the congressional Democrats well and to those who feared for the safety of the Republic that national politics were in a serious state of deadlock. Hampered by presidential opposition and by southern defection on a number of important fronts, the congressional Democrats were stymied. Two new housing bills were passed, only to be vetoed before a third watered-down measure was finally signed into law. No new legislation appeared to be forthcoming in what seemed to northern liberal Democrats two "must" areas—civil rights and area redevelopment (depressed areas). So impotent, in fact, were the Democrats that they proved unable to prevent substitution on the House floor of the tough Landrum-Griffin bill for a mild labor bill sponsored by Democratic leaders and its final passage into law late in the session. In the second session this state of deadlock persisted. The much discussed "Medicare" plan failed, as the much more conservative Kerr-Mills bill finally gained congressional and presidential approval. New school aid legislation died in the House Rules Committee after passage by both houses, and the new minimum wage bill failed to emerge from conference. An area redevelopment act finally passed only to meet the President's veto, which could not be overturned. Finally, after a long and arduous struggle, a new civil rights measure (The Civil Rights Act of 1960) passed only after it was rendered virtually meaningless (in the eyes both of supporters and opponents) by amendments supported by coalitions of Republicans and southern Democrats in both houses. Despite their swollen majorities—nearly 2 to 1 in both houses—the Democrats proved unequal to the combined opposition of the President and coalitions of Republicans and southern Democrats inside Congress.

The hairline victory of John F. Kennedy in the presidential election of 1960 altered this state of deadlock, in one respect at least, by returning the White House to Democratic control. The slim presidential victory, however, could not obscure the failure of the Democrats to maintain their congressional strength at the peak 1958 level. Interestingly, Kennedy's coattails were insufficiently strong to pull many of the congressmen who had been elected by marginal votes in 1958 back into office. A major source of the difficulties with Congress that were to plague the new President until his death in 1963 was thus apparent from the beginning; the Democratic margin of control in the House dropped from 283–153 in 1958 to 263–174 in 1960. Under these conditions success of the Kennedy legislative program would depend almost entirely on the behavior of the southern Democrats who had so often defected from Democratic majorities in the previous Congress. The record now clearly reveals that repeated defections of the southerners were more responsible than any other factor for the failure of the President to master his congressional majority during the period from 1961 to 1963.

A brief review of the two sessions of the Eighty-seventh Congress demonstrates that while the deadlock of the previous two years was mitigated somewhat, it was never really overcome.

Early in the first session the struggle over expansion of the notoriously obstructionist House Rules Committee, even though it was finally resolved to presidential satisfaction, augured badly for Kennedy's chances of success in days to come. Every ounce of Speaker Sam Rayburn's energies was apparently necessary to eke out a hairline victory over the usual coalition of conservative Republicans and southern Democrats.[3] In the remainder of the first session, though area redevelopment, minimum wage, and housing legislation was passed, the major aid to education bill was rejected by the Republican–southern Democratic coalition on the House floor in August, and "must" "Medicare" and tax revision measures were stalled completely. In the second session, although the tax revision bill finally passed, the Medicare plan was defeated on the floor of the Senate, and both the aid to higher education and urban affairs bills were defeated in the House. Despite vigorous presidential leadership, the Democrats had again proved unequal to the combined opposition of a determined Republican minority and defections in their own southern wing. The President's bold attempt to "get this country moving again," as he so often put it, was only partially successful.

To analyze the roll call voting of the Eighty-sixth and Eighty-seventh Congresses it is necessary to describe the behavior of the parties during these four years.[4] As previously stressed, one traditional concern of investigators of party behavior is party unity or cohesion. Both Julius Turner and V. O. Key, for example, employed Stuart Rice's index of cohesion to investigate the unity of the parties on roll call votes in selected

[3] See Milton C. Cummings and Robert L. Peabody, "The Decision to Enlarge the Committee on Rules," in Robert L. Peabody and Nelson W. Polsby (eds.), *New Perspectives on the House of Representatives* (Chicago: Rand McNally, 1963), 167–94.

[4] All roll call data in this chapter and in the remainder of this study have been compiled from the *Congressional Quarterly Almanac*, 1959, 1960, 1961, and 1962, hereinafter cited as *CQ Almanac*. Most often the data were published there in raw form. The various indices have been calculated by the author. It should be mentioned that references to southern Democrats include those from the eleven Confederate states. Border Democrats are classed as northern. When no other source is cited for data in tables, it should be assumed that the source is the *CQ Almanac*. In the analysis that follows, near-unanimous roll calls (those on which the minority amounted to less than 10 percent of the majority) have been omitted. This practice, instituted by Key, has its logic in the assumption that these matters of almost complete consensus reveal very little about party behavior.

sessions of the House of Representatives.[5] While the index of cohesion does not of itself reveal anything about party opposition, it is a useful device if an over-all view of party cohesion for a specific time period is desired. By averaging the index for selected groups over a session or series of sessions, some indication of the parties' ability to present a united front on roll call votes may be obtained. In Table 11 such average index of cohesion figures are presented for selected groups for the four sessions of the Eighty-sixth and Eighty-seventh Congresses.

TABLE 11

AVERAGE INDEX OF COHESION FOR SELECTED GROUPS:
HOUSE OF REPRESENTATIVES; BY SESSION, 1959–62†

| | Year | | | | Average, |
Group	1959	1960	1961	1962	All Sessions
Democrats	61.2	50.6	61.4	64.7	59.5
Republicans	60.6	51.0	54.1	53.6	54.8
So. Democrats	65.9	49.6	49.4	50.6	53.9
No. Democrats	73.7	73.0	81.2	84.2	78.0

†Near-unanimous roll calls (those on which the minority consisted of less than 10 percent of the majority) have been omitted.

As the table reveals, though there are some sizable deviations from session to session, the average index of cohesion for Democrats and Republicans, respectively, is 59.5 and 54.8—somewhat lower for both parties than in the six sessions examined by Julius Turner from 1921 to 1944. In general, the cohesion of the two parties differs little from the earlier sessions. Over the entire range of roll calls taken, the parties appear reasonably cohesive; approximately 80 percent of Democrats and somewhat more than 75 percent of Republicans voted with their respective parties on the average roll call vote.

An interesting perspective on Democratic behavior may be obtained by tabulating the average index of cohesion figures separately for northern and southern members of the party.[6] Table 11 reveals sharp differences in cohesion between these two groups. The average index of cohesion for northern Democrats alone is strikingly high—78.0 for the four sessions. At least on the average roll call taken during this period, northern

[5]See above, pp. 11, 41fn. 6.

[6]Throughout this chapter the practice will be followed of describing the behavior of Democrats, southern Democrats and northern Democrats. No attempt will be made to divide Republicans into comparable sectional groups.

Democrats were quite cohesive. Between 85 and 90 percent voted together on the average record vote. The cohesion of the Democrats, therefore, *when the southerners are subtracted from their ranks,* is nearly as high as that of the British parliamentary parties during the sessions of the House of Commons examined by Julius Turner.[7] In contrast, southern Democrats appear to be about as cohesive as the Republicans; somewhat more than 75 percent voted together on the average.

Table 12 puts cohesion of the parties in sharper focus. The question here involves the percentage of roll calls on which the selected party groups were able to maintain high cohesion (defined as an index of cohesion of 70 or above—85 percent or more members voting together). As the table reveals, the two parties differed hardly at all in this respect. Both were capable of maintaining this very high degree of unity on only a minority of roll calls—between 37 and 38 percent. The table is especially useful, however, in highlighting the previously cited differences between northern and southern Democrats. While southerners maintained high cohesion on only 36 percent of roll calls during the four sessions, northern Democrats maintained such cohesion on nearly three-fourths (74.3 percent) of these votes.

TABLE 12

HIGH COHESION VOTES: PERCENTAGE OF ROLL CALLS ON WHICH
SELECTED PARTY GROUPS MAINTAINED AN INDEX OF
COHESION OF 70 OR ABOVE; HOUSE OF
REPRESENTATIVES, BY SESSION,
1959–62†

Group	Year				Average, All Sessions
	1959	1960	1961	1962	
Democrats	44.0	25.3	39.8	41.0	37.5
Republicans	52.0	28.0	34.1	34.9	37.3
So. Democrats	56.0	30.7	27.3	30.1	36.0
No. Democrats	68.0	65.3	78.4	85.5	74.3

†Near-unanimous roll calls have been omitted.

While the index of cohesion demonstrates only one dimension of party behavior, it is a useful device by which to gauge the ability of the parties to present a united front in roll call voting. As these figures reveal, during the Eighty-sixth and Eighty-seventh Congresses the two parties re-

[7]Turner, *Party and Constituency,* 24.

mained nearly as cohesive as they were during the six earlier sessions studied by Julius Turner.[8] During the more recent sessions, however, Democrats would have been much more united if not for the rather general dissidence of a larger number of their southern members. Since no obvious sectional divisions can be observed for Republicans, the reasons for their failure to maintain greater unity will be examined later when the constituency characteristics of those members who defected regularly from majorities of their party are analyzed.

To this point the analysis has revealed nothing about party opposition in the Eighty-sixth and Eighty-seventh Congresses. Two questions may now be raised. How often were the parties opposed during the four sessions on which we have focused attention? To what extent were the parties able to maintain their cohesion when they opposed one another? Several approaches may be used to pinpoint various aspects of these two questions.

Although the party vote as used by Lowell and Turner, is a rather limited analytical device, it will be worthwhile to employ it briefly in gauging party opposition for the Eighty-sixth and Eighty-seventh Congresses to establish some comparability with material already examined. Table 13 records the number and percentage of party votes in the four sessions of these congresses. Interestingly enough, party voting seems to

TABLE 13

PARTY VOTING IN THE HOUSE:
BY SESSION, 1959–62†

Congress, Session, Year	Total Roll Calls	Party Votes	
		Number	Percent
86:1 (1959)	75	6	8.0
86:2 (1960)	75	2	2.7
87:1 (1961)	88	3	3.4
87:2 (1962)	83	5	6.0
Average Percentage of Roll Calls Party Votes for Four Sessions			5.0

†Near-unanimous roll calls have been omitted.

be a much rarer phenomenon today than during either the nineteenth century sessions studied by Lowell or the twentieth century sessions examined by Turner. During the entire period for which information is

[8]See above, p. 11.

available, in only one session of the House, 1928, was the level of party voting as low as in the period from 1959 to 1962. Whereas the average percentage of party votes in the two earlier periods amounted respective-

TABLE 14

PARTY OPPOSITION BY MAJORITIES:
PERCENT NUMBER AND PERCENTAGE OF HOUSE ROLL CALLS
ON WHICH 50 PERCENT OR MORE DEMOCRATS OPPOSED 50 PERCENT
OR MORE REPUBLICANS; BY SESSION, 1959–62†

Congress, Session, Year	Total Roll Calls	Number	Percent
86:1 (1959)	75	47	62.7
86:2 (1960)	75	49	65.3
87:1 (1961)	88	56	63.6
87:2 (1962)	83	55	66.3
Totals	321	206	64.2

†Near-unanimous roll calls have been omitted.

ly to 30.9 percent and 17.1 percent, the average in the recent sessions is 5 percent. Judgments about trends must be made with caution for there are many sessions for which we do not have this kind of information. However, since the average percentage of party votes for the five sessions studied by Turner (1944–48) is 14.6 percent,[9] it seems reasonable to infer that parties' ability to maintain 90 percent versus 90 percent opposition declined significantly during the 1950's.

The party vote, of course, demands quite a bit from the parties, so to speak. As has been noted exclusive reliance on this particular standard will nearly always dictate the conclusion that the congressional parties seldom oppose one another cohesively. In the period from 1959 to 1962, for example, the device is simply too insensitive to pick up a great deal of party opposition that other measurements will record. Since not all observers agree that the parties need to be opposed to this extent to be significantly different, it is helpful to employ additional methods of measurement. One such approach is to tabulate "majority opposition votes"— those on which a simple majority or more of Democrats opposed a simple majority or more of Republicans. (Application of this approach to data from Lowell's *Influence of Party Upon Legislation* in Chapter II revealed considerable party opposition.) Table 14 demonstrates that the parties

[9]See above, p. 11.

were opposed by majorities, or more, on nearly two-thirds (64.2 percent to be exact) of the roll calls analyzed for the four sessions of the Eighty-sixth and Eighty-seventh Congresses. Even though a particular observer

TABLE 15

AVERAGE INDEX OF COHESION

FOR SELECTED HOUSE PARTY GROUPS ON WHICH A MAJORITY

OF DEMOCRATS OPPOSED A MAJORITY

OF REPUBLICANS: BY SESSION, 1959–62†

Group	Year				Average, All Sessions
	1959	1960	1961	1962	
Democrats	70.1	49.9	61.0	63.7	61.2
Republicans	67.6	53.1	61.7	59.2	60.4
So. Democrats	68.2	49.5	44.3	49.9	53.0
No. Democrats	80.5	69.9	81.6	82.7	78.7

†Near-unanimous roll calls have been omitted.

may not be willing to accept majority opposition as sufficient evidence that the proposition, "the parties seldom differ," is inaccurate, Table 14 does reveal considerable party opposition. It would seem likely from all of the information reviewed that this sort of party opposition has been common throughout most of our history.

Another question of interest involves the ability of the parties to maintain cohesion when opposed to one another on these majority opposition votes. A simple means of determining this is to average the index of cohesion for all roll calls on which party majorities opposed one another. The result of such an analysis may be seen in Table 15. On these roll calls, the table reveals, the cohesion of both parties was actually slightly higher on the average than on those votes on which majorities of both parties agreed with one another. Calculating the index of cohesion in this manner eliminates the suspicion that where party opposition is not controlled in the analysis, then the index is inflated by high cohesion on matters of consensus between the two parties. It is now possible to say (at least for the Eighty-sixth and Eighty-seventh Congresses) that the cohesion of both party groups is higher where party opposition was a factor. Certainly, it is difficult to maintain that "the parties seldom differ," when, as this approach reveals, they opposed one another by majorities on nearly two-thirds of roll calls taken during these four sessions and at the same time maintained over 80 percent unity (index of cohesion above 60) . While there was little 90 percent versus 90 percent opposition during these four sessions, there was, however, a great deal of majority versus majority opposition accompanied by high cohesion.

Still another perspective on party opposition may be obtained by using the "modified party vote"—defined as a roll call on which 75 percent of one party opposed 75 percent of the other. While this standard is admittedly as arbitrary as the party vote, it is proposed with certain important political criteria in mind. While no argument will be made here that voters *do* perceive votes of this nature as party votes, it would seem reasonable to assume that this amount of opposition should satisfy most advocates of responsible legislative parties on at least two important grounds. First, if Democrats and Republicans had behaved in this manner throughout the Eighty-sixth and Eighty-seventh Congresses, the Democratic majority would have had no trouble whatever passing all of its programs. Second, this much differentiation of the parties' positions would seem to make their respective stands clear to those who study congressional voting. Since these major goals of "party reformers" can be obtained with less than 90 percent versus 90 percent opposition, it appears unnecessary to demand that much cohesive opposition. It seems sensible, rather, to adopt the modified party vote as a rough, arbitrary

TABLE 16

MODIFIED PARTY VOTES:
NUMBER AND PERCENTAGE OF ROLL CALLS
ON WHICH DEMOCRATS OPPOSED REPUBLICANS, BOTH
MAINTAINING AN INDEX OF COHESION OF
50 OR MORE (75 PERCENT UNITY) ; HOUSE OF
REPRESENTATIVES, BY SESSION, 1959–62†

Congress, Session, Year	Total Roll Calls	Number	Percent
86:1 (1959)	75	29	38.7
86:2 (1960)	75	16	21.3
87:1 (1961)	88	28	31.8
87:2 (1962)	83	29	34.9
Totals	321	102	31.8

†Near-unanimous roll calls have been omitted.

standard. On how many roll calls, then, from 1959 to 1962 did the parties satisfy this standard? Table 16 reveals that with the exception of the 1959 session the parties satisfied these criteria on 30 to 40 percent of roll calls taken. On the average, during these four sessions the parties conformed to the modified party vote on nearly a third of all roll calls analyzed. Again, it would seem rather difficult to maintain in the face of this information that "the parties seldom differed."

To this point this analysis has presented a general picture of party opposition and cohesion without discussing the substance of policy. In order to understand the policy differences between the parties in the Eighty-sixth and Eighty-seventh Congresses certain questions must be asked. On what kinds of issues were the parties most sharply opposed? Where were party differences most apparent? Least apparent? A reasonable way to approach these questions is to divide the roll calls taken during the four sessions from 1959 to 1962 into three categories—"modified party votes," "party opposition votes," and "party agreement votes." The roll calls falling into these three divisions may then be analyzed according to their policy content. In this manner it is possible to determine the kinds of issues on which the parties differed greatly, those on which differences are apparent but are not sufficient to satisfy the criteria of modified party voting, and finally, those on which majorities of both parties voted on the same side of the question. One virtue of such an analytical scheme is that *political* rather than *statistical* criteria are employed to separate the various classes of roll calls. As has been seen, those issues falling into the modified party vote category would seem to fit the model of party behavior proposed by advocates of responsible parties. Those issues, on the other hand, falling into the party agreement category constitute, politically speaking, the opposite end of a continuum, even if such a device as the index of likeness or the chi-square might indicate differences between the positions of the parties. Where a majority of both parties vote on the same side of a question, *politically* there is no party difference of fundamental importance.

Analysis of the policy content of roll calls falling into the first category—modified party votes—is very revealing. In each of the four sessions these issues are overwhelmingly of a domestic economic nature. For the most part, they are the highly controversial spending, regulatory, and welfare issues of the sort that Duncan MacRae in *Dimensions* included in his Fair Deal Scales. Noticeably absent from this category are foreign policy, civil rights, and civil liberties.[10] Clearly, the parties were most

---

[10]In three of the four sessions no foreign policy roll calls fall into this classification. In the second session of the Eighty-sixth Congress the House parties evidenced 75 percent versus 75 percent opposition on two foreign policy roll calls dealing with United Nations Bonds and a resolution expressing determination to resist the spread of communism from Cuba. The first of these has obvious spending overtones. A co-

sharply divided during the Eighty-sixth and Eighty-seventh Congresses on domestic "class" issues of the sort that have been prominent in national politics throughout the New Deal-Fair Deal-New Frontier-Great Society period. In this area, at least, there is no difficulty at all in placing the Democrats in the liberal category—favorable to spending, economic regulation, welfare, and expansion of the functions and activities of the national government—and Republicans in the conservative category—opposed to these measures. While no attempt will be made here to compile an exhaustive list of the roll calls falling into the modified party vote category, the following are typical:

HR 2256	(86:1) —Veterans' Housing Bill. A motion to recommit the bill and delete a section providing for a direct loan program.
HR 1011	(86:1) —Extension of Federal Airport Construction Act. Amendment to cut authorizations.
HR 3460	(86:1) —TVA Bonds. Authorize bonds to finance new power facilities. A motion to recommit the bill.
S 57	(86:1) —Housing Act of 1959. A motion to recommit the bill and substitute a much less extensive bill.
HR 7086	(86:1) —Amend Renegotiation Act of 1951 in order to recapture excess profits on defense contracts. A motion to recommit.
HR 3610	(86:1) —Amend 1948 Water Pollution Control Act. A motion to recommit the bill and require the states to match federal grants dollar for dollar.
HR 7509	(86:1) —Fiscal 1960 Public Works Appropriations Bill. A motion to recommit and cut five percent off each item of $5 million or more.
S 722	(86:2) —Area Redevelopment Act. A motion to recommit.
HR 12261	(86:2) —Farm Surplus Reduction Act of 1960. A motion to recommit and report back on the cutting of wheat production by twenty percent, retaining supports at seventy-five percent of parity.
H.Res.127	(87:1) —Resolution to increase the membership of the House Rules Committee from twelve to fifteen.
S1	(87:1) —Area Redevelopment Act. A motion to recommit, cutting authorizations, and deleting certain provisions.
HR 3935	(87:1) —Fair Labor Standards Act Amendments. Vote on accepting the conference report in which strong liberal provisions were restored.
HR 6094	(87:1) —Fixing of ceiling on appropriations for salaries of members

---

alition of Republicans and southern Democrats supported an amendment to bar the UN bonds until the General Assembly accepted the World Court's ruling on the financial obligation of U.N. members.

and employees of the Council of Economic Advisors. A motion to recommit, lowering the ceiling.

H.Res.305   (87:1) —A resolution disapproving the President's reorganization plan for the Federal Trade Commission.

HR 6028   (87:1) —Housing Act of 1961. A motion to recommit.

HR 8028   (87:1) —Authorization of funds for projects and training of personnel for controlling juvenile delinquency. An amendment to limit funds to the District of Columbia.

HR 6360   (87:2) —Authorization of a fourth Assistant Secretary of Congress to administer scientific and technological programs.

HR 8723   (87:2) —Strengthening of 1938 Welfare and Pension Plans Disclosure Act. A motion to recommit the bill and prohibit associate union memberships by the Labor Department's Pension and Welfare Division employees.

HR 10606   (87:2) —Public Welfare Amendments of 1962. Recommit and delete a provision increasing payments to the aged and the blind.

HR 11665   (87:2) —Amendments to the National School Lunch Act of 1946. Recommit and remove authorization allowing the Secretary of Agriculture to take into consideration the need of students for free or reduced-price lunches.

HR 1190   (87:2) —Increase the ceiling on the national debt. A motion to recommit and lower the ceiling.

S 167   (87:2) —Compel businesses to turn over to the Justice Department evidence to be used in anti-trust investigations. A motion to send the bill back to conference, insisting on the acceptance of House amendments.

HR 12392   (87:2) —Farm bill, extending 1962 wheat and feed grains programs for one year, setting new supports for corn, feed grains, etc.

HR 10904   (87:2) —Fiscal 1963 appropriations for Departments of Labor and Health, Education and Welfare. A motion to send the bill back to conference insisting on House disagreement with the Senate's increase of funds appropriated for the National Institutes of Health.

On these kinds of issues, at least, there can be no possibility of the conclusion that "the parties seldom differ." Cohesive opposition was common on domestic economic, regulatory, and welfare matters throughout the four sessions examined.

With respect to the tendency of southern Democrats to defect from party majorities that has been already noted, it is interesting to observe their behavior on these modified party vote roll calls. Table 17, which presents average index of cohesion data for the four sessions, indicates much lower unity for southern than northern Democrats in each case. Though the Democrats were usually able to carry along a majority of southerners on these votes, a considerable number of the latter defected on the average. Table 17, also strikingly highlights the very great unity of the two parties in the aggregate on a considerable number of roll calls during the four sessions. In fact, this is a close approximation of the sort of party behavior that is usually associated with the British parliamentary parties. Both Democrats and Republicans on the average were capable of maintaining between 85 and 90 percent unity on these roll calls, which amount to nearly a third of those examined.

TABLE 17

AVERAGE INDEX OF COHESION
ON MODIFIED PARTY VOTES:
HOUSE BY SESSION, 1959–62†

Congress, Session, Year	Democrats	Republicans	Southern Democrats	Northern Democrats
86:1 (1959)	79.3	78.0	66.5	86.7
86:2 (1960)	70.3	70.5	45.1	90.4
87:1 (1961)	73.5	75.9	45.7	92.5
87:2 (1962)	73.5	78.3	52.1	87.0
Average per Session	74.2	75.7	52.4	89.2

†Near-unanimous roll calls have been omitted.

The roll calls falling into the second category—"party opposition votes"—are quite similar in content to those just examined; by far, the greatest number of these votes were taken on domestic economic, regulatory, and welfare measures. There is no need to compile a sample of these roll calls, but it is important to note that many of them occurred on issues of major importance—for example, the Veterans' Housing Bill (1959), fiscal 1960 public works appropriations, substitution of the Landrum-Griffin bill (1959), the Area Redevelopment Bills (1960 and 1961), the School Construction Assistance Act (1960), Fair Labor Standards Act Amendments (1960 and 1961), the national debt ceiling (1961), several administrative reorganization plans (1961), the plan for a Department of Urban Affairs (1962), aid to education (1962), and Fair Labor Standards Act Amendments in the same year. Interestingly, though, the second category includes several roll calls on foreign policy matters—on the Foreign Investment Incentive Tax Act (1960), the Mutual Security Appropriations Acts (1960, 1961 and 1962), and the Trade

Expansion Act of 1962. And, although no civil rights roll calls fall into this category, a vote in 1959 on HR 3, a civil liberties measure (to limit federal pre-emption of subversive activities matters to those specifically designated by Congress), is included in this group.

In essence, this second group of roll calls is composed of policy questions on which party differences are clearly evident to the specialist observer, but are not great enough to satisfy what have been specified as reasonable minimum criteria for placating proponents of responsible parties. The reasons for the parties' shortcomings from this point of view are quite varied. On the domestic economic roll calls in this category the Democrats were plagued frequently with southern defections. On such important measures as the Housing Act of 1959, the substitution of the Landrum-Griffin bill in 1959, the Area Redevelopment Bill in 1960, the School Construction Act of 1960, the national debt ceiling (1960), the minimum wage (1961), the Emergency Education Act of 1961, the Department of Urban Affairs (1961), and aid to higher education (1962), the majority of the southern Democrats bolted to vote with conservative Republican majorities. On these same kinds of issues northern Democrats also found themselves divided quite often to the extent that their index of cohesion fell below 50 (75 percent unity). Roll calls taken on public works (1959), farm supports (1959), school aid (1960), farm surplus reduction (1960), reducing agricultural conservation funds (1961), wheat and feed grains programs (1961) and raising postal rates (1961) fall into this class. These roll calls indicate that northern Democrats were especially divided on questions involving farm policy. Republicans also often found themselves unable to present a united front on this category of domestic economic issues. On such important matters as veterans' housing (1959), general housing legislation (1599), public works (1959), area redevelopment (1960), school construction (1960), raising the national debt limit (1960 and 1962), area redevelopment (1961), agricultural conservation appropriations (1961), wheat and feed grains programs (1961) and extending fair labor standards provisions to children employed in agriculture (1962) they were unable to maintain an index of cohesion of 50. On the foreign policy roll calls, both of the parties were badly divided. Though Democrats were generally more favorable to internationalist policies than Republicans, both parties' records reveal substantial cleavage. In general, on these roll calls northern Democrats were highly favorable to internationalism. Republicans varied from support for internationalist policies during Eisenhower's Presidency to almost equal division or opposition to such policies in the two later sessions. Though southern Democrats were most often divided in this policy area, the majority consistently voted along "anti-internationalist" lines. On the single civil liberties issue in the majority opposition category (HR 3) in 1959, Democrats were very badly divided, while Republicans maintained over 75 percent unity in favor of the measure to prevent federal pre-emption of subversive activities matters. Southern Democrats in a most revealing manner maintained almost unanimous support of HR 3—rating an index of cohesion of 98 on both of these two roll calls.

The third category of roll calls—"party agreement votes"—cuts across all of the issue-areas that have been discussed, though fewer important matters of economic policy are apparent here. And where roll calls on such issues do fall into this classification, the vote usually reflects approval of final passage after important differences were settled in preliminary balloting. Though these party agreement votes are far too numerous to summarize in detail, a few brief generalizations about them are in order. First, a number of domestic economic, regulatory, and welfare issues became matters of party agreement after one or another group won out on preliminary decisions. Thus, for example, the highly emotional struggle over labor reform culminated in a party agreement vote in favor of the Landrum-Griffin bill once it became clear that this tough substitute bill could not be replaced by a more moderate measure. In like manner the controversy over amending the minimum wage provisions of the Fair Labor Standards Act in 1960 ended in a party agreement vote after a more conservative bill was substituted for the original Democratic bill in 1960.

A large majority of foreign policy roll calls taken during the Eighty-sixth and Eighty-seventh Congresses fall into the party agreement category. Though northern Democrats were usually favorable to internationalist policies, southern Democrats dissented from this position and Republicans vacillated considerably. Final passage of most foreign aid legislation, for example, came on votes on which both parties, though badly divided, affirmed their final support on party agreement votes. Most clearly, during the four sessions selected for examination, the positions of the two parties in this area were less than distinctly differentiated.

All important votes on civil rights during these years were decided on a party agreement basis. The positions of the parties may best be illustrated by focusing on votes taken during the passage of the Civil Rights Act of 1960. On the four roll calls taken on the bill in the House, rather cohesive majorities of Republicans voted with very cohesive groups of northern Democrats against a practically unanimous contingent of southern Democrats. On all of these roll calls both northern Democrats and Republicans maintained respectively an index of cohesion higher than 50. While there may have been differences between these groups in the area of civil rights during these sessions that might be revealed by examination of other actions in the House, these differences were not apparent in roll call voting. Insofar as the parties presented their record on civil rights publicly in recorded votes, they were agreed in favor of this mild voting rights bill that finally passed. These civil rights roll calls were purely sectional—not party—matters.

Civil liberties issues also fall mainly into the party agreement classification during the four sessions. While these votes are much more rare than those in the domestic economic and foreign policy areas, the relative positions of the two parties are highlighted by three important party agreement votes on these matters in the 1959 and 1961 sessions. On a 1959 roll call on which the question was adoption of an open rule for the consideration of HR 3, referred to earlier, Democrats divided almost equally, while Republicans strongly favored adoption of the rule. The respective indices of cohesion for the two parties are 6.2 and 85.2. As one might expect examination of the behavior of southern Democrats reveals the major source of Democratic disunity. Southern Democrats, in fact, voted unanimously in favor of the rule. On three roll calls (1959 and 1961) on bills to qualify the U.S. Supreme Court's ruling in the Mallory Case (pertaining to the length of time persons accused of a crime may be detained without arraignment), Democrats were almost equally divided. Republicans, however, were highly united in favor of modification of the Court's ruling. On these votes the index of cohesion for Democrats was in each case lower than 15, while that of the Republicans was in each instance higher than 75. Again, examination of the southern Democrats' behavior reveals the major source of Democratic disunity. On a motion to recommit the Mallory Rule Bill in 1959, southern Democrats were opposed unanimously to the proposed action, but on passage of the 1959 Mallory Bill, southern Democrats overwhelmingly favored passage, maintaining an index of cohesion of 95.6. Then on an attempt to pass a second Mallory Bill during the 1961 session of the Eighty-seventh Congress, the southerners again favored passage, maintaining an even higher index of 97.6.

On the basis of the evidence presented on a number of traditional questions about the parties—their cohesion, opposition, and positions on various policy questions—some tentative conclusions may now be ventured. First, it should be reiterated that the data in this chapter result from a case study of congressional voting during four recent sessions only. Since it has already been shown that the behavior of the parties has varied greatly from period to period, the present conclusions are strictly limited to the sessions under analysis. The necessity of historical specificity in accounts of congressional behavior must be reemphasized. When certain guesses about party behavior in broader time periods are ventured, inferences will be based on the findings of other studies devoted to recent sessions. Actually, the findings of a number of studies conducted since 1932 seem to suggest that the dimensions of congressional party behavior are delimited very largely by party realignments. Thus, while some changes are apparent in the behavior of the congressional parties over the years since 1932, a great many similarities are also apparent. It seems wise, therefore, to place inquiries into the performance of the congressional parties in the context of changes in the national party system as a whole. Especially with respect to domestic economic issues, it can be said that the dimensions of congressional voting have remained relatively stable throughout the era since the Smith-Roosevelt realignment of 1928–36.

Several kinds of evidence have been considered on "the differences between the parties" from 1959 through 1962. As indicated by the index of cohesion, for example, the unity of the parties ranged from about 75 percent for Republicans to 80 percent for the Democrats on the average roll call. This aspect of the parties' performance from 1959 through 1962 differs little from that during the twentieth century sessions examined by Julius Turner. Several standards have been employed to gauge party opposition. While various observers may dispute the appropriateness of one or another of these devices, each reveals something of worth. While there were very few party votes during the sessions studied, the parties opposed one another by simple majorities on nearly two-thirds of all roll calls analyzed. Moreover, party conflict satisfied a reasonable approximation of the prescriptive model proposed by the advocates of responsible party government on nearly a third of the roll calls analyzed. With respect to the substance of policy, the two parties differed quite sharply on a great many issues in the domestic economic area. Almost all of the roll calls in the modified party vote category fall into this classification. On foreign policy both parties were rather sharply divided during this period. Neither party took a consistently internationalist or anti-internationalist position. On civil rights and civil liberties matters, Democrats were, of course, badly divided, while Republicans were highly cohesive.

As has been noted, this kind of information is strictly factual, and will not of itself prove or disprove the partially normative proposition—"the parties are not significantly different." If the argument is about statistical significance, it can be quickly and easily settled. In this sense there are, of course, significant differences. Whether or not however the parties differ sufficiently to satisfy this or that observer is another matter. To some extent, perhaps, this analysis has succeeded in cutting through this problem with the modified party vote, which seems to approximate the model of cohesive opposition demanded by the party responsibility critics. If so, the parties behaved responsibly (at least in terms of voting) on nearly a third of the roll calls analyzed. It will be obvious, though, that various observers will continue to dispute this question. Why, some will ask, should the parties not be this cohesive on all roll calls? Why are the parties' positions not as distinct in the areas of foreign policy, civil rights, and civil liberties as they are in domestic economic matters? As long as different observers bring different values and expectations to bear on these questions, it is futile to expect to settle such arguments with facts. It is enough to hope that the factual and normative components of such evaluations of the parties' performance will be recognized as such. Then each observer is at least able to state his goals clearly and to evaluate the parties' behavior logically on the basis of factual propositions.

It is interesting to note that the parties' stands on policy matters during the Eighty-sixth and Eighty-seventh Congresses are similar in many respects to those in recent sessions examined by other observers such as Turner, Truman, Rossiter, Dahl, and Froman, whose studies have been cited. It would seem that the parties' stands on matters of economic policy have been relatively stable throughout the New Deal-Fair Deal-New Frontier period. Despite what seems to be an increasing tendency for southern Democrats to defect from party majorities since 1937, fairly cohesive majorities of both parties have taken opposite sides on important economic legislation throughout this entire era. These similarities of behavior in several sessions of Congress would seem to suggest that the policy dimensions of congressional party conflict are likely to remain fairly stable throughout the period from one electoral alignment to another.

Chapter IV

ANALYZING PARTY DIFFERENCES
ON MAJOR POLICY ISSUES

IN ORDER to differentiate between party groups in the Eighty-sixth and Eighty-seventh Congresses on matters of public policy, a series of cumulative (Guttman) scales has been constructed from roll call votes taken in the four sessions of these two Congresses. As has already been noted in discussing Duncan MacRae's use of scale analysis in *Dimensions of Congressional Voting*, this approach is especially helpful in roll call analysis for purposes of identifying dimensions of congressional voting and placing individual congressmen on these dimensions. The policy scales in this chapter provide a somewhat different and probably more accurate perspective, then, on the policy differences previously discussed. The concern here is not with individual congressmen but with the behavior of three party groups—northern Democrats, Republicans, and southern Democrats—as aggregates.

Scale analysis has become sufficiently familiar to political scientists that only a few words need be said about the procedure employed. (Those unfamiliar with the logic of scale analysis should consult Appendix I). First, the approach taken here to scaling roll call votes in the House is considerably simpler than that adopted by MacRae in *Dimensions*. Since the labor involved in MacRae's approach is prohibitive to a single researcher working without extensive financial support, a much simpler form of scale analysis, similar to that employed by Charles D. Farris in another study of roll call voting in the House, has been chosen.[1] Since an attempt was made to scale only those roll calls dealing with specific major policy issues (such as housing and aid to education), the dimensions revealed in the scales are considerably narrower than those revealed in

[1]Charles D. Farris, "A Scale Analysis of Ideological Factors in Congressional Voting," *Journal of Politics*, XX (May, 1958), 308–38.

MacRae's scales.[2] Second, since a major purpose is to reveal differences between party groups as well as intra-party cleavages, scales were constructed for all congressmen rather than for the two parties separately. (It will be remembered that MacRae's procedure was designed for a different purpose, which led him to construct scales for the two parties separately.[3]) Since the scales are cumulative, they present a more accurate picture of roll call voting than would simple summation or percentagizing of "yea" and "nay" votes on the various policy matters considered. Though no claim is made for unidimensionality in a precise sense in these scales, their cumulative element does provide some assurance that congressmen perceived the policy matters in question in a similar manner. The scales, then, provide a means whereby the members of the three party groups analyzed may be ranked ordinally as being more or less liberal or conservative. This rather simple mode of scale analysis reveals a great deal about the comparative behavior of the three party groups selected for analysis. By distributing the members of these groups in the seventeen scales, a more accurate focus than that provided in Chapter III may be obtained on party differences regarding major policy questions. As will become apparent, the results of this analysis are complementary to the findings spelled out in that chapter. In all of the four policy areas under consideration—domestic economic, regulatory and welfare matters, foreign affairs, civil liberties and civil rights—the scales reveal striking differences in party behavior.

The "Labor Scale," based on four roll calls taken during the passage of the Landrum-Griffin Act in the 1959 session of the Eighty-sixth Congress illustrates the very great differences characterizing the three party groups on labor reform at this time.[4] Table 18 presents a frequency distribution

[2]As noted in Chapters I and II, decisions on the importance of various policy questions are fraught with certain hazards. Various observers will differ in their judgment of these matters. It would seem, however, that in the eyes of both parties and nearly all students of congressional behavior, *these* issues were of major importance. Of course, some other questions regarded by some observers as major issues will not be treated here.

[3]See above, p. 26, 67.

[4]On this and the other scales that follow a few members of each party were omitted. Some died or resigned during the various sessions. Others were ill for long periods or absent for other reasons. Data for these congressmen were not gathered and punched on cards, even though they may have voted on a number of roll calls during the various sessions. In the construction of the individual scales, some congressmen were again excluded for reasons of absence or failure to record a vote. A few others in some cases were not placed on the scales when they recorded more than one error as defined in the literature of scaling. See Appendix I for a more detailed explanation of errors. The result of these various exclusions is that the totals for the three party groups vary from scale to scale.

of scale scores for the three groups on the Labor Scale. The most striking feature of the table is the virtual unanimity of Republicans and
southern Democrats on this matter; 87.1 percent of Republicans and
84.5 percent of southern Democrats scored 5 (most conservative) on the
scale. Northern Democrats, on the other hand, are present in substantial
numbers in each of the score categories. Over 65 percent of northern
Democrats scored 1 or 2 on the scale, whereas less than 4 percent of Republicans and only 1 percent of southern Democrats were liberal enough
to rate such a score. Clearly, a large proportion of northern Democrats
maintained a steadfast opposition to even the passage of the bill. Others
voted for passage after it became apparent that the tough Landrum-Griffin
substitute bill could not be recommitted. Most southerners and Republicans, on the other hand, voted both for the substitute and against its
recommittal. The conclusion is plain that while most northern Democrats
were pro-labor, Republicans and southern Democrats were overwhelmingly in the anti-labor category.

TABLE 18

FREQUENCY DISTRIBUTION OF HOUSE PARTY GROUPS
ON THE LABOR SCALE; 86TH CONGRESS

Scale Score	Northern Democrats		Republicans		Southern Democrats	
	Number	Percent	Number	Percent	Number	Percent
1 (most liberal)	50	28.1	1	0.7	0	0.0
2	66	37.1	4	2.7	1	1.0
3	15	8.4	4	2.7	1	1.0
4	35	19.7	9	6.1	11	11.3
5	10	5.6	128	87.1	82	84.5

The issue of area redevelopment came before the House in both the
Eighty-sixth and the Eighty-seventh Congresses. The Area Redevelopment Scale for the first of these Congresses is presented in Table 19.
While it is far from ideal, consisting as it does of votes on only two roll
calls, it does reveal clearly the differences in behavior of the three party
groups. The congressmen who scored 1 voted against recommittal and for
passage of the bill. A score of 2 represents a vote for recommittal, but
also for passage. A score of 3 indicates votes for recommittal and against
passage. Table 19 leaves no doubt about the differences in party behavior
on these questions. The overwhelming majority of northern Democrats

scored 1, while an overwhelming majority of Republicans and a very thin majority of southern Democrats scored 3.

TABLE 19

FREQUENCY DISTRIBUTION OF HOUSE PARTY GROUPS
ON THE AREA REDEVELOPMENT SCALE; 86TH CONGRESS

Scale Score	Northern Democrats		Republicans		Southern Democrats	
	Number	Percent	Number	Percent	Number	Percent
1 (most liberal)	161	90.4	23	15.6	21	21.6
2	4	2.2	0	0.0	17	17.5
3	5	2.8	123	83.7	49	50.5

Clearly, northern Democrats were largely liberal on this question. Republicans were mainly conservative, and southern Democrats were, as a group, ambiguous but leaned heavily toward the most conservative stand. Nearly 70 percent of the latter voted either for recommittal of the bill or for both recommittal and against final passage.

When area redevelopment legislation came before the House again during the Eighty-seventh Congress, the positions of the three groups, as indicated by Table 20, were not greatly altered, though some changes are apparent. The second Area Redevelopment Scale, which is based on

TABLE 20

FREQUENCY DISTRIBUTION OF HOUSE PARTY GROUPS
ON THE AREA REDEVELOPMENT SCALE; 87TH CONGRESS

Scale Score	Northern Democrats		Republicans		Southern Democrats	
	Number	Percent	Number	Percent	Number	Percent
1 (most liberal)	147	96.1	30	18.0	40	43.0
2	1	0.7	11	6.6	12	12.9
3	2	1.3	12	7.2	34	36.1
4	1	0.7	114	68.3	1	1.1

three roll calls, again reveals very great differences in the behavior of the party groups. An overwhelming number of northern Democrats are placed in Scale Score 1, indicating votes for acceptance of a conference report, for passage of the bill, and against recommittal. On the other hand, almost 70 percent of the Republicans scored 4 on the scale, indicating consistent votes in the other direction. The record of the southern Democrats appears considerably more ambiguous in the Eighty-seventh Congress. The percentage of southerners scoring in the most liberal category doubles from the first to the second scale, but a large proportion—36.1 percent of the group—is to be found in scale score 3, indicating votes against the conference report, against recommittal, but yet also against passage. Since it is somewhat unusual to find a group opposed to an important piece of legislation voting in greater numbers against recommittal than for passage, it would seem reasonable to infer that many southerners wanted to help the leadership at least to the extent of preventing recommittal, but felt they could not support final passage of the legislation. The record in these two Congresses, then, places northern Democrats as very liberal, Republicans as very conservative, and southern Democrats as ambiguous on the matter of area redevelopment. In the Eighty-seventh Congress, however, the southerners seemingly became more liberal on this issue, perhaps due to the presence of a Democratic President.

Measures involving federal aid to education came before the House during both the Eighty-sixth and Eighty-seventh Congresses. Table 21, which provides frequencies for the three party groups on the first Aid to Education Scale, clearly indicates their disparate behavior. Northern Democrats, as in the case of the other domestic economic issues examined here, scored overwhelmingly in the most liberal scale category, reflecting their votes for passage, against a conservative substitute bill, and against recommittal. In contrast, large majorities of both Republicans and southern Democrats are grouped in scale scores 3 and 4, indicating votes both for recommittal and the conservative substitute before passage, or for consistent opposition—votes for recommittal, the substitute bill, and against final passage.

On the second Aid to Education Scale, Table 22, the pattern of behavior for all of the groups remained very nearly the same. The scale, based on three roll calls on recommittal, sending the bill to conference, and final passage, places almost nine-tenths of the northern Democrats in the most liberal category. Again, large majorities of Republicans and southern Democrats are placed in scores 2 and 3, as a result of their support of a recommittal motion or a vote against final passage. Northern Democrats, then, were strongly in favor of federal aid to education in both the Eighty-sixth and Eighty-seventh Congresses. Both Republicans and southern Democrats were considerably more conservative—inclined to recommit the bills in question, at least for purposes of reducing various programs or to oppose federal aid altogether.

Two Minimum Wage Scales were constructed—one for each Congress

TABLE 21

FREQUENCY DISTRIBUTION OF HOUSE PARTY GROUPS
ON THE AID TO EDUCATION SCALE; 86TH CONGRESS

Scale Score	Northern Democrats		Republicans		Southern Democrats	
	Number	Percent	Number	Percent	Number	Percent
1 (most liberal)	161	90.4	26	17.7	0	0.0
2	7	3.9	3	2.0	8	8.2
3	7	3.9	50	34.0	72	74.2
4	1	0.6	58	39.5	10	10.3

TABLE 22

FREQUENCY DISTRIBUTION OF HOUSE PARTY GROUPS
ON THE AID TO EDUCATION SCALE; 87TH CONGRESS

Scale Score	Northern Democrats		Republicans		Southern Democrats	
	Number	Percent	Number	Percent	Number	Percent
1 (most liberal)	137	89.5	29	17.4	12	12.9
2	9	5.9	75	44.9	41	44.1
3	1	0.7	55	32.9	32	34.4

examined. The first scale, presented in Table 23, is based on votes on a conservative substitute for the more liberal committee bill and on final passage of the 1960 legislation amending the Fair Labor Standards Act. Again, the virtual unanimity of the northern Democrats is strikingly apparent. Less than a fifth of Republicans and southern Democrats, by contrast, took as liberal a position. The two latter groups are to be found distributed mainly in scores 2 and 3. The largest group of both Republicans and southern Democrats is to be found in scale score 2, which reflects their votes for the conservative substitute, later passed by a conservative coalition vote. A considerable proportion of both groups was conservative enough to vote also against the conservative substitute bill on final passage.

Table 24 distributes the scale scores of members of the three party groups on the second Minimum Wage Scale. The results are based on four roll calls—a motion to recommit, a conservative substitute, acceptance of a conference report, and passage of the amended bill. As in all of the scales examined so far, northern Democrats are clustered at the

TABLE 23

FREQUENCY DISTRIBUTION OF HOUSE PARTY GROUPS
ON THE MINIMUM WAGE SCALE; 86TH CONGRESS

Scale Score	Northern Democrats		Republicans		Southern Democrats	
	Number	Percent	Number	Percent	Number	Percent
1 (most liberal)	161	90.4	27	18.4	13	13.4
2	7	3.9	86	58.5	47	48.5
3	6	3.4	33	22.4	35	36.1

liberal end of the scale—in this case in the most liberal scale score of 1. Nearly 80 percent of Republicans by contrast are scored at 4 and 5, as a result of votes in favor of recommittal and the conservative substitute, and against the conference report, or as a result of total opposition to any change in the minimum wage laws whatever. While southern Democrats were obviously more ambiguous than Republicans in their opposition (nearly a fifth of the southerners are in the most liberal rank), a clear majority of their numbers is to be found in the two

TABLE 24

FREQUENCY DISTRIBUTION OF HOUSE PARTY GROUPS
ON THE MINIMUM WAGE SCALE; 87TH CONGRESS

Scale Score	Northern Democrats		Republicans		Southern Democrats	
	Number	Percent	Number	Percent	Number	Percent
1 (most liberal)	141	92.2	20	12.0	18	19.4
2	7	4.6	5	3.0	6	6.5
3	2	1.3	8	4.8	12	12.9
4	1	0.7	96	57.5	19	20.4
5	1	0.7	35	21.0	35	37.6

most conservative scores of 4 and 5, as a result of votes for recommittal, the substitute bill, against the conference report, and, in some cases, against final passage of the legislation.

Two scales were constructed from roll calls dealing with public housing issues which came before the House during these years—one for
the Eighty-sixth and the other for the Eighty-seventh Congress. A look
at the first of these scales (Table 25), based on four roll calls taken
during the 1959 session, reveals once more the impressive unity of the
northern Democratic congressional party. The results of this scale are
very similar to those of the other scales examined to this point. Whereas nearly nine-tenths of northern Democrats are clustered in the most
liberal scale rank, an almost exactly equal proportion of Republicans
are located in the most conservative rank. A majority of southerners are
located in the two most conservative ranks, 4 and 5, although a some-

TABLE 25

FREQUENCY DISTRIBUTION OF HOUSE PARTY GROUPS
ON THE HOUSING SCALE; 86TH CONGRESS

Scale Score	Northern Democrats		Republicans		Southern Democrats	
	Number	Percent	Number	Percent	Number	Percent
1 (most liberal)	153	86.0	6	4.1	34	35.7
2	18	10.1	4	2.7	7	7.2
3	3	1.7	4	2.7	6	6.2
4	4	2.2	126	85.7	44	45.4

what higher proportion than usual are found in rank 1, along with the
great majority of their northern confreres.

The second Housing Scale (for the Eighty-seventh Congress) demonstrates the relative liberalism of the southerners on this as compared with other specific domestic economic issues that we have examined. This scale, based on three roll calls taken during 1961, places
a majority of southern Democrats with their northern brothers (an
overwhelming portion of their numbers, as usual) in the most liberal
score, showing their opposition to recommittal and support of final
passage. In Table 26 Republicans, as usual, are found at the conservative end of the scale. Again, there would seem to have been an increase
in southern support for housing legislation in the Eighty-seventh Congress. Perhaps it is once more reasonable to infer that the presence of
a Democratic President in the White House had some effect on their behavior.

The final remaining scale in the domestic area is the Welfare Scale
for the Eighty-seventh Congress. The issue before the House was passage

of public welfare amendments in 1962. The scale, the results of which are presented in Table 27, is based on two votes—one on passage and the other on recommittal with instructions to delete a provision increasing payments to the aged and the blind. Northern Democrats, as usual,

TABLE 26

FREQUENCY DISTRIBUTION OF HOUSE PARTY GROUPS
ON THE HOUSING SCALE; 87TH CONGRESS

Scale Score	Northern Democrats		Republicans		Southern Democrats	
	Number	Percent	Number	Percent	Number	Percent
1 (most liberal)	142	92.8	6	3.6	51	54.8
2	1	0.7	18	10.8	4	4.3
3	4	2.6	141	84.4	35	37.6

score in the liberal category, but both Republicans and southern Democrats score somewhat more heavily at the liberal end of the scale than on most of the other domestic economic scales examined. Here a clear majority of southern Democrats score in the first rank. Republicans are fairly evenly divided between ranks 2 and 3. Southern Democrats seem to have been rather strongly in favor of these liberalizing amendments to federal welfare programs, which, after all, must have been popular with a great majority of their constituents. The largest group of Republicans interestingly falls into the second rank on the scale, indicating their vote first to recommit, then to pass a measure that must have been regarded as too popular to oppose.

TABLE 27

FREQUENCY DISTRIBUTION OF HOUSE PARTY GROUPS
ON THE WELFARE SCALE; 87TH CONGRESS

Scale Score	Northern Democrats		Republicans		Southern Democrats	
	Number	Percent	Number	Percent	Number	Percent
1 (most liberal)	141	92.2	17	10.2	61	65.6
2	3	2.0	73	43.7	8	8.6
3	0	0.0	65	38.9	3	3.2

In the area of foreign affairs four Foreign Aid Scales were constructed—one for each session of the Eighty-sixth and Eighty-seventh Congresses.

A great many roll calls, of course, were taken on foreign aid during this period, and since the percentages of congressmen voting "yea" and "nay" on many of them were quite similar, roll calls were selected for the scales that provided the greatest variety of cutting points. Another person scaling these same roll calls undoubtedly could produce a slightly different scale, but since the purpose of this analysis is not to place individual congressmen with respect to their public records, this procedure would still seem to provide a fairly sound basis for investigating the behavior of the aggregate party groups. Table 28, presenting the distribution of scale scores for the 1959 session of the Eighty-sixth Congress, reveals that the patterns discovered in the domestic scales are not precisely duplicated in the area of foreign aid. To be sure, northern and southern Democrats are found in about the same proportions in the liberal and conservative ranges of the scale, but Republicans are much more divided than usual. In fact they are almost bipolarized; two large and fairly equal groups of Republicans are to be found in both the most liberal and the most conservative ranks of the scale. Apparently, Republicans were much more divided in matters of foreign policy than in domestic economic matters. Table 29, which presents the distribution of scale scores for the 1960 Foreign Aid Scale practically duplicates Table 28. Again, the distributions are similar to those in the area of domestic economic policy with the same exception. The Republicans are again placed throughout the scale in a U-like distribution, revealing their deep cleavages on the question of foreign aid or internationalism.

TABLE 28

FREQUENCY DISTRIBUTION OF HOUSE PARTY GROUPS
ON THE FOREIGN AID SCALE—1959; 86TH CONGRESS

Scale Score	Northern Democrats		Republicans		Southern Democrats	
	Number	Percent	Number	Percent	Number	Percent
1 (most liberal)	151	84.8	76	51.7	25	25.8
2	2	1.1	5	3.4	5	5.2
3	3	1.7	3	2.0	2	2.1
4	20	11.2	58	39.5	64	66.0

Table 30, which provides the results of the distribution of party members in the three groups on the 1961 Foreign Aid Scale indicates that voting patterns in this area did not change appreciably during the first year of John F. Kennedy's presidency. The distributions described in the foregoing two tables are very nearly duplicated. Again, Republicans reveal their deep cleavages on the issue of foreign aid.

TABLE 29

FREQUENCY DISTRIBUTION OF HOUSE PARTY GROUPS
ON THE FOREIGN AID SCALE—1960; 86TH CONGRESS

Scale Score	Northern Democrats		Republicans		Southern Democrats	
	Number	Percent	Number	Percent	Number	Percent
1 (most liberal)	98	55.1	70	47.6	4	4.1
2	44	24.7	15	10.2	27	27.8
3	6	3.4	7	4.8	1	1.0
4	25	14.0	50	34.0	60	61.9

TABLE 30

FREQUENCY DISTRIBUTION OF HOUSE PARTY GROUPS
ON THE FOREIGN AID SCALE—1961; 87TH CONGRESS

Scale Score	Northern Democrats		Republicans		Southern Democrats	
	Number	Percent	Number	Percent	Number	Percent
1 (most liberal)	132	86.3	61	36.5	27	29.0
2	11	7.2	4	2.4	8	8.6
3	4	2.6	23	13.8	21	22.6
4	1	0.7	58	34.7	30	32.3

The final Foreign Aid Scale for the 1962 session of the Eighty-seventh Congress reveals no pronounced alteration in the patterns of party distribution, except perhaps a slight shifting of Republicans toward a more conservative position on foreign aid (Table 31). Now a majority of the group is to be found in the most conservative score on the scale. It will be noted, though, that the essential bipolarity of the Republican distribution is still apparent, since slightly over 40 percent of Republicans are placed in the first two ranks of the scale. Throughout this entire period, then, northern Democrats reveal a strong attachment to foreign aid or internationalism, while southern Democrats, despite their liberal minority on this question, are generally found at the conservative end of the scales. Republicans, seemingly have been unable to unite on this question in recent years. The House congressional party apparently contains two very diverse groups—one as firmly committed to foreign aid internationalism as the other is opposed. This finding, of course, is quite consistent with the material which was discussed in Chapters I and II of this study.

TABLE 31

FREQUENCY DISTRIBUTION OF HOUSE PARTY GROUPS
ON THE FOREIGN AID SCALE—1962; 87TH CONGRESS

Scale Score	Northern Democrats		Republicans		Southern Democrats	
	Number	Percent	Number	Percent	Number	Percent
1 (most liberal)	136	88.9	34	20.4	25	26.9
2	5	3.3	33	19.8	10	10.8
3	0	0.0	6	3.6	0	0.0
4	11	7.2	85	50.9	54	58.1

In contrast to the four Foreign Aid Scales examined, the Trade Expansion Scale, based on three roll calls taken on the lowering of tariff barriers in 1962, reveals a slightly different kind of distribution of party groups. Table 32 demonstrates that while the northern Democrats are, as usual, very much united in favor of lower tariffs and Republicans are rather badly split on this question, the southern Democrats are much more liberal as a group on this question than on matters involving foreign aid. A firm majority of the southerners score in the most liberal

TABLE 32

FREQUENCY DISTRIBUTION OF HOUSE PARTY GROUPS
ON THE TRADE EXPANSION SCALE; 87TH CONGRESS

Scale Score	Northern Democrats		Republicans		Southern Democrats	
	Number	Percent	Number	Percent	Number	Percent
1 (most liberal)	136	88.9	42	25.1	55	59.1
2	0	0.0	43	25.7	10	10.8
3	15	9.8	81	48.5	22	23.7

category along with the overwhelming number of northern Democrats. Perhaps in this area, at least, a portion of traditional southern internationalism remains in an era when the southerners have turned quite sharply away from internationalism in matters of foreign aid.

Turning now to Table 33, and the area of civil liberties, differences between the three party groups may be seen in this scale, which is based on three roll calls for HR 3, a bill to limit federal preemption of subversive activities matters. Obviously, in this area, except for a small band of dissident Republicans, liberalism is an exclusively northern Democratic phenomenon. Nearly 70 percent of northern Democrats score in the most liberal category on the scale, reflecting their total opposition to leaving subversive activities matters in the hands of the states or perhaps reflecting their opposition to a frontal attack on the United States Supreme Court. Very heavy majorities of Republicans and southern Democrats score at the conservative end of the scale. It is clear that if the House

TABLE 33

FREQUENCY DISTRIBUTION OF HOUSE PARTY GROUPS
ON THE CIVIL LIBERTIES SCALE; 86TH CONGRESS

Scale Score	Northern Democrats		Republicans		Southern Democrats	
	Number	Percent	Number	Percent	Number	Percent
1 (more liberal)	122	68.5	15	10.2	0	0.0
2	28	15.7	16	10.9	1	1.0
3	17	9.6	111	75.5	96	99.0

TABLE 34

FREQUENCY DISTRIBUTION OF HOUSE PARTY GROUPS
ON THE CIVIL RIGHTS SCALE; 86TH CONGRESS

Scale Score	Northern Democrats		Republicans		Southern Democrats	
	Number	Percent	Number	Percent	Number	Percent
1 (most liberal)	139	78.1	121	82.3	0	0.0
2	23	12.9	9	6.1	4	4.1
3	14	7.9	14	9.5	91	93.8

is to take libertarian positions on this or similar matters, the number of congressmen in the various groups will have to be altered substantially, for there is a large anti-civil libertarian majority built into present party alignments. It is not difficult to see why Americans who are concerned about these matters have had to look elsewhere in recent years for their salvation.

In a fourth and final area of policy—civil rights (Table 34) —an altogether different situation prevails than any to be seen in scales dealing with the other policy areas. Civil rights, at least in terms of roll call voting in the 1960 session of the House of Representatives, appears to be a matter of consensus between the northern Democrats and the Republicans. While it seems clear that the major impetus for this kind of legislation in recent years has come from liberal, northern Democrats, Civil Rights represents an issue which the northerners of both parties cannot afford to oppose. Aside from the obvious rectitude of the Negro's cause in light of dominant American political norms, it seems clear that neither party has felt able to ignore the Negro political strength in northern metropolitan areas. On roll calls on civil rights from 1959 through 1962 the southern Democrats voted as a true sectional minority, opposed by the overwhelming majorities of the combined northern Democratic and Republican parties. Lest one should feel a certain unwarranted sympathy for the southerners' plight, however, it should be pointed out that the Civil Rights Act of 1960, passed through the efforts of the moderate Democratic leaders and the Republicans, was but a token civil rights measure. Though the two parties voted together, they did little of importance in this area with their combined power in 1960.

The scale analysis of party differences in the Eighty-sixth and Eighty-seventh Congresses provides an alternative but complementary perspective on the policy positions of the three selected party groups discussed in Chapter III. Distributions of northern Democrats, southern Democrats, and Republicans on cumulative scales constructed for four recent sessions of the House have revealed striking differences in the voting behavior of these groups. In all four of the policy areas examined here, northern Democrats were found to be nearly unanimously liberal. In domestic economic, regulatory, and welfare matters Republicans were found nearly always grouped in the most conservative scores on the various scales. On questions of civil liberties that arose during the four sessions examined, the Republicans were almost unanimously conservative. However, on civil rights' roll call voting, their position was hardly distinguishable from that of the northern Democrats. Concerning foreign aid issues, the Republicans in the Eighty-sixth and Eighty-seventh Congresses evidenced little unity. On the four Foreign Aid Scales they distributed themselves rather consistently in a bipolar pattern with nearly equal groups favoring both the most liberal and the most conservative policy positions. Southern Democrats on these scales reveal the rather sharp cleavages separating them from the overwhelming number of northern Democrats in all policy matters examined. On domestic issues, foreign aid, civil rights, and civil liberties, southern Democrats were vastly more conservative than their northern colleagues.

Chapter V

THE SOUTHERN DEMOCRATS
AND THE CONSERVATIVE COALITION

ANALYSIS of party behavior in the Eighty-sixth and Eighty-seventh Congresses has revealed that southern defection from Democratic majorities was the most common cause of Democratic disunity in the period from 1959 through 1962. In all four policy areas examined in Chapters III and IV—domestic economic, regulatory, and welfare issues; foreign policy; civil rights; and civil liberties—southern Democrats manifested a strong tendency to bolt from positions taken by the northern majority of the party. On domestic issues and matters concerning foreign policy and civil liberties the southerners commonly joined in substantial numbers with conservative Republicans to vote against the liberal stands taken by most northern Democrats. In the fourth area—civil rights—the southerners stood alone as a true sectional minority, opposed by majorities of both Democrats and Republicans.

Since no major effort has been made to describe the behavior of southern Democrats in the House since V. O. Key's classic analysis in *Southern Politics* (1949),[1] their actions in the two Congresses selected for analysis here would seem to call for a new treatment. The data analyzed in this chapter reveal that southern dissidence from policy positions taken by the majority of congressional Democrats has greatly increased since the four sessions on which Professor Key based his analysis. In the years from 1959 through 1962 the "conservative coalition," which Key argued had a much exaggerated reputation in the sessions he examined, constituted a phenomenon of undeniable importance. In a very real sense voting lines in the House during this period were most commonly of a coalitional rather than a party nature on many of the most important matters

---

[1] Key, *Southern Politics*, 369–82.

in three policy areas—domestic issues, foreign policy, and civil liberties. On these issues it was a common matter for the great majority of northern Democrats and a handful of liberal Republicans to find themselves opposed by a coalition of conservative Republicans and southern Democrats. Such coalition voting muddied the waters of congressional party politics considerably during this period.

Stung by such defeats in the House as the substitution of the weak Landrum-Griffin Bill by a coalition of Republicans and southern Democrats in 1959, trade union commentators have recently regarded coalition voting as an especially important problem. Commenting on the conservative coalition in 1960, the liberal union publication the *American Federationist* noted disapprovingly that "a coalition of conservative forces from both the Democratic and Republican parties . . . has shaped the nation's political direction for the last twenty-three years." [2] In 1961, William Schnitzler, also writing for the *Federationist,* argued that the coalition was largely responsible for the failure of most Americans to understand the basic issues of national politics. Because it has worked behind the scenes, he argued, and "because of its two party nature the coalition is a politically irresponsible group. It cannot be called to account as a whole by the voters." [3] Another liberal-labor commentator, William Phillips (at that time head of the House Democratic Study Group's staff), commented in 1961:

A clear understanding of the conservative Republican-southern Democratic coalition and the crucial part it plays in the formulation of legislation is necessary to understand the operation of Congress today. . . . The real alignment in the House on important roll-call votes reveals an almost even split between conservative and liberal forces—190-200 conservative Republicans and southern Democrats and 195–205 liberal Democrats, moderate southern and border state Democrats and liberal Republicans. The remaining numbers shift from one side to the other, depending on the issue.[4]

In addition, reflecting a preference for party responsibility, Phillips noted that "in many respects the conservative coalition in Congress today is in itself a separate 'political party' within the existing party framework. It bears little allegiance to party labels or party principles, nor

2"The Real Power in Congress—A 23-Year-Old Coalition," *American Federationist,* April, 1960, p. 4.

3William Schnitzler, "Usurpers of Power—The Conservative Coalition," *American Federationist,* December, 1961, p. 11.

4William Phillips, "Congress: A Study in Political Realities," *American Federationist,* February, 1961, p. 13.

does it usually respond to presidential leadership in the formulation of legislation in the public interest . . . and except for rare occasions, it is content with its role of obstructionism and the status quo." [5]

The success of the coalition in the case of labor legislation in 1959 and the failure of the House to move on civil rights early in 1960 brought the issue of Republican-southern Democratic cooperation to the floor of the House itself, where Congressman Emmanuel Celler (Dem., New York), chairman of the Judiciary Committee, charged that a "deal" had been made between Republicans and southern Democrats to provide southern votes against all welfare legislation in exchange for Republican support in blocking the passage of civil rights legislation.[6] On the same day Congressman Frank Thompson (Dem., New Jersey), arguing that the coalition actually controlled the House on a number of important matters, read into the *Congressional Record* a lengthy research paper on the history of the coalition.[7] The bi-party group, he argued, had recently become more visible as it tightened its lines during the first session of the Eighty-sixth Congress, but its work actually began as early as 1937. "When the Court [the United States Supreme Court] upheld the [Wagner] Act in April, 1937, it became clear to many conservatives in the industrial North and the low-wage farm areas of the South that only by forging a bi-partisan conservative alliance in Congress could they hope to stem the tide of new dealism, with its growing emphasis on the needs of city dwellers, minority groups, workers, small farmers, and other underprivileged segments of the population." Over the years, Thompson went on to say, the coalition had won a number of crucially important victories. During 1937, for example, it succeeded in blocking the passage of the Fair Labor Standards bill for an entire session. In the Seventy-sixth Congress it forced investigation of the NLRB and passed the Hatch Act, which prevented federal employees from engaging in politics. During the war years the coalition managed to pass the Smith anti-strike bill, created the House Committee on Un-American Activities, and "watered down" the price control and excess profits programs. In the postwar years the group succeeded in excluding farm labor from NLRB jurisdiction, turned over the U.S. Employment Service to the control of the states, and further weakened price control legislation. With the election of the Republican

[5]*Ibid.,* 14.

[6]The immediate issue was the failure of Republicans to sign a discharge petition to dislodge the Civil Rights Bill from the Rules Committee. See *Congressional Record,* 86th Cong., 2nd Sess., 1425.

[7]*Ibid.,* 1440–42.

Eightieth Congress in 1946, Thompson said, the biparty alliance achieved perhaps its greatest victory with the passage of the Taft-Hartley Act and its successful overturning of the President's veto of the act. Throughout Truman's Presidency the group remained active, emasculating or blocking altogether such Fair Deal measures as aid to education, civil rights, housing, farm programs, and FEPC. During the Eisenhower years from 1953 through 1958, the coalition was responsible for turning over offshore oil resources to several coastal states, weakening housing legislation, defeating aid to education legislation, and generally weakening or blocking attempts to expand other regulatory and welfare programs.

"Over the years since 1937," Thompson said, "the Republican-southern Democratic voting coalition has operated with varying degrees of effectiveness, being most successful on legislation dealing with education, social welfare, labor, regulation of business, public works, resource development, civil rights, immigration, taxes and other economic issues, and those where states' rights have been involved." [8]

It should be clear that concern of this nature over the operation of the conservative coalition in the House is motivated by the liberal policy stance of these commentators. Most obviously, biparty conservative cooperation has been viewed in a very different light by those whose political values dispose them to oppose the New Deal-Fair Deal issues that Representative Thompson discusses. If the coalition is an obstacle to the passage of such measures, and if, as it may be inferred, it obfuscates responsibility for the conduct of the political process in Congress, conservatives may be expected to regard it generally as a good rather than a bad institution. So it is, as has been noted, with the party responsibility argument in general. With few exceptions, it will be found that liberals are inclined to favor responsible parties and conservatives to oppose them. The purpose of this analysis is not to argue for one or another of these positions, but to describe the coalitional nature of voting in the House of Representatives from 1959 through 1962. If this description is accurate, it may be employed as one element of an evaluation of party behavior; but, as Chapters I and II of this study have stressed, differing political values, applied to the facts about the congressional parties, may lead logically to very different evaluations.

What, then, does analysis of roll call voting reveal about the southern Democrats and the conservative coalition in the Eighty-sixth and Eighty-seventh Congresses? The index of likeness—a simple, traditional device—has been used to compare the southern Democrats to northern Demo-

8*Ibid.*, 1442.

crats and Republicans, respectively, on all roll calls during the four sessions selected.[9] Also, the major lines of Key's treatment in 1949 have been retraced to demonstrate that application of his techniques to the four sessions indicates the increased importance of the conservative coalition in recent years. Additional perspective on the rise of the coalition and its continued activity is obtained through frequency distributions of the index of party loyalty for northern and southern Democrats.[10] Finally, a number of peak coalition roll calls are examined in order to determine the nature of the policy questions that most commonly brought southern Democrats and Republicans together.

Table 35 shows the number and percentage of roll calls on which southern Democrats were more "like" Republicans than northern Democrats in the four sessions of the Eighty-sixth and Eighty-seventh Congresses.[11]

TABLE 35

ROLL CALLS ON WHICH SOUTHERN DEMOCRATS
WERE MORE LIKE REPUBLICANS THAN NORTHERN DEMOCRATS;
HOUSE OF REPRESENTATIVES; BY SESSIONS, 1959–62[a]

Congress, Session, Year	Total Roll Calls	Number	Percent
86:1 (1959)	75	31	41.3
86:2 (1960)	75	43	57.3
87:1 (1961)	88	45	51.1
87:2 (1962)	83	36	43.4
Totals	321	155	48.3

[a]Near-unanimous roll calls have been omitted.

The ambiguity of the southerners on the entire range of roll calls analyzed is amply demonstrated by the fact that the percentage of votes falling into this category never falls below 40 in any session. Even more

[9]The index of likeness, it will be remembered, is calculated by subtracting the percentage of one grouping voting for a measure from the percentage of another and subtracting the difference from 100.

[10]The index of party loyalty, discussed above, is simply the percentage of times a legislator supported his party when majorities of the two parties opposed one another.

[11]The quotation marks indicate that the word is being used in the special sense of the index of likeness.

striking is the fact that during two of the sessions (1960 and 1961) southern Democrats were more like Republicans than their northern colleagues on a majority of roll calls analyzed. On a very sizable proportion of the total roll calls analyzed in these four sessions, southern Democratic voting behavior followed the same pattern. Of course, many of the roll calls included in the totals in Table 35 fall into the "party agreement" category.

While it is important to look at the behavior of the southerners on these roll calls, it is more revealing to examine their actions on roll calls where they had the alternative of aligning themselves with either a majority of Democrats or a majority of Republicans, when the two parties were opposed to one another. Table 36 focuses on southern Democratic behavior under these conditions by presenting the number and percentage of votes on which the southern Democrats were more like Republicans than northern Democrats when simple majorities of the two parties opposed one another. While the percentage of these votes drops off somewhat from the levels of Table 35, the affinity of southern Democrats for coalition voting is still clearly apparent. On more than a third of these majority opposition votes, the southern Democratic minority was more like the Republicans than their northern party brethren.

TABLE 36

MAJORITY OPPOSITION ROLL CALLS ON WHICH SOUTHERN
DEMOCRATS WERE MORE LIKE REPUBLICANS THAN
NORTHERN DEMOCRATS; HOUSE OF
REPRESENTATIVES, BY
SESSION, 1959–62†

Congress, Session, Year	Total Roll Calls	Number	Percent
86:1 (1959)	47	11	23.4
86:2 (1960)	49	22	44.9
87:1 (1961)	56	21	37.5
87:2 (1962)	55	19	34.5
Totals	207	73	35.3

†Near-unanimous roll calls have been omitted.

The affinity of the southerners for Republican-like voting during these years is placed in a still clearer light by Table 37, showing the number and percentage of modified party vote roll calls on which they were more like Republicans than northern Democrats.[12] The roll calls of maximum party cleavage are isolated in each session under examination. If, as has been shown, southern Democrats continued to be more like Republicans on matters involving economic, regulatory, and welfare policies, a very serious problem for the Democrats during these sessions

TABLE 37

MODIFIED PARTY VOTE ROLL CALLS ON WHICH SOUTHERN
DEMOCRATS WERE MORE LIKE REPUBLICANS THAN
NORTHERN DEMOCRATS; HOUSE OF
REPRESENTATIVES, BY
SESSION, 1959–62†

Congress, Session, Year	Total Roll Calls	Number	Percent
86:1 (1959)	29	4	13.8
86:2 (1960)	16	5	31.3
87:1 (1961)	28	6	21.4
87:2 (1962)	29	4	13.8
Totals	102	19	18.6

†Near-unanimous roll calls have been omitted.

will have been revealed. As Table 37 clearly demonstrates, while the percentage of roll call votes falling into the "more like Republicans" category continues to drop off as party opposition is increased, the percentage remaining is still substantial in all of the sessions. On nearly 20 percent of these highly partisan modified party votes, southern Democrats were closer to Republicans than to the northern members of their own party. Even as party opposition increased, then, the southerners continued their defection in voting on a substantial number of roll calls.

The three tables just presented have already indicated a great deal of conservative coalition voting by southern Democrats in the Eighty-sixth and Eighty-seventh Congresses. This pattern of coalition behavior may be clarified even more by examining certain other data for the four sessions along with comparable data compiled by Professor Key for earlier House sessions (1933, 1937, 1941, and 1945).[13]

[12]Modified party votes, as defined above, are those on which 75 percent of one party oppose 75 percent of the other.

[13]Key, *Southern Politics*, 371–78. I have interspersed new material for the four sessions 1959–62 while following Key's analysis.

Table 38 presents data amassed by Key for the four sessions between 1933 and 1945 and data collected by the author for the four later sessions chosen for this study. Key's purpose in presenting this material was to demonstrate that majorities of southern Democrats opposed majorities of Republicans on 70.5 percent of roll calls analyzed for the four

TABLE 38

HOUSE ROLL CALLS WITH A MAJORITY OF SOUTHERN DEMOCRATS
OPPOSING A MAJORITY OF REPUBLICANS:
BY SESSIONS; 1933–62†

Congress, Session, Year‡	Total Roll Calls	Roll Calls With Majority in Disagreement	
		Number	Percent
73:1 (1933)	56	47	83.9
75:1 (1937)	77	50	64.9
77:1 (1941)	67	50	74.6
79:1 (1945)	75	47	62.7
Totals	275	194	70.5
86:1 (1959)	75	50	66.7
86:2 (1960)	75	39	52.0
87:1 (1961)	88	44	50.0
87:2 (1962)	83	46	55.4
Totals	321	179	55.8

†Near-unanimous roll calls have been omitted in all sessions.
‡Data for the first four sessions are from V. O. Key, Jr., *Southern Politics* (New York: Vintage Books, n.d.) , 371.

sessions. Under these conditions, he argued, coalition behavior could hardly have been as common as some commentators had supposed.[14] Comparable figures for the Eighty-sixth and Eighty-seventh Congresses, however, indicate a sharp drop in the number of roll calls on which majorities of Republicans and southern Democrats opposed one another. Whereas, on the average, 70.5 percent of roll calls in Key's sessions pitted southern Democrats and Republicans against one another, only 55.8 percent did so from 1959 through 1962.

Table 39 takes a somewhat different approach to the same question by examining roll calls on which southern cohesion was especially high

[14]*Ibid.*, 371.

(evidencing an index of cohesion of 80 or more—90 percent unity).
Key's point was that when southern Democrats were extremely cohesive
they were much more likely to vote with a majority of northern Democrats than against them. Again, the opposite occurrence in the more recent sessions is apparent. Whereas, in Key's sessions, southern Democrats
voted with northern Democrats on 101 of 112 of these roll calls, they
voted similarly on 41 of 49 in the four recent sessions. Not only has there
occurred a drop in agreement with northern Democrats on the southern
high cohesion roll calls, but the percentage on these roll calls of the
total analyzed has also declined drastically. Whereas the southerners
were highly cohesive on 40.7 percent of the roll calls analyzed for the
earlier sessions, they were similarly cohesive only on 15.3 percent from
1959 through 1962.

TABLE 39

HOUSE ISSUES OF HIGH SOUTHERN DEMOCRATIC COHESION
IN OPPOSITION TO REPUBLICAN MAJORITIES:
BY SESSIONS; 1933–62†

Congress, Session, Year‡	Total Roll Calls	Roll Calls of High Southern Cohesion		Number on Which So. Dem. Majority Agreed with Non-So. Dem. Majority	Dis- agreed
		Number	Percent		
73:1 (1933)	56	28	50.0	28	0
75:1 (1937)	77	25	32.5	20	5
77:1 (1941)	67	35	52.2	32	3
79:1 (1945)	75	24	32.0	21	3
Totals	275	112	40.7	101	11
86:1 (1959)	75	18	24.0	18	0
86:2 (1960)	75	13	17.3	6	7
87:1 (1961)	88	7	8.0	6	1
87:2 (1962)	83	11	13.3	11	0
Totals	321	49	15.3	41	8

†Near-unanimous roll calls have been omitted in all sessions.
‡Data for the first four sessions are from V. O. Key, Jr., *Southern Politics* (New
York: Vintage Books, n.d.), 372.

Table 40 presents data for another approach taken by Key to the
question of the conservative coalition. How often do actual majorities

of both southern Democrats and Republicans vote together against a majority of northern Democrats? The answer, Key wrote, is—not very often. In the 1933 session not a single coalition vote appeared. In 1937 the coalition materialized on only 9.7 percent of the roll calls analyzed. Though the percentages for the two sessions in the 1940's were higher, the average for the four sessions under consideration amounts only to 10.2 percent. The comparable data for the four later sessions examined indicate that on the average conservative coalition voting is more than twice as common as in Key's sessions. In three of the four sessions the coalition appeared on more than a fifth of all roll calls analyzed. In 1960 the group formed on more than a fourth of the roll calls analyzed. The conclusion is plain that the coalition was a much more important phenomenon in the four more recent sessions. Where a sectional minority of a party is capable of voting with the opposition party on more than a fifth of all roll calls taken over a period of four sessions, it is hard to deny that coalitional voting is of fundamental importance.

TABLE 40

HOUSE ROLL CALLS ON WHICH
MAJORITIES OF SOUTHERN DEMOCRATS AND REPUBLICANS
OPPOSED A MAJORITY OF NORTHERN DEMOCRATS:
BY SESSION; 1933–62†

Congress, Session, Year‡	Total Roll Calls	Number	Percent
73:1 (1933)	56	0	0.0
75:1 (1937)	77	7	9.1
77:1 (1941)	67	9	13.4
79:1 (1945)	75	12	16.0
Totals	275	28	10.2
86:1 (1959)	75	11	14.7
86:2 (1960)	75	21	28.0
87:1 (1961)	88	23	26.1
87:2 (1962)	83	17	20.5
Totals	321	72	22.4

†Near-unanimous roll calls have been omitted in all sessions.
‡Data from the first four sessions are from V. O. Key, Jr., *Southern Politics* (New York; Vintage Books, n.d.) , 375.

A final comparison of Professor Key's data with those of the present study appears in Table 41. It measures the relative solidarity of northern and southern Democrats when both opposed majorities of Republicans. Key's conclusions are clear: when both groups of Democrats

TABLE 41

RELATIVE SOLIDARITY OF SOUTHERN AND NORTHERN DEMOCRATS
IN THE HOUSE WHEN MAJORITIES OF EACH GROUP
OPPOSED A MAJORITY OF REPUBLICANS: 1933–62†

| Congress, Session, Year‡ | Total Roll Calls | Southern and Northern Democrats Against Republicans | | |
		Number	Higher SD Cohesion	Higher NSD Cohesion
73:1 (1933)	56	44	38	6
75:1 (1937)	77	41	27	14
77:1 (1941)	67	39	36	3
79:1 (1945)	75	40	24	16
Totals	275	164	125	39
86:1 (1959)	75	40	13	25
86:2 (1960)	75	23	10	13
87:1 (1961)	88	37	5	32
87:2 (1962)	83	39	5	33
Totals	321	139	33	103

†Near-unanimous roll calls have been omitted in all sessions.
‡Data for the first four sessions are from V. O. Key, Jr., *Southern Politics* (New York: Vintage Books, n.d.) , 377.

opposed majorities of Republicans, the southern Democrats were the more cohesive group in a large majority of cases.[15] On 164 such votes, the southerners were more cohesive than their northern colleagues. The data for the later sessions present a strikingly different picture. Of the 139 roll calls on which majorities of southern Democrats and northern Democrats opposed majorities of Republicans, northern Democrats were more cohesive in 103 cases. For the later sessions, Key's findings are precisely reversed. Not only did southern Democrats vote more often with Republicans against northern Democrats, but also when the preponderance of both Democratic groups opposed Republican majorities, the northern

[15]*Ibid.*, 376.

Democrats were more cohesive than their southern counterparts in an overwhelming percentage of cases.

Although the conservative coalition appeared to Professor Key as a highly overrated phenomenon in the four House sessions he examined, the use here of identical procedures has revealed that coalition voting greatly increased between 1933 (Key's first session) and 1959. Again, it is obvious that party behavior in the House of Representatives is seldom subject to time-proof generalizations. While a descriptive generalization may be perfectly valid for one period, (e.g., when majorities of southern and northern Democrats oppose majorities of Republicans, southern Democrats are most often more cohesive than northern), it may be totally invalid for another. This is precisely the case with the generalization cited. Obviously something has happened since the beginning of the New Deal period to cause southern Democrats to bolt with much greater frequency from positions taken by northern party members.

The historical dimension of conservative coalition voting is apparent to some extent in Table 40, which reveals that the number of roll calls on which majorities of southern Democrats and Republicans opposed majorities of northern Democrats increased from none to 7, to 9, to 12, in four sessions from 1933 to 1945. It would seem that the conservative alliance was of negligible importance before 1937, but rose gradually in the sessions throughout the 1940's to a position of greater potency. By

TABLE 42

FREQUENCY DISTRIBUTION OF NORTHERN AND SOUTHERN DEMOCRATS;
INDEX OF LOYALTY:
HOUSE OF REPRESENTATIVES; 1930–31†

Range of Index of Loyalty	Northern Democrats		Southern Democrats	
	Number	Percent	Number	Percent
Below 75.1	11	18.0	2	2.0
75.1–80.0	13	21.3	4	4.0
80.1–85.0	8	13.1	4	4.0
85.1–90.0	6	9.8	24	24.2
90.1–95.0	13	21.3	36	36.4
95.1–100	10	16.4	29	29.3
Totals	61	100	99	100

†Source: Julius Turner, *Party and Constituency: Pressures on Congress* (Baltimore: Johns Hopkins Press, 1951), 136.

TABLE 43

FREQUENCY DISTRIBUTION OF NORTHERN AND SOUTHERN DEMOCRATS;
INDEX OF LOYALTY:
HOUSE OF REPRESENTATIVES, 1944†

Range of Index of Loyalty	Northern Democrats		Southern Democrats	
	Number	Percent	Number	Percent
Below 75.1	12	11.3	66	61.1
75.1–80.0	7	6.6	14	13.0
80.1–85.0	7	6.6	10	9.3
85.1–90.0	16	15.1	9	8.3
90.1–95.0	26	24.5	5	4.6
95.1–100	38	35.8	4	3.7
Totals	106	100	108	100

†Source: Julius Turner, *Party and Constituency: Pressures on Congress* (Baltimore: Johns Hopkins Press, 1951), 137.

1945, majorities of southern Democrats and Republicans voted together against northern Democrats on 16 percent of roll calls analyzed. While comparable data for the period between 1945 and 1959 are not available, it seems reasonable to assume tentatively that the coalition remained at least as important as in 1945 during the intervening Congresses.

Another perspective on the rise and continued activity of the conservative coalition may be gained through frequency distributions of the index of party loyalty, which is no more than the percentage of times an individual congressman voted with a majority of his party when majorities of the two parties opposed one another. Since this measurement of party loyalty coincides exactly with the *Congressional Quarterly's* "Party Unity Scores" which are available for the four recent sessions examined, it is worthwhile to compare the loyalty of northern and southern Democrats by analyzing the frequency with which both groups fell into various divisions of the index of loyalty (or Party Unity Scores). Table 42 presents such a distribution for the two groups of Democrats in the 1930–31 session examined by Julius Turner in *Party and Constituency*. The table is revealing; it clearly indicates that during this session southern Democrats were far more loyal to party majorities than their northern colleagues. Examination of the table reveals that whereas the southerners cluster in the three most loyal groups (85.1–100) northern Democrats are scattered over the entire range. Nearly a fifth of northern Democrats fall into the range below 75.1, whereas only 2 percent of southerners are to be found below 75.1.

Table 43, which presents identical data from Turner's *Party and Constituency* for the 1944 session, reveals with unusual clarity that a change has taken place in the intervening years. The table strikingly documents the rise of the conservative coalition. The distributions of the index of loyalty have been altered almost beyond recognition. Southern Democrats are clustered in the lower ranges of loyalty. Whereas only 2 percent were in the range below 75.1 in the 1930–31 session, 61.1 percent are to be found there in 1944. Clearly the rise of the coalition can be placed in the time period between these two sessions. At the same time, Table 43 indicates that northern Democrats became a great deal more loyal to party majorities. Examination of the two tables (42 and 43) will reveal a considerable shifting of their numbers toward the upper ranges of loyalty.

Frequency distributions of the Party Support Scores reveal in similar manner the comparative party loyalty of southern and northern Democrats in the Eighty-sixth and Eighty-seventh Congresses. Since these scores are calculated by the *Congressional Quarterly* in such a manner that absences artifically tend to depress congressmen's scores on this measurement, the following tables should be accepted with caution. Probably all of the scores for both southern and northern Democrats are lower than they would have been if they had been calculated under a system that would take absences into account. However, if it is assumed, and such an assumption seems reasonable, that the absence rates of southern and northern Democrats are about the same, this conveniently available data facilitate the same mode of analysis that Julius Turner employed in the preceding two tables. Table 44, which presents comparative party loyalty data for northern and southern Democrats in 1959, demonstrates, as did Table 26 for the 1944 session, that a majority of southern Democrats are clustered in the lowest range of party loyalty. Almost 60 percent of the southerners as against nearly 20 percent of northerners are to be found below 75. Approximately 10 percent of southerners are above 90 as against nearly 40 percent of the northern Democrats. The 1960 figures, though the loyalty of both groups drops off somewhat in this session, indicate the continued comparative disloyalty of the southern members.

Table 45 places nearly 80 percent of the southern Democrats in the ranges of loyalty below 75, as against 45.1 percent of northern members. As Table 46 reveals, the situation remained unchanged in the first

TABLE 44

FREQUENCY DISTRIBUTION OF NORTHERN AND SOUTHERN DEMOCRATS;
PARTY UNITY: HOUSE OF REPRESENTATIVES, 1959†

Range of Index of Loyalty	Northern Democrats		Southern Democrats	
	Number	Percent	Number	Percent
Below 75	27	18.8	57	58.8
75–79.9	17	11.8	12	12.4
80–84.9	22	15.3	7	7.2
85–89.9	21	14.6	11	11.3
90–94.9	38	26.4	10	10.3
95–100	19	13.2	0	0.0
Totals	144	100	97	100

†Data are from the *Congressional Quarterly Almanac,* 1959.

TABLE 45

FREQUENCY DISTRIBUTION OF NORTHERN AND SOUTHERN DEMOCRATS;
PARTY UNITY: HOUSE OF REPRESENTATIVES, 1960†

Range of Index of Loyalty	Northern Democrats		Southern Democrats	
	Number	Percent	Number	Percent
Below 75	65	45.1	76	78.4
75–79.9	25	17.4	11	11.3
80–84.9	31	21.5	7	7.2
85–89.9	14	9.7	1	1.0
90–94.9	9	6.3	2	2.1
95–100	0	0	0	0
Totals	144	100	97	100

†Data are from the *Congressional Quarterly Almanac,* 1960.

session of the Eighty-seventh Congress in 1961. Though the party loyalty of northern Democrats picked up considerably over that of the 1960 session, the dissidence of the southern group is even more pronounced. During the first year of John F. Kennedy's Presidency, more than 80 percent of southern Democrats were in the ranges of loyalty below 75 as compared with 18.3 percent of the northern group. While over 50 percent of northern party members scored in the ranges above 75, only 9.7 percent of the southerners fell into the same ranges. The distribution of

TABLE 46

FREQUENCY DISTRIBUTION OF NORTHERN AND SOUTHERN DEMOCRATS;
PARTY UNITY: HOUSE OF REPRESENTATIVES, 1961†

Range of Index of Loyalty	Northern Democrats		Southern Democrats	
	Number	Percent	Number	Percent
Below 75	22	18.3	77	82.8
75–79.9	11	9.2	3	3.2
80–84.9	25	20.8	4	4.3
85–89.9	22	18.3	4	4.3
90–94.9	27	22.5	3	3.2
95–100	13	10.8	2	2.2
Totals	120	100	93	100

†Data are from the *Congressional Quarterly Almanac,* 1961.

TABLE 47

FREQUENCY DISTRIBUTION OF NORTHERN AND SOUTHERN DEMOCRATS;
PARTY UNITY: HOUSE OF REPRESENTATIVES, 1962†

Range of Index of Loyalty	Northern Democrats		Southern Democrats	
	Number	Percent	Number	Percent
Below 75	32	26.7	81	87.1
75–79.9	19	15.8	3	3.2
80–84.9	23	19.2	2	2.2
85–89.9	18	15.0	6	6.5
90–94.9	10	8.3	1	1.1
95–100	18	15.0	0	0
Totals	120	100	93	100

†Data are from the *Congressional Quarterly Almanac,* 1962.

support scores for 1962 evidences a similar pattern of Democratic behavior.

Table 47 indicates that southern Democrats, again, are clustered in the ranges below 75, while northerners are to be found throughout the various ranges. In this session nearly 90 percent of southerners are to be found in the ranges of loyalty below 75. While these data, taken from *Congressional Quarterly* computations, should be accepted with some caution, there is no difficulty in interpreting their meaning. In each of the four recent sessions examined, southern Democrats were much less likely to support Democratic majorities than their northern colleagues. The continued existence of the romance between southern Democrats and Republicans is amply confirmed by these figures.

It has been seen that the coalition came into existence between 1930 and 1944, but the causes of its rise have not been revealed. Perhaps by examining the policy issues on which the coalition most commonly appeared during the Eighty-sixth and Eighty-seventh Congresses, it may be possible to uncover some clues to the causes of southern disaffection with the northern Democrats in the House. The approach here will be to isolate the peaks of southern discontent by examining conservative coalition roll calls—those on which a majority of southern Democrats joined a majority of southern Democrats joined a majority of Republicans to vote against a majority of northern Democrats. In these votes the high points of coalition behavior are revealed. Identification of the policy matters on which the southerners are aroused to the point of leaving the party temporarily to vote with the opposition will provide at least some basis for speculation about the causes of the coalition's rise and continued existence.

Since 72 percent of these conservative coalition votes were taken during the period from 1959 through 1962, it will not be feasible to discuss each vote in detail. It will be sufficient to summarize briefly the kinds of policy issues on which the biparty alliance formed during the four sessions analyzed.

It is readily apparent that some of the most important economic, regulatory, and welfare legislation considered during this period was subject to conservative coalition votes. For example, the Housing Act of 1959, the Labor-Management Reporting and Disclosure Act of 1959, area redevelopment legislation in 1960 and 1961, the School Construction Assistance Act of 1960, fair labor standards amendments in 1960, 1961 and 1962, the Emergency Education Act of 1961, the President's reorganization plan for the NLRB in 1961, the vote on increasing the membership of the House Rules Committee in 1961, the admission of migratory Mexican farm laborers in 1961, and the President's plan for a Department of Urban Affairs and Housing in 1962 all occasioned one or more conservative coalition votes. These are obviously isolated samples of some of the most important domestic issues facing Congress during these years. It will be apparent to most readers that this legislation is typical of the urban-oriented, regulatory, and welfare measures that have constituted the very heart of New Deal, Fair Deal, New Frontier, and Great Society programs. On these policy issues involving labor, regulation of the economy, and social welfare the southerners reveal most clearly their alienation from the northern congressional party by aligning themselves with Republicans to protest the entire thrust of national Democratic domestic policies in recent years.

Several foreign policy roll calls also reflect conservative coalition votes during recent years. Examination of the entire range of foreign policy roll calls, moreover, indicates that there would have been many more such votes if only the Republicans had been more cohesive in opposition to internationalist policies. These sessions evidence a strong protest from the southerners on foreign policy—one directed at Democratic internationalism in general, it would seem. During the four sessions in question, conservative coalition votes occurred on matters involving the United Nations in 1962, authorization of payment to Philippine citizens for damages during World War II (1962), and foreign aid in 1961 and 1962. Most clearly, the absence of coalition roll calls on foreign aid in the 1959 and 1960 sessions is attributable not to the southerners but to the Republicans, who were somewhat more internationalist during the Eisenhower Presidency. Since the 1930's something has been responsible for what would seem to be a general southern congressional revolt against the internationalism of the northern Democratic party.

Given their rarity (such issues are seldom raised on the floor of the House), it is striking how many civil liberties issues provoked coalition votes during these sessions. Five roll calls on these issues—on federal preemption of subversive activities matters and the famous "Mallory Rule"—occurred in one session in 1959. In 1961 the coalition formed again to attempt to pass yet another measure on the Mallory Rule. It would seem, then, that these questions held a certain inordinate fascination for the southern Democrats.

Identification of the peak issues on which the southern Democrats expressed their alienation from the northern party provides at least a tentative basis for speculation on the causes of the coalition's rise and continued existence through the four sessions discussed. It has been shown that the southerners have been in a general state of revolt in recent sessions. Their alienation cuts deeply across major issues of domestic economic regulation and welfare, foreign policy, civil liberties and, of course, civil rights, though the latter area has not been subject to conservative coalition voting—at least on roll calls. The crux of the problem seems to lie in the difficulty the largely rural Anglo-Saxon South has experienced in coexisting with the urban, labor, and minority group-oriented northern party since the middle 1930's, once the direction of the New Deal became clear to southern congressmen. The South's attachment to the Democratic Party since the Civil War, after all, had been largely a matter of two things—the weight of tradition and a convenient means to preserve a racial caste system. It would seem reasonable to infer that as the agreement (conscious or not) between northern and southern Democrats on race relations was destroyed after 1935, that attachment became obsolete.

Moreover, the economic populism of the rural South, which buttressed the traditional attachment to the party in the 1930's, has largely declined under the influence both of new southern affluence and the civil rights revolution. The latter, as economic conservatives in the region know full well, has served to divert the attention of the region's less affluent whites from economic to racial issues. When it is understood that the rural south has felt largely bypassed by the urban revolution and that the northern Democrats have moved closer to the interests and concerns of the northern metropolis, the dissidence of southern congressmen on New Deal-Fair Deal-New Frontier economic issues becomes more easily understood.

Southern conservatism on questions of foreign affairs in recent House sessions is somewhat more difficult to account for, but it seems reasonable to suggest that the rise of the race issue is at the root of this phenomenon also. At least one participating observer, former Congressman Frank E. Smith of Mississippi, has attributed the recent southern revolt against internationalism to the revival of racial politics in the South.[16] In recent years, he argues, the white southerner has come to see the world situation in the perspective of American race relations. American foreign aid, the United Nations, and internationalism in general have become objects of suspicion in the post-World War II period as the southerner has found little support abroad for his domestic policies in a new world of non-white developing nations and anti-colonialist sentiments.

Southern conservatism on the two civil liberties issues raised in the Eighty-sixth and Eighty-seventh Congresses would seem to be of rather obvious origin. Both issues interestingly reveal overt hostility to the United States Supreme Court and the libertarian direction that institution has taken under the leadership of Chief Justice Earl Warren. Moreover, both issues must have seemed closely related to race relations in the southerners' minds. HR 3, of course, was largely a states' rights issue. But, perhaps more important, it involved the rights of the states

16See Frank E. Smith, *Look Away From Dixie* (Baton Rouge: Louisiana State University Press, 1965), 17–30. See also his *Congressman From Mississippi* (New York: Pantheon Books, 1964), *passim*. Congressman Jamie Whitten, for example, in his successful campaign against Smith called the moderate Congressman "the only Mississippi Congressman to vote for such Kennedy Administration measures as: Foreign Aid [and the] Special U.N. Appropriation (Congo Operation)." The allusion to African chaos in the latter case was probably not lost on Mississippi electors. See *Congressman From Mississippi*, 288–89.

to handle various subversives in their own manner. Since there can be no doubt whatever that "communism," "subversion," and "integration" have been closely related concepts in many parts of the South since 1954, the racial overtones of these issues seem clear. The furor over the Mallory Case, likewise, would seem to have been provoked by a number of similar factors. After all, Mallory was a Negro and a rapist. Again, it is not difficult for anyone familiar with the association of these factors in the southern mind since 1954—integration, rape, crime in the streets, coddling of criminals, and finally, Earl Warren—to see the connections that must have triggered such a fierce southern reaction to the Supreme Court's ruling in the Mallory Case.

In recent sessions of the House, then, southern Democratic voting behavior indicates the disaffection of the south from the northern members of the party on most of the major policy questions examined. Such evidence of southern revolt in the House is but a small portion of a larger picture. A number of indicators—for example, Republican presidential voting and the renewed vitality of local Republican parties—in addition to conservative coalition voting in the House suggest that large areas of the South have for all practical purposes left the national Democratic Party. For years, a process of political realignment seems to have been in progress, the end product of which may eventually be some kind of a two-party South.[17]

Commenting on charges from the House floor of a "deal" between southern Democrats and Republicans, Representative Thomas B. Curtis (Rep., Missouri) indicated that there is more than one way to assess the coalition's activities. The real "deal," he argued, is the dishonest alliance between northern and southern Democrats for the purpose of winning power (presumably the Presidency and control of both Houses of Congress).[18] In a sense the point is well taken. Obviously, were it not for the advantages of patronage and the control of a disproportionate number of congressional committees, the most alienated of southerners (particularly those whose reelection seemed certain) in the House and Senate would long ago have left the party to join the Republicans.

If these speculations are accurate, examination of the constituency characteristics of loyal and disloyal southerners should provide additional clues to southern Democratic disaffection. Such an examination does provide considerable support for the position taken in this chapter.

[17]See Allan P. Sindler (ed.), *Change in the Contemporary South* (Durham, N.C., Duke University Press, 1963), *passim*.
[18]*Congressional Record*, 86th Cong., 2nd Sess., 700–702.

Chapter VI

CONSTITUENCY CHARACTERISTICS
AND ELECTION

As a first step toward explaining the differences between the parties (or, viewed from another perspective, influences on the congressman) the present chapter inquires into the relationship between a number of socio-economic constituency characteristics and the election of party representatives. Such an inquiry begs a fundamental question about the logic of attempts by some roll call analysts to compare the influence of party and constituency on voting behavior. The difficulty lies in the inseparability of these two supposedly distinct variables in this type of analysis. Julius Turner, for example, has attempted to compare both party and constituency pressures on roll call votes.[1] Yet, he could have done so only if he had succeeded in separating these two factors. Close scrutiny of his procedures in *Party and Constituency* has revealed that the two variables are *not* effectively separated. The difficulty is actually very fundamental. Turner identified the force he called party by membership alone, and supposed that he had isolated a truly independent variable. It can be shown, however, that the selection of Democrats and Republicans in congressional elections is highly associated with certain socio-economic characteristics of the various constituencies. Since there is such a pronounced tendency for certain types of constituencies to select Democrats and for other types to select Republicans, in a very real sense the congressional parties are in large part reflections of constituency characteristics. If, for example, nearly all 80 percent or more urban constituencies in a given election choose Democrats, the party variable reflects the constituency variable to such an extent that the two cannot be completely separated in roll call analysis.

[1]See above, pp. 17–23, *passim.*

115

In recognition of this difficulty the analysis here will take a somewhat different course. First, in the present chapter the constituency basis
of the congressional parties in the Eighty-sixth and Eighty-seventh Congresses is examined. To a very great extent, it will become clear, the two
congressional parties reflect the socio-economic characteristics of the constituencies. Chapter VII will focus on the relationship of selected constituency characteristics to deviation from party voting. This exercise reveals
that constituency factors will account in part for some deviant party behavior. Party members from atypical constituencies are rather more likely
in some cases to be disloyal to party majorities than their colleagues from
more typical districts. There are, however, many party differences that
cannot be adequately explained by aggregate constituency characteristics.
Many congressmen from atypical districts are highly loyal. Others from
typical districts are more disloyal. Party behavior must be considered
therefore as more than the simple reflection of constituency differences.
While no claim is made that party pressures are proved effective by differences in voting behavior that cannot be accounted for by constituency
characteristics, these differences do indicate that party is an independent
force in Congress.

Attempts to explain party differences for which constituency characteristics will not account might be based on a great many hypotheses. Undoubtedly, party leaders often succeed in eliciting the cooperation of
congressmen whose constituencies are atypical. Or selection processes in
these atypical constituencies may serve to recruit congressmen who are
committed to programs of their respective parties. It also seems likely
that the congressman responds to a certain segment within his constituency that is only very imperfectly indicated by the aggregate characteristics of his district. Or the policy preferences of the electorate may vary
significantly from constituency to constituency even where aggregate
characteristics are quite similar. Quite possibly, too, the congressman
perceives the "interest" of his constituency selectively through the lens
of his own preconceptions. These are only a few of the possibilities that
must be considered by students of congressional voting. The point here
is that none of these suggestions can be adequately explored through the
comparison of roll call voting with the aggregate characteristics of congressional districts. Further understanding will require other modes of
analysis.

What, then, can be learned about the constituency basis of the congressional parties? What kinds of constituencies tend to elect Democrats?
Which tend to elect Republicans? In order to investigate these questions
five separate indicators of the aggregate socio-economic status of con-

gressional districts have been chosen—urban-rural population, owner-occupied housing, nonwhite population, blue collar labor, and median family income.[2] By presenting frequency distributions of Democrats and Republicans elected in constituencies falling into various percentage ranges of these variables, it can be shown that party representation in the Eighty-sixth and Eighty-seventh Congresses was closely related to these constituency characteristics. Certain types of constituencies today, it seems, are much more likely to elect Democrats, while others are much more likely to elect Republicans. The congressional parties, as aggregates, reflect the disparate socio-economic characteristics of the constituencies from which their members emerge.

In this analysis the South (defined as the eleven Confederate states) has been omitted. Since the choice of congressmen in the southern states was limited traditionally to members of the Democratic Party during the period of this study, the choice of Democratic rather than Republican congressmen would not be expected to reflect constituency characteristics to any great extent. It may be that constituency factors are related to the party loyalty of southern Democrats, but it is a foregone conclusion that the dimensions of party choice in House elections in the South are quite different from those in the North. While the one-party system may now be breaking down in the South, that system still prevails for all practical purposes in House of Representatives elections.

Tables 48 and 49 represent frequency distributions of Democrats and Republicans elected in constituencies falling into various ranges of the percentage of urban population. In the case of the Eighty-sixth Congress there is little association apparent between urbanism and choice of Demo-

[2]These data are taken from three separate sources. Percentages of urban and rural population in congressional districts are taken from the *Congressional Quarterly Weekly Report*, February 2, 1962, pp. 153–69. Data on percentages of nonwhite population and owner-occupied housing are from *The Congressional District Data Book, Districts of the Eighty-seventh Congress*. Data on blue collar labor and median incomes were compiled by the author and Mr. James Farganis, while both were graduate students in residence at Cornell University. In an operation of great laboriousness these data were pieced together from U.S. Census figures (1960) from counties and census tracts. Data for each unit of each congressional district were punched on Hollerith cards and processed in the Cornell University Computing Center. This operation, incidentally, involved one of the great tragedies of political research (in the eyes of the author, of course), since the U.S. Bureau of the Census approximately a year after its completion published a greatly expanded version of *The Congressional District Data Book* from which much of this information might have been taken. See *The Congressional District Data Book, Districts of the Eighty-eighth Congress*. Blue collar labor refers to the combined occupational categories, "craftsmen, foremen and kindred workers," "operatives and kindred workers," "private household workers," "private household workers," "service workers," and "laborers except mine" from the *U.S. Censuses of Population and Housing: 1960*.

cratic representatives except in the highest range (over 80 percent), where slightly over four-fifths of the seats went to Democrats. A much closer relationship prevails between urbanism and party representation in the Eighty-seventh Congress. In the second of the two Congresses examined the most rural constituencies (under 20 percent urban) preferred Republicans to Democrats in nearly two-thirds of the cases, while the most urban (over 80 percent) chose Democrats in well over four-fifths of the cases. Clearly, the association between urbanism and party representation varies

TABLE 48

FREQUENCY DISTRIBUTION OF SEATS
HELD BY HOUSE DEMOCRATS AND REPUBLICANS
BY URBAN POPULATION, 86TH CONGRESS†

Percent Urban Population	Number of Constituencies‡	Elected Democrats		Elected Republicans	
		Number	Percent	Number	Percent
Under 20	127	61	48.0	66	52.0
20–40	82	43	52.4	39	47.6
40–60	29	16	55.2	13	44.8
60–80	20	9	45.0	11	55.0
Over 80	60	49	81.7	11	18.3

†Data on the percentages of urban population in the constituencies are from the *Congressional Quarterly Weekly Report,* February 2, 1962.
‡Southern Democrats and Republicans are excluded.

TABLE 49

FREQUENCY DISTRIBUTION OF SEATS
HELD BY HOUSE DEMOCRATS AND REPUBLICANS
BY URBAN POPULATION, 87TH CONGRESS†

Percent Urban Population	Number of Constituencies‡	Elected Democrats		Elected Republicans	
		Number	Percent	Number	Percent
Under 20	131	47	35.9	84	64.1
20–40	80	34	42.5	46	57.5
40–60	26	13	50.0	13	50.0
60–80	19	10	52.6	9	47.4
Over 80	58	49	84.5	9	15.5

†Data on percentages of urban population in the constituencies are from the *Congressional Quarterly Weekly Report,* February 2, 1962.
‡Southern Democrats and Republicans are excluded.

over time, but the tendency in both of these Congresses for more urban constituencies to elect Democrats should be noted. It would seem that many of the more rural congressional districts which elected Democrats in the Democratic landslide of 1958 returned to what must be assumed to be their more normal Republican preferences in the congressional election of 1960. While there is nothing like a one-to-one relationship, it does seem apparent that urbanism and party representation are related. In 1960, which seems to have been a much more normal election year than 1958, this relationship is especially apparent.

The relationship of owner-occupied housing in the constituencies to party representation in the House is shown in Tables 50 through 53. The first and second of these four tables present frequency distributions of party choice for all northern constituencies. With few exceptions these tables reveal a negative association between the percentage of owner-occupied housing in the constituencies and preference for Democratic representation. In the upper ranges (where most constituencies are located) the association between percentage of owner-occupied housing and party choice is relatively weaker, but in the lower ranges it is immediately apparent. In both the Eighty-sixth and Eighty-seventh Congresses, districts characterized by less than 60 percent owner-occupied housing elected Democrats approximately twice as frequently as Republicans. Tables 52 and 53, which present exactly comparable data for Urban-Suburban constituencies (those with less than 40 percent rural population), demonstrate convincingly that the relationship between the percentage of owner-occupied housing and Republican preferences is much stronger

TABLE 50

FREQUENCY DISTRIBUTION OF SEATS
HELD BY HOUSE DEMOCRATS AND REPUBLICANS
BY PERCENTAGE OF OWNER-OCCUPIED HOUSING, 86TH CONGRESS†

Percent Owner-Occupied	Number of Constituencies‡	Elected Democrats		Elected Republicans	
		Number	Percent	Number	Percent
Under 20	13	12	92.3	1	7.7
20–40	23	18	78.3	5	21.7
40–60	52	33	63.5	19	36.5
60–80	220	111	50.5	109	49.5
Over 80	10	4	50.0	6	50.0

†Data on percentages of owner-occupied housing are from the *Congressional District Data Book, Districts of the Eighty-seventh Congress.*
‡Southern Democrats and Republicans are excluded.

TABLE 51

FREQUENCY DISTRIBUTION OF SEATS
HELD BY HOUSE DEMOCRATS AND REPUBLICANS
BY PERCENTAGE OF OWNER-OCCUPIED HOUSING, 87TH CONGRESS†

Percent Owner-Occupied	Number of Constituencies‡	Elected Democrats		Elected Republicans	
		Number	Percent	Number	Percent
Below 20	14	13	92.9	1	7.1
20–40	21	17	81.0	4	19.0
40–60	51	35	68.6	16	31.4
60–80	218	83	38.1	135	61.9
Over 80	10	5	50.0	5	50.0

†Data on percentages of owner-occupied housing are from the *Congressional District Data Book, Districts of the Eighty-seventh Congress.*
‡Southern Democrats and Republicans are excluded.

in these city-dominated congressional districts. While the lower ranges of the distributions remain largely unchanged (apparently, most low owner-occupancy districts are city districts), the upper ranges are altered significantly when the rural districts are excluded from the analysis. In Tables 52 and 53 the relationship between owner-occupancy and party choice is quite clear. In the case of the Eighty-seventh Congress, as owner-occupancy increases, preference for Republican representatives increases with but a single exception in the highest range of owner-occupancy. In the lowest ranges of owner-occupancy Democrats are preferred 9 to 1, whereas in the highest ranges preferences for the two parties are either about equal or slightly favorable to the Republicans. The percentage of owner-occupied housing with some exceptions is a fairly good indicator, it would seem, of the social status of congressional districts. Though there are some obvious difficulties here (former Representative and now New York Mayor John Lindsay's "Silk Stocking" 17th District in New York City is relatively very low in owner-occupied housing, for example), low percentages of owner-occupied property seem nearly always to indicate low socio-economic status. These low-status districts are strong in their preference for Democratic representation. High owner occupancy, it seems, is not necessarily an indicator of high status, and consequently there is less association apparent in the higher ranges in the four tables presented here. The tables show clearly, however, that owner-occupancy and Democratic representation in the House are highly negative in association.

TABLE 52

FREQUENCY DISTRIBUTION OF SEATS
HELD BY HOUSE DEMOCRATS AND REPUBLICANS
IN URBAN-SUBURBAN CONSTITUENCIES BY OWNER-OCCUPIED HOUSING, 86TH CONGRESS†

Percent Owner- Occupied	Number of Constituencies‡	Elected Democrats		Elected Republicans	
		Number	Percent	Number	Percent
Below 20	13	12	92.3	1	7.7
20–40	23	18	78.3	5	21.7
40–60	44	27	61.4	17	38.6
60–80	66	34	51.5	32	48.5
Over 80	6	2	33.3	4	66.7

†Data on percentages of owner-occupied housing are from the *Congressional District Data Book, Districts of the Eighty-seventh Congress.*
‡Southern Democrats and Republicans are excluded.

TABLE 53

FREQUENCY DISTRIBUTION OF SEATS
HELD BY HOUSE DEMOCRATS AND REPUBLICANS
IN URBAN-SUBURBAN CONSTITUENCIES BY OWNER-OCCUPIED HOUSING, 87TH CONGRESS†

Percent Owner- Occupied	Number of Constituencies‡	Elected Democrats		Elected Republicans	
		Number	Percent	Number	Percent
Below 20	14	13	92.9	1	7.1
20–40	21	17	81.0	4	19.0
40–60	43	29	67.4	14	32.6
60–80	64	27	42.2	37	67.8
Over 80	6	3	50.0	3	50.0

†Data on percentages of owner-occupied housing are from the *Congressional District Data Book, Districts of the Eighty-seventh Congress.*
‡Southern Democrats and Republicans are excluded.

Another useful indicator of social status in northern congressional districts is the percentage of nonwhite persons in the population. While low percentages of nonwhite population are not good indicators of high economic and social status, the reverse is almost always the case. High percentages of nonwhite persons almost always indicate low status, American residential patterns being what they are. It is not surprising, then, to find in Tables 54–57 a very high positive association between percentage of nonwhite population and Democratic representation both for all northern congressional districts and for city-dominated districts alone. Tables 54 and 55 reveal this relationship for all northern districts. In each table the relationship is clear. As the percentage of nonwhites increases, the percentage of districts electing Democrats increases. In the city-dominated districts (containing less than 40 percent rural population), this relationship becomes even clearer, as Tables 56 and 57 demonstrate. In the urban-suburban districts, 10 percent or more nonwhite population seems to be accompanied by over-

TABLE 54

FREQUENCY DISTRIBUTION OF SEATS
HELD BY HOUSE DEMOCRATS AND REPUBLICANS
BY NONWHITE POPULATION, 86TH CONGRESS†

Percent Nonwhite	Number of Constituencies‡	Elected Democrats		Elected Republicans	
		Number	Percent	Number	Percent
Below 10	248	119	48.0	129	52.0
10–20	39	30	76.9	9	23.1
20–30	15	11	73.3	4	26.7
30–40	9	8	88.9	1	11.1
Over 40	10	10	100.0	0	0.0

†Data on percentages of nonwhite population are from the *Congressional District Data Book, Districts of the Eighty-seventh Congress.*
‡Southern Democrats and Republicans are excluded.

TABLE 55

FREQUENCY DISTRIBUTION OF SEATS
HELD BY HOUSE DEMOCRATS AND REPUBLICANS
BY NONWHITE POPULATION, 87TH CONGRESS†

Percent Nonwhite	Number of Constituencies‡	Elected Democrats		Elected Republicans	
		Number	Percent	Number	Percent
Below 10	248	97	39.1	151	60.9
10–20	36	27	75.0	9	25.0
20–30	12	12	100.0	0	0.0
30–40	9	8	88.9	1	11.1
Over 40	9	9	100.0	0	0.0

†Data on percentages of nonwhite population are from the *Congressional District Data Book, Districts of the Eighty-seventh Congress.*
‡Southern Democrats and Republicans are excluded.

whelming preference for Democratic representation. In both Congresses, districts falling into the ranges above 10 percent were represented by Democrats in over 70 percent of cases. Above 20 percent, Democratic representation was practically certain. This heavy preference for the Democrats is probably explained both by the preferences of the nonwhite residents themselves and by those of the low-status white people who live in the same areas. There is little doubt, for example, that the variable employed—percentage of nonwhite population—is highly correlated with

TABLE 56

FREQUENCY DISTRIBUTION OF SEATS
HELD BY HOUSE DEMOCRATS AND REPUBLICANS
IN URBAN-SUBURBAN CONSTITUENCIES BY NONWHITE POPULATION, 86TH CONGRESS†

Percent Nonwhite	Number of Constituencies‡	Elected Democrats		Elected Republicans	
		Number	Percent	Number	Percent
Below 10	97	47	48.5	50	51.5
10–20	26	19	73.1	7	26.9
20–30	10	9	90.0	1	10.0
30–40	9	8	88.9	1	11.1
Over 40	10	10	100.0	0	0.0

†Data on percentages of nonwhite population are from the *Congressional District Data Book, Districts of the Eighty-seventh Congress.*
‡Southern Democrats and Republicans are excluded.

TABLE 57

FREQUENCY DISTRIBUTION OF SEATS
HELD BY HOUSE DEMOCRATS AND REPUBLICANS
IN URBAN-SUBURBAN CONSTITUENCIES BY NONWHITE POPULATION, 87TH CONGRESS†

Percent Nonwhite	Number of Constituencies‡	Elected Democrats		Elected Republicans	
		Number	Percent	Number	Percent
Below 10	96	45	46.9	51	53.1
10–20	24	17	70.8	7	29.2
20–30	10	10	100.0	0	0.0
30–40	8	8	100.0	0	0.0
Over 40	9	9	100.0	0	0.0

†Data on percentages of nonwhite population are from the *Congressional District Data Book, Districts of the Eighty-seventh Congress.*
‡Southern Democrats and Republicans are excluded.

such other indicators of socio-economic status as percentage of owner-occupied housing, blue collar labor, and median incomes. As has been noted, American residential patterns being what they are, Negroes are certain to be located in greatest number in urban, low-status areas. These areas, as the tables reveal, manifest strong Democratic preferences in the election of representatives to both the Eighty-sixth and Eighty-seventh Congresses.

A very effective indicator of the economic and social status of congressional constituencies would seem to be blue collar labor or those people employed in such occupations as laborer, household worker, operative, and craftsman. This population characteristic in the various congressional districts provides a strong basis for inferences about the policy preferences prevailing among the electorate. The expectation, of course, is that percentage of blue collar or working class population should be strongly and positively associated with preferences for Democratic representation, and this is amply borne out by the data in Tables 58–61. Tables 58 and 59 present data relating blue collar labor to Democratic representation for all northern congressional districts. The relationship, even when rural areas are included in the distribution, is so strong that it requires little interpretation. As the percentage of working class population increases, the percentage of Democrats elected also increases. The tendency for high status and farm areas to prefer Republicans and low status areas to prefer Democrats is especially clear at the extremes where the preference in one direction or the other runs better than 2 to 1 for both the Eighty-sixth and Eighty-seventh Congresses. In the urban areas, as expected, the association of working class population and Democratic representation is even more clear. In the city-

TABLE 58

FREQUENCY DISTRIBUTION OF SEATS
HELD BY HOUSE DEMOCRATS AND REPUBLICANS
BY BLUE COLLAR LABOR, 86TH CONGRESS†

Percent Blue Collar	Number of Constituencies‡	Elected Democrats		Elected Republicans	
		Number	Percent	Number	Percent
Below 40	24	8	33.3	16	66.7
40–50	84	41	48.8	43	51.2
50–60	142	78	54.9	64	45.1
Above 60	68	51	75.0	17	25.0

†Data on Blue Collar labor were computed by author.
‡Southern Democrats and Republicans are excluded.

TABLE 59

FREQUENCY DISTRIBUTION OF SEATS
HELD BY HOUSE DEMOCRATS AND REPUBLICANS
BY BLUE COLLAR LABOR, 87TH CONGRESS†

Percent Blue Collar	Number of Constituencies‡	Elected Democrats		Elected Republicans	
		Number	Percent	Number	Percent
Below 40	25	5	20.0	20	80.0
40–50	84	38	45.2	46	54.8
50–60	138	62	44.9	76	55.1
Over 60	67	48	71.6	19	28.4

†Data on Blue Collar labor were computed by author.
‡Southern Democrats and Republicans are excluded.

dominated districts, where blue collar labor exceeds 50 percent of the population, Democrats were elected in more than 60 percent of the cases. Where blue collar workers exceed 60 percent of the population, Democratic representation was again almost a foregone conclusion. Democrats were elected in these working class districts nearly nine times out of ten. Inspection of Tables 60 and 61 leaves no doubt whatever about the class basis of House representation in northern urban areas. These areas manifest a very strong preference for party representatives who, we must infer, seemed to these constituents most likely to serve their economic interests.

The final constituency characteristic whose relationship to party representation in the House is examined here is median family income. Again, it seems evident that these data present a very strong indication of the socio-economic status of the various constituencies and thus as

TABLE 60

FREQUENCY DISTRIBUTION OF SEATS
HELD BY HOUSE DEMOCRATS AND REPUBLICANS
IN URBAN-SUBURBAN CONSTITUENCIES BY BLUE COLLAR LABOR, 86TH CONGRESS†

Percent Blue Collar	Number of Constituencies‡	Elected Democrats		Elected Republicans	
		Number	Percent	Number	Percent
Below 40	9	2	22.2	7	77.8
40–50	39	15	38.5	24	61.5
50–60	77	54	70.1	23	29.9
Above 60	37	32	86.5	5	13.5

†Data on Blue Collar labor were computed by author.
‡Southern Democrats and Republicans are excluded.

solid a foundation as is likely to be found in aggregate data for inferences about the policy preferences of the electorate. Again, the expectation is that median income will be strongly negative in association with Democratic representation. Since incomes in the various constituencies probably correlate very highly with the status of occupations, a distribution quite similar to that prevailing in the four tables immediately foregoing—but in the opposite direction—would be expected. Tables 62–65 present frequency distributions of Democrats and Republicans elected in constituencies ranging from $2,500 income or lower through $8,000 or above. In each of the cases the actual median has been assigned to the nearest even $500 class. In both sets of tables—62 and 63, presenting distributions for all northern constituencies, and 63 and 64, presenting comparable distributions for urban-suburban constituencies alone—a strong negative relationship between district median income and Democratic representation is apparent. For all northern constituencies, as Tables 62 and 63 demonstrate, this relationship is especially clear at the extremes of the distribution. For the city-dominated districts alone, ranging from $4,000 to $8,000 incomes and above, the negative relationship of median income to Democratic representation is crystal clear. Again, Tables 64 and 65, presenting data for the urban-suburban constituencies, leave no doubt about the high association of socio-economic status and party representation in northern urban areas. To a very great extent congressional Democrats and Republicans in the Eighty-sixth and Eighty-seventh Congresses reflected the disparate socio-economic status of the constituencies their members represented.

Clearly, these socio-economic constituency factors were strongly related to party representation in the Eighty-sixth and Eighty-seventh Con-

TABLE 61

FREQUENCY DISTRIBUTION OF SEATS
HELD BY HOUSE DEMOCRATS AND REPUBLICANS
IN URBAN-SUBURBAN CONSTITUENCIES BY BLUE COLLAR LABOR, 87TH CONGRESS†

Percent Blue Collar	Number of Constituencies‡	Elected Democrats Number	Elected Democrats Percent	Elected Republicans Number	Elected Republicans Percent
Below 40	9	3	33.3	6	66.7
40–50	39	15	38.5	24	61.5
50–60	74	49	66.2	25	33.8
Above 60	36	32	88.9	4	11.1

†Data on Blue Collar labor were computed by author.
‡Southern Democrats and Republicans are excluded.

TABLE 62

FREQUENCY DISTRIBUTION OF SEATS
HELD BY HOUSE DEMOCRATS AND REPUBLICANS
BY MEDIAN FAMILY INCOME, 86TH CONGRESS†

Median Income	Number of Constituencies‡	Elected Democrats		Elected Republicans	
		Number	Percent	Number	Percent
Under $2,500	1	0	0.0	1	100.0
$3,000	3	3	100.0	0	0.0
3,500	6	5	83.3	1	16.7
4,000	23	18	78.3	5	21.7
4,500	15	8	53.3	7	46.7
5,000	22	12	54.5	10	45.5
5,500	62	35	56.5	27	43.5
6,000	59	33	55.9	26	44.1
6,500	58	36	62.1	22	37.9
7,000	33	19	57.6	14	42.4
7,500	19	5	26.3	14	73.7
8,000 or above	17	4	23.5	13	76.5

†Data on median incomes were computed by author.
‡Southern Democrats and Republicans are excluded.

TABLE 63

FREQUENCY DISTRIBUTION OF SEATS
HELD BY HOUSE DEMOCRATS AND REPUBLICANS
BY MEDIAN FAMILY INCOME, 87TH CONGRESS†

Median Income	Number of Constituencies‡	Elected Democrats		Elected Republicans	
		Number	Percent	Number	Percent
Under $2,500	1	0	0.0	1	100.0
$3,000	3	3	100.0	0	0.0
3,500	6	5	83.3	1	16.7
4,000	24	14	58.3	10	41.7
4,500	19	8	42.1	11	57.9
5,000	24	8	33.3	16	66.7
5,500	60	28	46.7	32	53.3
6,000	54	31	57.4	23	42.6
6,500	55	31	56.4	24	43.6
7,000	33	17	51.5	16	48.5
7,500	19	5	26.3	14	73.7
8,000 or over	16	3	18.8	13	81.2

†Data on median incomes were computed by author.
‡Southern Democrats and Republicans are excluded.

gresses. The more urban, nonwhite, and blue collar the constituency, the more likely was that constituency to be represented by a Democrat. The higher the percentage of owner-occupied housing and the median income, the more a district was apt to have chosen a Republican. The meaning of these relationships seems quite clear. At least in recent years, lower status, urban congressional districts in the North have constituted the bedrock of the aggregate Democratic congressional constituency, while the rural and more affluent urban areas have formed the core of the Republican constituency. Such a relationship is probably true for any Congress since 1932. The earlier assertion that the congressional parties reflect constituency factors to the extent that party and constituency cannot be completely separated in roll call analysis has been amply documented.

It would seem that the major dimensions of partisan policy conflict in Congress are set by party alignments which weight the two congressional parties respectively in favor of certain aggregate groups in the population. Since 1932, it must be assumed, the congressional Democrats have been weighted heavily in favor of urban, blue collar districts (and thus in favor of nonwhite and other minority groups who are also likely to be found there). Congressional Republicans, on the other hand, have been so heavily weighted in favor of rural and higher status urban areas (and thus in favor of the white, old stock elements to be found

TABLE 64

FREQUENCY DISTRIBUTION OF SEATS
HELD BY HOUSE DEMOCRATS AND REPUBLICANS
IN URBAN-SUBURBAN CONSTITUENCIES BY MEDIAN FAMILY INCOME, 87TH CONGRESS†

Median Income	Number of Constituencies‡	Elected Democrats		Elected Republicans	
		Number	Percent	Number	Percent
$4,000	2	2	100.0	0	0.0
4,500	5	5	100.0	0	0.0
5,000	5	4	80.0	1	20.0
5,500	13	13	100.0	0	0.0
6,000	24	20	83.3	4	16.7
6,500	40	26	65.0	14	35.0
7,000	29	13	44.8	16	55.2
7,500	16	3	18.8	13	81.2
8,000 or over	14	3	21.4	11	78.6

†Data on median incomes were computed by author.
‡Southern Democrats and Republicans are excluded.

there). While it will not be argued here that all observed differences between the parties can be explained by these diverse "centers of gravity," it does seem beyond question that these links between the constituencies and the congressional parties account for a good portion of Democratic liberalism and Republican conservatism, especially on questions of domestic economic policy. The major policy struggles of our domestic politics since 1932 have involved urban-oriented welfare and regulatory legislation formulated primarily to meet the needs of lower-status people in the vast urban, industrial areas. While housing, labor, welfare, minimum wage, and health measures have been viewed favorably by the residents of these areas, they must have been regarded as either irrelevant, useless, or dangerous to many rural and suburban people. It must be assumed that a great deal of the divergent behavior of congressional Democrats and Republicans can be explained by divergent policy preferences prevailing in these different kinds of constituencies. It must also be noted, however, that in a great many of the constituencies there is little apparent association of socio-economic characteristics and party representation. Toward the middle of each of the distributions presented, very little association is apparent. And even at the extremes of these distributions many constituencies do not follow the expected pattern. In the case of these constituencies it is by no means clear that Democratic or Republican voting differences can be explained by con-

TABLE 65

FREQUENCY DISTRIBUTION OF SEATS
HELD BY HOUSE DEMOCRATS AND REPUBLICANS
IN URBAN-SUBURBAN CONSTITUENCIES BY MEDIAN FAMILY INCOME, 86TH CONGRESS†

Median Income	Number of Constituencies‡	Elected Democrats		Elected Republicans	
		Number	Percent	Number	Percent
$4,000	2	2	100.0	0	0.0
4,500	4	4	100.0	0	0.0
5,000	5	5	100.0	0	0.0
5,500	14	14	100.0	0	0.0
6,000	25	20	80.0	5	20.0
6,500	42	27	64.3	15	35.7
7,000	29	15	51.7	14	48.3
7,500	16	3	18.8	13	81.2
8,000	15	3	25.0	12	75.0

†Data on median incomes were computed by author.
‡Southern Democrats and Republicans are excluded.

stituency interests (defined, of course, as inferred attitudes of the electorate). Many Democrats, for example, were elected to the Eighty-sixth and Eighty-seventh Congresses from rural areas. Loyal party voting on the part of these congressmen in non-farm, economic, and regulatory matters is not easily explained in terms of constituency interests. Likewise, many Republicans were elected from urban areas where levels of blue collar labor and incomes might lead the observer to suppose that the policy preferences of the electorate on these same issues would be relatively liberal. Again, loyal Republican voting on the part of these representatives is not readily explained by reference to constituency interests.

The domestic economic conservatism of many southern Democrats in the House, discussed earlier, would also seem to be basically related to the socio-economic characteristics of their constituencies and, inferentially, the opinions prevailing therein. Many southern Democratic districts, of course, resemble very closely (in terms of the socio-economic factors discussed) northern Republican districts. In the one-party South, rural and suburban areas that in the North would almost certainly elect Republicans elect Democrats as a matter of tradition. It is hardly surprising that these Democrats are more conservative than their northern colleagues from urban, low status areas. It must be assumed that suburban and rural southerners, much like their social counterparts in the North, have viewed the major domestic policies of the New Deal-Fair Deal-New Frontier either as unnecessary innovations at best, or as dangerous threats to an established order at worst. When it is remembered that those southerners with the strongest reasons to be attached to Democratic policies—the Negroes—have in many parts of the South traditionally been disfranchised and excluded from the political process, the conservatism of many southern congressmen is not difficult to comprehend.

Differences in party behavior relating to foreign affairs and civil liberties would seem to be less directly related to the constituency differences examined, but there is some evidence suggesting that such connections do exist. Distributions of public opinion data for various geographical areas, for example, have revealed that rural areas have ranked far behind the cities in internationalism in recent years.[3] While the reasons behind this fact are not altogether well understood, it is known that rural residence is highly correlated with conservatism in this policy area. Rural areas are also found to rank quite low on matters involving civil liberties. Here,

[3]See Key, *Public Opinion and American Democracy*, 114.

again, the connection would seem reasonably clear. Little, it seems, in the experience of the rural or small town American disposes him to tolerate dissent or deviation from accepted community norms.[4] In both of these latter areas, since it must be supposed that most constituents are less concerned about foreign policy and civil liberties matters than about domestic economic issues, it would seem that party behavior has more to do with the representative's outlook than with expressed preferences of the electorate.

A good many of the observed differences between House northern Democrats and Republicans during the Eighty-sixth and Eighty-seventh Congresses would seem to be rooted in the characteristics of the constituencies their members represented. Even if there were no organizational party pressures at all, it would seem that the differing constituency bases of the two congressional parties would account for many of their differences. This point having been established, it becomes appropriate to investigate the relationship of selected constituency characteristics to party loyalty and disloyalty. Such an exercise will indicate that while these factors will account in part for variations in party voting behavior, they will by no means serve to explain that behavior entirely. There are, it seems, many intra-party differences in voting behavior for which aggregate constituency characteristics will not account.

---

[4]See Samuel A. Stouffer, *Communism; Conformity and Civil Liberties* (New York: John Wiley and Sons, Science Editions, 1966), 130 and 109–30, *passim*. It should also be noted that when level of education is controlled, the South is less tolerant on civil liberties matters than any northern region. See *ibid.*, 120–22.

Chapter VII

CONSTITUENCY CHARACTERISTICS
AND INTRA-PARTY VOTING DIFFERENCES

As CHAPTER II of this study has shown, several investigators have concerned themselves with party and constituency as influences on congressional voting.[1] With the exception of Julius Turner's unique attempt to compare the influence of party and constituency,[2] the writings of these observers have much in common. In each study intra-party voting differences have been conceptualized as dependent variables to be explained—at least in part—by constituency characteristics. The supposition of these writers has been that aggregate constituency factors hold one of the major keys to the explanation of intra-party voting differences. Turner, for example, investigated the effects of atypical constituency characteristics on party loyalty.[3] Duncan MacRae similarly studied the relationship of voting scale scores for Democrats and Republicans to section and the occupational status of constituencies.[4] Lewis A. Froman attempted to demonstrate that the liberalism of Democrats and Republicans (measured by *Congressional Quarterly* Kennedy Support Scores) was related to four constituency characteristics in the case of the first session of the Eighty-seventh Congress.[5] Finally, David Truman examined the constituency characteristics of members of the various blocs identified in *The Congressional Party*.[6]

A similar analysis is undertaken here of constituency factors and party voting during the Eighty-sixth and Eighty-seventh Congresses. In this

1See above, 55–61, *passim.*
2*Ibid.,* 17–23, *passim.*
3*Ibid.*
4*Ibid.,* 27–30.
5*Ibid.,* 58.
6*Ibid.,* 35.

chapter northern Democrats, northern Republicans, and southern Democrats are examined in turn so that deviation from party voting may be viewed in relation to selected constituency factors—urban population, percentage of blue collar labor, and median income for the northern groups, and urban population and percentage of nonwhite population for the southern Democrats. Another constituency factor, section, is partially controlled for the Democrats by dividing the party into northern and southern groups. In the absence of any objective way to divide northern Democrats and Republicans into further sectional groupings, further remarks about sectional influences will be limited to identifying the geographic location of extremely deviant scale types in each of the parties in a number of specific policy areas. While this procedure is not the most sophisticated that might be imagined, it seems preferable to dividing the nation into sections on the basis of arbitrarily drawn lines.[7] In the case of each of the three groups mentioned the analysis will focus on the same question: to what extent can deviation from party voting be explained by constituency factors? No assumption is made that the rather crude analysis employed here adequately captures the subtle interplay of factors related to congressional voting. In fact, other techniques and approaches *must* be employed if the understanding of party and constituency influences on voting in Congress is to be improved.

It has been shown in the previous chapter that Democratic representation in the Eighty-sixth and Eighty-seventh Congresses was positively related to urban population, percentage of nonwhite population, and percentage of blue collar labor, and negatively related to median income and percentage of owner-occupied housing. It would seem reasonable to suppose, then, that intra-party voting differences might also be related to these same factors. A great many northern Democrats were elected, however, from constituencies that might be considered atypical. The supposition is justifiable, therefore, that these representatives find it somewhat more difficult to support their party when majorities of Democrats oppose majorities of Republicans. In other words Democrats from Republican-like constituencies and Republicans from Democratic-like constituencies

[7]The problem of dividing the nation into sections for the purposes of roll call analysis has been raised above. See page 29. There would seem to be little difficulty in demarcating "the South," although even here various practices are employed (Oklahoma, Missouri, Kentucky, West Virginia and Maryland are sometimes included, sometimes excluded). Beyond this point, however, troubles are legion. Is Ohio a midwestern or northeastern state? Should the coastal western states be divided into two sections or treated as one? Many more questions of this sort must be dealt with. There would seem to be no authoritative way to resolve them here.

would tend to deviate from party voting more often than those members of each party who represented more typical districts. To investigate this possibility for northern Democrats in the case of the Eighty-sixth and Eighty-seventh Congresses, party opposition (as measured by the *Congressional Quarterly's* Party Opposition Scores) [8] will be considered in relation to three of the constituency characteristics already discussed—urban population, blue collar labor, and median income—for one session of each Congress included in this study. If party opposition is to be accounted for in terms of constituency characteristics, Democrats from rural areas, from low blue collar districts, and from high income districts should be much more disloyal than those from urban, high blue collar, and low income areas.

Table 66 presents a frequency distribution of northern Democrats who were relatively loyal (those voting with majorities on more than three quarters of roll calls on which a majority of Democrats opposed a majority of Republicans) and those who were relatively disloyal (those opposing their party majority on more than a quarter of these roll calls) by percentage of urban population in their constituencies. If rural population were highly related to defection from northern Democratic ranks when majorities of the two parties opposed one another, the Democratic deviants should be found at the top of the table in the lower ranges of urban population. But, in fact, they are not. In neither the 1960 nor the 1962 session does the table reveal a pronounced tendency for rural Dem-

TABLE 66

FREQUENCY DISTRIBUTION OF PARTY OPPOSITION SCORES
FOR NORTHERN DEMOCRATIC CONGRESSMEN BY
URBAN POPULATION, 86TH AND 87TH CONGRESSES

Percent Urban	Party Opposition Score, 1960				Party Opposition Score, 1962			
	Below 25		Above 25		Below 25		Above 25	
	No.	Percent	No.	Percent	No.	Percent	No.	Percent
0–20	55	90.2	6	9.8	41	87.2	6	12.8
20–40	41	95.3	2	4.7	32	94.1	2	5.9
40–60	12	75.0	4	25.0	11	91.7	1	8.3
60–80	9	100.0	0	0.0	9	90.0	1	10.0
80–100	46	93.9	3	6.1	49	100.0	0	0.0

[8]The "Party Opposition Score" as calculated by the *CQ* is defined as the percentage of roll calls on which majorities of the two parties oppose one another, on which the congressman *opposes* his party majority. The information employed here is taken from *CQ Almanac*, Vol. 16 (1960), 140–41; and Vol. 18 (1962), 764–65.

ocrats to be more disloyal to party majorities than their urban colleagues. Lest it be thought that the distributions presented are influenced by the choice of cut-off points on Party Opposition Scores, it should be said that dichotomizing the Democrats' scores at any other point has little effect on the outcome. When other factors are left uncontrolled, then, rural Democrats are found to be little, if any, less loyal to party majorities than their urban counterparts. Northern Democrats in these sessions were nearly all highly loyal when majorities of the two parties opposed one another, and those few who did defect on more than a quarter of these roll calls were spread throughout the various ranges of urban population.

Tables 67 and 68 should disclose any relationship between party disloyalty and low percentages of blue collar labor in the constituencies for the Eighty-sixth and Eighty-seventh Congresses, respectively. Again, if such a relationship existed, the deviants among the northern Democrats should be clustered in the lower ranges of blue collar labor. The tables, however, reveal no very impressive relationship. In the 1960 session of the Eighty-sixth Congress (Table 67) only those Democrats from the lowest range manifest some tendency to be more disloyal than those in the highest range. When rural-urban differences are held constant by eliminating those Democrats from Urban-Suburban constituencies (those characterized by less than 40 percent rural population), it becomes apparent that the relationship between defections from party majorities and percentage of blue collar labor is no stronger in the urban areas. There is little alteration of this situation in Table 68, which presents comparable data for the 1962 session of the Eighty-seventh Congress. In fact, in direct contrast to the hypothesis that northern Democrats from relatively low blue collar

TABLE 67

FREQUENCY DISTRIBUTION OF PARTY OPPOSITION SCORES
FOR NORTHERN DEMOCRATIC CONGRESSMEN BY
BLUE COLLAR LABOR, 86TH CONGRESS

Percent Blue Collar Labor	Party Opposition Score, 1960			
	All Northern Democrats		Urban-Suburban Democrats	
	Below 25 No. Percent	Above 25 No. Percent	Below 25 No. Percent	Above 25 No. Percent
Under 40	5 62.5	3 37.5	1 50.0	1 50.0
40–50	39 95.1	2 4.9	15 100.0	0 100.0
50–60	71 91.0	7 9.0	40 90.9	4 9.1
Over 60	48 94.1	3 5.9	29 90.6	3 9.4

TABLE 68

FREQUENCY DISTRIBUTION OF PARTY OPPOSITION SCORES
FOR NORTHERN DEMOCRATIC CONGRESSMEN BY
BLUE COLLAR LABOR, 87TH CONGRESS

Percent Blue Collar Labor	Party Opposition Scores, 1962							
	All Northern Democrats				Urban-Suburban Democrats			
	Below 25		Above 25		Below 25		Above 25	
	No.	Percent	No.	Percent	No.	Percent	No.	Percent
Under 40	5	100.0	0	0.0	3	100.0	0	0.0
40–50	35	92.1	3	7.9	5	83.3	1	16.7
50–60	56	91.8	5	8.2	19	95.0	1	5.0
Over 60	46	95.8	2	4.2	19	95.0	1	5.0

districts would be more disloyal than those from districts falling into the higher ranges, those Democrats in the lowest range were the most loyal of all. When the rural districts (over 40 percent rural) are eliminated, all the representatives from the extremely atypical Democratic Urban-Suburban constituencies appear in the relatively more loyal group. Again, it should be noted that whatever cutting points of Party Opposition Scores are chosen, the distributions in Tables 67 and 68 are not noticeably altered. In neither the second session of the Eighty-sixth nor the Eighty-seventh Congress, then, is there a pronounced tendency of Democrats from low blue collar constituencies to be more disloyal than their colleagues from more heavily blue collar districts.

The frequency distributions of the loyalty and disloyalty of the northern Democrats, whose constituencies fall into various divisions based on median income data, are shown in Tables 69 and 70. If there were any relationship prevailing between defections to the opposition when majorities of the two parties opposed one another and the income status of constituencies, the northern Democratic should cluster at the bottom of these tables in the high income ranges. As the tables clearly reveal, there is no such relationship either for all northern Democrats or for Urban-Suburban Democrats alone. Only in the case of the second session of the Eighty-sixth Congress, when rural constituencies are excluded from the analysis, is there even the slightest tendency in the highest range for party opposition to increase. In neither the Eighty-sixth nor the Eighty-seventh Congress, then, does there appear a relationship for northern Democrats between the income status of constituencies and voting with the opposition party against a majority of one's own party. Those northern Democrats who represented relatively affluent constituencies—whether rural or

TABLE 69

FREQUENCY DISTRIBUTION OF PARTY OPPOSITION SCORES
FOR NORTHERN DEMOCRATIC CONGRESSMEN BY
MEDIAN FAMILY INCOME, 86TH CONGRESS

	Party Opposition Score, 1960							
	All Northern Democrats				Urban-Suburban Democrats			
Median	Below 25		Above 25		Below 25		Above 25	
Income	No.	Percent	No.	Percent	No.	Percent	No.	Percent
$3,000	2	66.7	1	33.3	....	....	....	....
3,500	5	100.0	0	0.0	....	....	....	....
4,000	15	83.3	3	16.7	2	100.0	0	0.0
4,500	7	87.5	1	12.5	3	100.0	0	0.0
5,000	12	100.0	0	0.0	5	100.0	0	0.0
5,500	33	94.3	2	5.7	14	100.0	0	0.0
6,000	29	87.9	4	12.1	16	80.0	4	20.0
6,500	34	94.4	2	5.6	25	92.6	2	7.4
7,000	18	94.7	1	5.3	14	93.3	1	6.7
7,500	5	100.0	0	0.0	3	100.0	0	0.0
8,000	3	75.0	1	25.0	2	66.7	1	33.3

TABLE 70

FREQUENCY DISTRIBUTION OF PARTY OPPOSITION SCORES
FOR NORTHERN DEMOCRATIC CONGRESSMEN BY
MEDIAN FAMILY INCOME, 87TH CONGRESS

	Party Opposition, 1962							
	All Northern Democrats				Urban-Suburban Democrats			
Median	Below 25		Above 25		Below 25		Above 25	
Income	No.	Percent	No.	Percent	No.	Percent	No.	Percent
$3,000	2	66.7	1	33.3	....	....	....	....
3,500	5	100.0	0	0.0	....	....	....	....
4,000	12	85.7	2	14.3	2	100.0	0	0.0
4,500	6	75.0	2	25.0	5	100.0	0	0.0
5,000	8	100.0	0	0.0	4	100.0	0	0.0
5,500	26	92.9	2	7.1	12	92.3	1	7.7
6,000	31	100.0	0	0.0	20	100.0	0	0.0
6,500	30	96.8	1	3.2	25	96.2	1	3.8
7,000	14	87.5	2	12.5	12	92.3	1	7.7
7,500	5	100.0	0	0.0	3	100.0	0	0.0
8,000	3	100.0	0	0.0	3	100.0	0	0 0

urban—evidenced little if any tendency to defect to the opposition more often than their colleagues from more typical Democratic constituencies.

The conclusion seems clear that opposition to Democratic majorities, when majorities of both parties opposed one another during the Eighty-sixth and Eighty-seventh Congresses, cannot be explained to any great extent by the aggregate socio-economic characteristics of the relatively disloyal representatives' constituencies. As a group, northern Democrats were very cohesive in both Congresses examined. Those few who did defect to the opposition with some regularity do not, however, consistently appear in the rural, low blue collar, and high income categories. Rather, these relatively less loyal members of the party are represented in nearly all ranges of the variables considered. It should be noted at this point, moreover, that these defectors do not seem to be clustered in any obvious geographic area.

Another means of relating constituency characteristics of northern Democrats to their voting behavior is available through isolation of what might be called the extreme deviants on the same major socio-economic, civil liberties, and foreign policy matters scaled in Chapter IV. Although little relationship has been apparent between Party Opposition Scores and the constituency characteristics examined, it is possible that defectors among the northern Democrats who rated Republican-like scale scores on these issues represented atypical constituencies. This proposition may be tested by examination of the constituency characteristics of those northern Democrats who placed in the most conservative category. In fact, such an exercise reveals some relationship between rural, low blue collar, midwestern, and border state constituencies, and extreme disloyalty.

On the Labor Scale for the Eighty-sixth Congress eight of ten northern Democratic deviants represented heavily rural constituencies, and all but one of their districts were located in the Midwest or border areas. The only urban members who defected represented cities in border states—Maryland and Oklahoma. On the Area Redevelopment Scale for the Eighty-sixth Congress three of five extreme variants represented heavily rural districts in the border and western areas. The urban Democrats in this group represented cities in Oklahoma and Utah. The single extreme conservative among the northern Democrats on the Area Redevelopment Scale for the Eighty-seventh Congress represented a rural constituency in Upstate New York. The only extreme defector on the Aid to Education Scale for the Eighty-sixth Congress spoke for a rural constituency in the Midwest. A rural, border Democrat similarly rated the only extreme conservative score on this same issue in the Eighty-seventh Congress. On the Minimum Wage Scales for the Eighty-sixth and Eighty-seventh Congresses five of six extreme conservatives came from rural districts in the Midwest, while the other, who appeared on both scales at the extreme, represented a border state city. The Housing Scales for the Congresses examined reveal five extreme northern Democratic conservatives, three of whom appeared in the most conservative group on both scales. All but one of these men represented rural constituencies in a border state or in the Midwest. One, whose name appears quite frequently as an extreme deviant, spoke for a border state city. The Civil Liberties Scale for the Eighty-sixth Congress includes seventeen northern Democratic extreme deviants. All represented border and midwestern constituencies, and all but two of these constituencies are heavily rural. Of twenty extreme conservatives on the Foreign Aid Scale for 1959, half were from the Midwest, six were from border states, and three from western states. Only a single one of these Democrats spoke for a district in the Northeast. All but one of these extremely anti-foreign aid Democrats came from heavily rural areas. The single exception represented a midwestern city. Although the nature of the deviant conservative group among the northern Democrats is somewhat different on each of the scales examined, there is some consistency in the characteristics of the constituencies these congressmen represented. In each of the three major areas examined—domestic regulatory and welfare issues, civil liberties, and foreign aid—sectionalism is clearly apparent. In the deviant group on several of the scales the Midwest and the border states are obviously overrepresented, while there are almost no extreme deviants from the Northeast, and none at all from the coastal areas of the Northeast or West. The vast majority of these northern Democratic conservatives represented rural areas. Urban congressmen in this group came from midwestern, border, or interior western states. It should be noted, however, that this analysis does not establish that rural, midwestern, and border Democrats were disloyal as a group. Clearly, this is not the case. There were, for example, fifty or more (depending on how sectional lines are drawn) midwestern and border Democrats among the congressmen included in the analysis for the Eighty-sixth Congress whose constituencies were over 40 percent rural. Most of these representatives, though their constituencies were apparently quite similar to those of the extreme deviants, never fell into the extreme groups on the scales examined. The same can be said for those northern Democratic representatives who spoke for such constituencies during the Eighty-seventh Congress.

What has been shown, then, is that those Democrats who *did* deviate considerably from the positions taken by the vast majority of their colleagues on selected major issues came largely from the same kinds of border and midwestern constituencies. While no relationship seems to exist between Party Opposition Scores and the constituency characteristics examined, a relationship *does* appear between extreme deviance on the scales examined and rural, relatively low blue collar population, and midwestern and/or border location. While Democrats as a whole were quite cohesive during the Congresses examined, those members of the party who *did* deviate from the position of their colleagues on the scales examined very largely spoke for constituencies characterized by these factors.

In Chapter VI it was demonstrated that Republican representation in the Eighty-sixth and Eighty-seventh Congresses was negatively related to urban and nonwhite population and percentage of blue collar labor, and positively related to median income and percentage of owner-occupied housing. It would seem reasonable to suppose, as in the case of northern Democrats, that these factors are also related to intra-party voting differences—that Republicans from atypical constituencies characterized by high levels or urban, nonwhite and blue collar population, by low median income, and low levels of owner-occupied property would be more disloyal to party majorities than those from more typical Republican constituencies. This proposition may be tested by considering the Party Opposition Scores of northern Republicans during the two Congresses in relation to the same three constituency characteristics employed in our analysis of northern Democrats—urban population, blue collar labor, and median income. If the disloyalty of northern Republicans is to be explained to any great extent by constituency characteristics, those members of the party who spoke for urban areas, for high blue collar districts, and for low income districts should have been more disloyal than those from more typical Republican constituencies.

Table 71, with urban population controlled, presents a frequency distribution of northern Republicans' Party Opposition Scores for the 1960 and 1962 sessions of the Eighty-sixth and Eighty-seventh Congresses, respectively. If rural Republicans, as such, were significantly more disloyal to majorities of their party when majorities of Democrats and Republicans opposed one another, the relatively disloyal group (those whose Party Opposition Score is above 25) should tend to cluster at the bottom of the table in the higher ranges of urban population. Again, as in the case of the northern Democrats, there is no indication of such a relationship prevailing. To be sure, the highest range of urban population does contain a higher percentage of disloyal party members than any other, but aside from this group the table reveals no clear relationship. The lowest range of urban population, for example, for both Congresses contains more relatively disloyal northern Republicans than the third and fourth ranges

TABLE 71

FREQUENCY DISTRIBUTION OF PARTY OPPOSITION SCORES
FOR NORTHERN REPUBLICAN CONGRESSMEN BY
URBAN POPULATION, 86TH AND 87TH CONGRESSES

Percent Urban	Party Opposition Score, 1960				Party Opposition Score, 1962			
	Below 25		Above 25		Below 25		Above 25	
	No.	Percent	No.	Percent	No.	Percent	No.	Percent
0–20	50	74.6	17	25.4	68	80.9	16	19.1
20–40	21	55.3	17	44.7	29	63.0	17	37.0
40–60	11	84.6	2	15.4	10	76.9	3	23.1
60–80	9	81.8	2	18.2	9	100.0	0	0.0
80–100	6	54.5	5	45.5	4	44.4	5	55.6

which contain sizable elements of urban population. Aside from the few party members who represented districts that were from 80 to 100 percent urban, there would seem to be little tendency for the more urban Republicans to join forces with the Democrats against majorities of their own party.

Tables 72 and 73 present Party Opposition Scores for northern Republicans whose constituencies fall into various divisions of percentage of blue collar labor. Again, it would seem reasonable to suppose that the relatively disloyal members of the party would tend to cluster at the bottom of these tables in the higher ranges of percentage of blue collar labor. In fact, for reasons which are not at all apparent, this is the case for all northern Republicans and for Urban-Suburban Republicans alone (Table 72) during the Eighty-sixth Congress, but no trace of such a relationship prevails for the Eighty-seventh Congress (Table 73). In the first of these two tables there is a definite tendency for the Republicans from more working class constituencies to defect to the Democratic side when majorities of the two parties opposed one another. This tendency is especially clear at the extremes of the distributions for both the total group and for city Republicans alone. In the second table, however, this pronounced relationship disappears completely. In the case of the Eighty-seventh Congress the most urban Republicans were actually more loyal as a group than the most rural members of the party. Certainly, the vagaries of congressional voting amply indicate that these relationships vary considerably from time to time and suggest that such startling shifts in behavior be investigated in more narrowly focused studies.

Tables 74 and 75 present Party Opposition Scores for northern Republicans whose constituencies fall into various divisions based on median

TABLE 72

FREQUENCY DISTRIBUTION OF PARTY OPPOSITION SCORES
FOR NORTHERN REPUBLICAN CONGRESSMEN BY
BLUE COLLAR LABOR POPULATION, 86TH CONGRESS

Percent Blue Collar Labor	Party Opposition Score, 1960							
	All Northern Republicans				Urban-Suburban Republicans			
	Below 25		Above 25		Below 25		Above 25	
	No.	Percent	No.	Percent	No.	Percent	No.	Percent
Under 40	13	81.2	3	18.8	6	85.7	1	14.3
40–50	31	72.1	12	27.9	17	70.8	7	29.2
50–60	48	75.0	16	25.0	21	77.8	6	22.2
Over 60	5	29.4	12	70.6	2	40.0	3	60.0

TABLE 73

FREQUENCY DISTRIBUTION OF PARTY OPPOSITION SCORES
FOR NORTHERN REPUBLICAN CONGRESSMEN BY
BLUE COLLAR LABOR POPULATION, 87TH CONGRESS

Percent Blue Collar Labor	Party Opposition Score, 1962							
	All Northern Republicans				Urban-Suburban Republicans			
	Below 25		Above 25		Below 25		Above 25	
	No.	Percent	No.	Percent	No.	Percent	No.	Percent
Under 40	15	78.9	4	21.1	3	50.0	3	50.0
40–50	33	71.7	13	28.3	18	66.7	9	33.3
50–60	69	76.7	21	23.3	13	56.5	10	43.5
Over 60	16	84.2	3	15.8	2	66.7	1	33.3

family income. If the hypothesis is to be accepted that congressional party members from atypical constituencies are more disloyal than those from more typical constituencies, the relatively disloyal group should be clustered at the top of the table in the lower ranges of median income. For the Eighty-sixth Congress, as Table 74 reveals, there is a tendency in this direction, although many exceptions are apparent. For both the total northern Republican group and within the Urban-Suburban category the representatives in the highest ranges of median family income are shown to have been more loyal than those in the lower ranges. This relationship between low income and Party Opposition Scores, however, largely disappears in the case of the Eighty-seventh Congress (Table 75). In neither the total group nor the Urban-Suburban group alone are the members whose constituencies fall into the higher ranges of income more loyal

TABLE 74

FREQUENCY DISTRIBUTION OF PARTY OPPOSITION SCORES
FOR NORTHERN REPUBLICAN CONGRESSMEN BY
MEDIAN FAMILY INCOME, 86TH CONGRESS

	Party Opposition Score, 1960							
	All Northern Republicans				Urban-Suburban Republicans			
Median	Below 25		Above 25		Below 25		Above 25	
Income	No.	Percent	No.	Percent	No.	Percent	No.	Percent
$2,500	0	0.0	1	100.0	....	....	....	....
3,000	....	....	....	....	....	....	....	....
3,500	0	0.0	1	100.0	....	....	....	....
4,000	3	60.0	2	40.0	....	....	....	....
4,500	5	71.4	2	28.6	....	....	....	....
5,000	6	60.0	4	60.0	....	....	....	....
5,500	17	65.4	9	34.6	....	....	....	....
6,000	18	69.2	8	30.8	3	60.0	2	40.0
6,500	16	72.7	6	27.3	9	60.0	6	40.0
7,000	10	71.4	4	28.6	10	71.4	4	28.6
7,500	10	71.4	4	28.6	10	76.9	3	23.1
8,000	11	84.6	2	15.4	10	83.3	2	16.7

TABLE 75

FREQUENCY DISTRIBUTION OF PARTY OPPOSITION SCORES
FOR NORTHERN REPUBLICAN CONGRESSMEN BY
MEDIAN FAMILY INCOME, 87TH CONGRESS

	Party Opposition Score, 1962							
	All Northern Republicans				Urban-Suburban Republicans			
Median	Below 25		Above 25		Below 25		Above 25	
Income	No.	Percent	No.	Percent	No.	Percent	No.	Percent
$2,500	1	100.0	0	0.0	....	....	....	....
3,000	....	....	....	....	....	....	....	....
3,500	1	100.0	0	0.0	....	....	....	....
4,000	10	100.0	0	0.0	....	....	....	....
4,500	10	100.0	0	0.0	....	....	....	....
5,000	11	68.8	5	31.2	0	0.0	1	100.0
5,500	27	84.4	5	15.6	....	....	....	....
6,000	17	73.9	6	26.1	2	50.0	2	50.0
6,500	17	70.8	7	29.2	9	64.3	5	35.7
7,000	11	73.3	4	26.7	11	68.8	5	31.2
7,500	7	50.0	7	50.0	7	53.8	6	46.2
8,000	8	61.5	5	38.5	7	63.6	4	36.4

than those in the lower. In the very lowest ranges of income, in fact, Republicans were more loyal than those in the higher divisions. Some small relationship seems to remain for the Urban-Suburban group alone, but it is certainly not impressive. Again, the analysis has produced a rather mystifying conclusion—that a relationship of sorts exists between low income and northern Republic Party Opposition in the case of the Eighty-sixth Congress, while little such relationship is apparent in the Eighty-seventh Congress.

As in the analysis of Democratic Party Opposition Scores, it would appear that northern Republican differences during the two Congresses are not highly related to the aggregate constituency factors examined. Very little relationship is apparent between Party Opposition and urban population, and relationship of such opposition to blue collar labor and median family income is weak at best and, at times, almost entirely absent. Although northern Republicans were somewhat less cohesive as a group than northern Democrats during the two Congresses examined, there is little evidence that members of the party from atypical districts defected to the opposition more frequently than those from more typical constituencies when majorities of the two parties opposed one another. Therefore, since over half of the relatively more disloyal group (Party Opposition Score above 25) came from northeastern states (28 of 40, for example, in the 1962 session), it would seem that sectionalism is a factor in Republican disloyalty. It should be noted, however, that even the midwestern Republicans (whose loyalty is often supposed to be greater than that of members from other areas of the nation) are generously represented in the relatively disloyal group during both sessions. Though northeastern members of the party were the most disloyal, disloyalty was by no means limited to this group.

As with the northern Democrats, a more accurate view of extreme Republican deviance in specific policy areas may be obtained by examining the constituency characteristics of those party members who scored in the most liberal category possible on the scales presented in Chapter IV. Such an analysis does reveal a relationship between northeastern sectional location and, in some cases, urban and suburban population and Republican deviance.[9]

On the Area Redevelopment Scales for the Eighty-sixth and Eighty-seventh Congresses there is a clear sectional tendency apparent; twelve of twenty extreme irregulars represented northeastern constituencies on the

[9]Suburban population data were taken from the *CQ Weekly Report*, February 2, 1962, pp. 153–69.

first scale, and twenty of twenty-seven represented such constituencies on the second. While urban representatives do not seem to be more disloyal than those from rural areas, it is apparent that most of the rural representatives in the extreme liberal category spoke for constituencies that were characterized by high percentages of blue collar labor. On the Aid to Education Scales for both Congresses the tendency of Republicans from the Northeast to defect to the opposition is again quite apparent; twenty of twenty-six extreme deviants on the first scale and twenty-three of twenty-eight on the second spoke for northeastern districts. Inspection of the percentage of urban, suburban, and rural population in the constituencies of these extreme liberal Republicans suggests no relationship between this factor and Republican liberalism. Sectional influence is again obviously apparent in the two Minimum Wage Scales for the Eighty-sixth and Eighty-seventh Congresses. Of twenty-seven Republican extreme defectors on the first scale, eighteen represented northeastern districts. Of twenty deviants on the second scale, nineteen represented northeastern districts. Such voting on these scales is also obviously related to urban and suburban population. An overwhelming number of these liberal Republicans represented constituencies characterized by high levels of urban and/or suburban population. Republican liberals on the two Housing Scales for the Congresses under examination were almost exclusively from the Northeast. Only a single representative from another area—the coastal West—rated an extreme liberal place on these scales. Again, the influence of urban population is quite apparent. Every representative in the deviant category on the question of housing spoke for a constituency with large percentages of urban and/or suburban population. On the Welfare Scale for the Eighty-seventh Congress the extreme liberal group again reveals the influence of section. Thirteen of seventeen in this group represented northeastern districts. No urban-rural relationship is revealed in the characteristics of these congressmen's constituencies. The Civil Liberties Scale for the Eighty-sixth Congress demonstrates with unmistakable clarity that extreme civil libertarian sympathies in the Republican group at this time were almost exclusively limited to northeastern members, whose constituencies for the most part were heavily urban or suburban. Of fifteen men in this group, twelve spoke for districts with more than 40 percent urban and suburban population. On the Foreign Aid Scales sectional differences among the Republicans are again clearly apparent. Since the party was badly divided on this question, there is no position that can be called a party position. When, however, the constituency characteristics of the extreme liberal and conservative groups on the scales are examined, sectional differences are clearly apparent. On the

1959 scale, for example, members of the party from the Northeast who scored in the most liberal rank outnumbered those in the most conservative rank by a ratio of 5 to 1. In the Midwest on the other hand, extreme conservatives outnumbered extreme liberals by almost 2 to 1. All border state Republicans appeared in the most conservative category. In the West the liberal group outnumbered the conservatives by a margin of 3 to 2. Here again, urban-rural or socio-economic differences in the constituencies are not apparent. In all of the scales examined, therefore, a tendency is apparent for northeastern Republicans to fall into the extreme liberal group more often than party members from other areas of the nation. In some of the scales urban and suburban population seems also to have some relationship to Republican liberalism. In summary, then, it may be said that the socio-economic factors considered seem to bear little relationship to Republican Party Opposition Scores, but examination of the constituency characteristics of those relatively disloyal members does reveal a tendency for northeastern members of the party to be more disloyal than those from other areas. This same sectional tendency is apparent in deviant Republican scores on the scales examined. At times deviance on these scales seems to be related also to urban and suburban population and to lower socio-economic status, but these latter factors are much less clearly linked to Republican liberalism than is section. Something that is not evident in the aggregate socio-economic characteristics of their constituencies apparently disposes northeastern Republicans to liberal positions on these matters. Many of the northeastern defectors, for example, represented heavily rural areas which differ in no apparent way from the same type of area in other parts of the nation. There would seem to be little alternative but to accept the tentative conclusion, suggested also by other studies examined, that northeastern Republicans *as such* are somewhat more liberal than those from other areas of the nation.

It has been shown that southern Democrats in the Eighty-sixth and Eighty-seventh Congresses were much more conservative than their northern party colleagues in all of the policy areas examined and that they often defected in substantial numbers to take Republican-like positions on domestic economic questions as well as on those involving civil liberties and foreign aid. The question now arises as to what extent can intra-southern Democratic voting differences be explained by constituency characteristics? In light of what is generally known about southern politics in recent years,[10] it would seem reasonable to suppose that southern

10See especially V. O. Key's description of rural, black belt conservatism in

Democratic congressmen from rural areas with high Negro population would be more conservative than those who spoke for urban constituencies with few Negroes. This supposition may be tested in two ways. First, southern Democratic Party Opposition Scores may be compared with percentages of urban population and nonwhite population in the various constituencies. Second, the constituency characteristics of the most conservative southerners on the scales presented in Chapter V may be examined.

Table 76 presents Party Opposition Scores for southern Democrats for two sessions of the Eighty-sixth and Eighty-seventh Congresses in relation to the percentage of urban population. There is, it seems, some relationship between urban population and Party Opposition for both sessions examined, though that relationship is not as strong as might be

TABLE 76

FREQUENCY DISTRIBUTION OF PARTY OPPOSITION SCORES
FOR SOUTHERN DEMOCRATIC CONGRESSMEN BY
URBAN POPULATION, 86TH AND 87TH CONGRESSES

Percent Urban	Party Opposition Score, 1960				Party Opposition Score, 1962			
	Below 25		Above 25		Below 25		Above 25	
	No.	Percent	No.	Percent	No.	Percent	No.	Percent
0–10	10	23.8	32	76.2	14	35.0	26	65.0
10–20	8	57.1	6	42.9	7	53.8	6	46.2
20–30	3	27.3	8	72.7	5	41.7	7	58.3
30–40	6	60.0	4	60.0	2	22.2	7	77.8
40–50	4	57.1	3	42.9	5	83.3	1	16.7
50 +	8	61.5	5	38.5	7	58.3	5	41.7

expected. Between the extremes in the ranges of the percentage of urban population there is an obvious difference in voting behavior. In the highest ranges of urban population nearly two-thirds of the southerners are in the relatively more loyal group (Party Opposition Score of less than 25); in the lowest range over two-thirds are in the relatively less loyal group. Between these extremes, however, there is no consistent relationship apparent between urban population and party loyalty. Obviously, many rural southerners were highly loyal to Democratic majorities in the Eighty-sixth and Eighty-seventh Congresses, while many from urban areas were more disloyal.

Southern Politics, 10–12 and 666–67, *et passim*. See also his argument that urban Southern congressmen are more loyal to party majorities than those from rural constituencies, 378–82.

Table 77, which presents data on Party Opposition Scores for the 1960 and 1962 sessions, again points to the "on again-off again" quality of relationships between aggregate constituency characteristics and roll call voting behavior. In the 1960 session there is an unmistakably clear relationship of southern Democratic Party Opposition and the percentage of nonwhite population. As nonwhite population increases, the percentage of representatives falling into the relatively less loyal category also increases without exception. In the low-Negro areas the loyal southerners outnumber the disloyal by a ratio of more than 2 to 1, while all of the representatives from areas 40 percent or more Negro appear in the relatively more disloyal group. In the 1962 session, for reasons which are not at all apparent, this relationship largely disappears. And, strangely, the group of southern congressmen in the lowest range of Negro population, 71.4 percent of whom were in the relatively more loyal group of southerners during the first session, are to be found mainly (75 percent) in the less loyal group for the second session. There is very little that can be said with certainty in the face of these mystifying shifts in behavior save that

TABLE 77

FREQUENCY DISTRIBUTION OF PARTY OPPOSITION SCORES
FOR SOUTHERN DEMOCRATIC CONGRESSMEN BY
NONWHITE POPULATION, 86TH AND 87TH CONGRESSES

Percent of Nonwhite	Party Opposition Score, 1960				Party Opposition Score, 1962			
	Below 25		Above 25		Below 25		Above 25	
	No.	Percent	No.	Percent	No.	Percent	No.	Percent
0–10	10	71.4	4	28.6	3	25.0	9	75.0
10–20	13	65.0	7	35.0	14	70.0	6	30.0
20–30	10	31.3	22	68.7	11	36.7	19	65.3
30–40	4	26.7	15	73.3	9	47.4	10	52.6
Over 40	0	0.0	10	100.0	3	27.3	8	72.7

their occurrence serves as a needed reminder that generalizations about congressional voting must be limited to specific time periods. It would be more comforting, however, if some reason, or reasons, for their occurrence could be uncovered.

In summary, then, it can be said that although there is some relationship between both the percentages of nonwhite population and urban population and southern Democratic Party Opposition Scores, that relationship is not as strong as might be expected.

As in the case of the northern Democrats and Republicans examined, additional perspective may be gained by examining the behavior of southern Democrats on the scales presented in Chapter IV. Here the extreme conservatives on the scales will be isolated to see if there is some uniformity in the characteristics of these members' constituencies. Again, the expectation is that these extreme Democratic deviants should represent rural and high nonwhite constituencies. On the Labor Scale for the Eighty-sixth Congress, however, little constituency influence is apparent in southern Democratic behavior; practically the entire southern group is clustered in the most conservative category on the scale. Nearly all southern Democrats—regardless of their constituency characteristics—were in the anti-labor group in the Eighty-sixth Congress. On the issue of area redevelopment a majority of southern Democrats in the Eighty-sixth Congress are to be found in the most conservative category also. Although some urban-rural difference is noticeable in the constituency characteristics of these defectors, that difference is not striking. Nearly two-thirds of southern Democrats from constituencies consisting of less than 50 percent urban and/or suburban population are present in this category as compared with slightly less than half of those from majority urban and/or suburban districts. Differences with respect to the percentage of nonwhite population are also apparent, but again not striking. Over 70 percent of the "black belt" southern Democrats (defined as those from districts 40 percent or more Negro) scored in the extreme conservative category in comparison to slightly less than half of those members with less than 20 percent nonwhite population in their constituencies. On the same issue, a very different pattern of southern Democratic behavior is manifested in the scale constructed for the Eighty-seventh Congress. Here the largest group of southerners is located in the most liberal category along with a majority of northern Democrats, and only one southerner is to be found in the most conservative scale category. This single deviant represented a black belt rural district.

On the Aid to Education scale for the Eighty-seventh Congress approximately one-fifth of the urban southerners are placed in the extreme conservative category as opposed to only one-eighth of the southerners representing rural or predominantly rural districts. Nor is the influence of nonwhite population apparent in this case. In fact, proportionately, southerners from low nonwhite constituencies (20 percent or less) outnumber those from black belt districts in the most extreme conservative category. On the Aid to Education Scale for the Eighty-seventh Congress extreme conservatism *is* related, apparently, to both rural and nonwhite population. Only one-seventh of the southerners who represented predominately urban and/or suburban areas are to be found in the most conservative scale rank in comparison with approximately one-third of those who spoke for more rural constituencies. Slightly less than two-thirds of the black belt Democrats rated placement in the most conservative category in contrast to less than one-third of those from low nonwhite districts.

On both Minimum Wage Scales there is a clear relationship between both the rural and nonwhite factors and extreme conservatism. In the scale for the Eighty-sixth Congress less than one-tenth of the southern Democrats from predominantly urban and/or suburban areas rated placement in the most conservative scale group in contrast to nearly half of those from more rural constituencies. On the second scale this pattern is only very slightly altered. On the Eighty-sixth Congress scale over 70 percent of the black belt group is to be found in the extreme conservative rank in comparison to just slightly more than a quarter of the low nonwhite group. Again, this situation is only very slightly altered in the case of the scale for the Eighty-seventh Congress.

For the Eighty-sixth and Eighty-seventh Congresses' Housing Scales there is again a clear relationship between both urban and nonwhite population and placement in the most conservative category. On both of these scales there are, proportionately, more southern Democrats from rural and black belt districts than from urban and low nonwhite districts. On the first scale slightly more than a quarter of the urban and/or suburban southerners appear in the most conservative rank in comparison to over half of those from more rural districts. Roughly the same proportion of both groups is to be found also in the most conservative category for the Eighty-seventh Congress. On the first scale over 50 percent of the black belt representatives, as compared with just over 35 percent of those from low nonwhite constituencies, are located in the most conservative category. On the second scale approximately twice as many black belt southerners, proportionately, as those from low nonwhite districts appear in the extreme conservative scale position.

Of three extreme southern Democratic conservatives on the Welfare Scale for the Eighty-seventh Congress, all spoke for rural areas, but there is no uniformity apparent with respect to the percentages of nonwhite population in their constituencies.

Finally, on the question of foreign aid, a relationship appears on the scales between both the urban and nonwhite factors and placement in the extreme conservative category. On the 1959 Foreign Aid Scale, for example, just above a third of 50 percent urban and/or suburban group among the southern Democrats are located in the most conservative category as compared to nearly 77 percent of those from more rural constituencies.

Over 80 percent of those from the black belt group rated placement in the most conservative scale rank in contrast to just over half of those from low nonwhite districts.

The results of the foregoing analysis of southern Democratic behavior based on the policy scales presented in Chapter IV are, unfortunately, rather baffling. It can only be said that extreme southern Democratic conservatism is at times linked to rural and high nonwhite population, but at other times there would appear to be no relationship between these factors. In one case—aid to education—a relationship appears, but one that runs precisely counter to what might be expected from the hypothesis that rural, black belt southerners ought to be more conservative than those from urban and low nonwhite areas. Linkage between the constituency factors examined and voting behavior on the scales seems to shift from issue to issue. On policy matters involving housing, minimum wage, and foreign aid, rural and high nonwhite population are both clearly linked to conservatism. On the issue of welfare, only the influence of rural population is apparent. Both factors are weakly linked to southern conservatism on the issue of area redevelopment. On the other hand, in labor matters no voting differences were apparent during the Eighty-sixth Congress, despite the great constituency differences that characterized the southern Democratic delegation in the House. And finally, in the matter of aid to education both factors examined are *negatively* related to conservatism during one Congress and *positively* related during the other. To say the least, these results are extremely cryptic.

Several observers of congressional voting behavior have investigated the relationship of aggregate constituency characteristics to intra-party voting differences on the basis of the assumption that constituency factors might account for these differences. It would be encouraging to argue here that this assumption has been borne out—that constituency factors account for a major portion of deviation from party voting. Unfortunately, the studies on this question have yielded rather ambiguous results, which suggest *some relationship, at times,* between constituency factors and intra-party differences. But by no means do these factors adequately explain all, or even the major portion, of the behavior in question. At times, as in the case of sectional cleavage in the Democratic Party, the several studies yield relatively uniform findings. In other instances, as with the attempts to investigate the association of socio-economic status and intra-party differences, the results have been less than clear at best and openly contradictory at worst. Consequently, there would seem to be no simple answer to the question: Will constituency characteristics account for party irregularity? A summary of findings on this question, however, may be offered at this point. If such a summary leaves the matter of constituency influence in some doubt, it should at least constitute a necessary step in the direction of further inquiry.

The constituency factors employed commonly in studies conducted by Turner, MacRae, Truman, and Froman, and also in this study, may be broken down into four classes for purposes of analysis: (1) urban and rural population; (2) socio-economic differences; (3) sectional differences; and (4) political competition. Results of several studies pertinent to the first three factors can now be summarized.

Three of the studies—this one and those by Turner and Froman—offer somewhat contradictory results on the question of urban-rural differences and party voting. Normally, since 1932, the expectation of most observers of the congressional parties has been that rural Democrats and urban Republicans would tend to be more disloyal than other members of their respective parties on roll call votes. Julius Turner in *Party and Constituency* found this expectation accurate in part. In both the 1937 and 1944 sessions urban Democrats were significantly more loyal to party majorities than those from rural constituencies. On the other hand, urban and rural Republicans differed significantly in the 1944 session but not in the 1937 session.[11] The reason for this shift in Republican behavior is by no means obvious. Lewis A. Froman in *Congressmen and Their Constituencies* found in an investigation of a single recent session that the percentage of urban population in the constituencies was related to liberalism (defined as *Congressional Quarterly's* Kennedy Domestic Support score) for both northern Democrats and Republicans.[12] The evidence that may be drawn from our present inquiry into this matter in the case of the Eighty-sixth and Eighty-seventh Congresses is somewhat mixed. While there is some tendency for northern Republicans from 80 percent urban constituencies to rate higher Party Opposition Scores than those from less urban areas, there is no relationship of this kind for northern Democrats. For southern Democrats, considered alone, there is again some relationship between urban population and intra-group differences, but apparently only for those southerners in the most rural and most urban groups. Examination of scale positions in specific issue-areas above reveals even more ambiguous results. On all of the scales examined there is a clear tendency for rural Democrats to fall disproportionately into the extreme deviant group. By contrast, on only three of the scales—minimum wage

[11]Turner, *Party and Constituency*, 83–87.
[12]Froman, *Congressmen and Their Constituencies*, 92–93.

regulations, housing, and civil liberties—are urban Republicans more inclined to take the extreme liberal position than other members of their party. Finally, urban population seems to be related to southern Democratic liberalism on some of the scales but not on others. Only on matters involving minimum wage regulations, housing, and foreign aid would there seem to be an unambiguous positive relationship between urban constituency and southern Democratic liberalism.

In sum, the relationship prevailing between urban and rural constituency and intra-party voting differences remains in considerable doubt. In Turner's analysis urban-rural differences are clearly apparent for Democratic voting behavior, but less clearly for the Republicans. Froman's study supports the supposition that rural Democrats and urban Republicans are less likely than other members of their parties to take typical party positions on roll call votes, but that analysis is based on questionable statistical procedures, and consequently must be regarded with some skepticism.[13] The present study yields ambiguous results. At times the influence of urban-rural differences is apparent, and at times it is not. In no case can it be argued on the basis of data presented in this study that urban-rural differences account for a major proportion of intra-party voting differences during the Eighty-sixth and Eighty-seventh Congresses.

With respect to socio-economic constituency characteristics and intra-party differences, this study and the studies by MacRae and Froman present anything but clear results. It will be remembered that MacRae in *Dimensions* attempted to relate occupational characteristics of the various House constituencies to scale positions with rather mixed results.[14] Higher percentages of farmers, for example, seemed to dispose both Democratic and Republican representatives to more conservative behavior in domestic economic matters. Similarly, farm population appeared to be related to conservatism for Democrats in the area of race relations, but not for Republicans. In foreign policy matters, this relationship was reversed; farm population was associated slightly with conservatism for Republicans, but not for Democrats. In the more urban areas, despite the strong feeling of most observers that socio-economic status would be reflected in intra-party differences, the percentage of professional and managerial employees in the various constituencies was found to be very slightly, if at all, related to voting behavior in any of the policy areas examined. Froman, by contrast, found a rather weak correlation of one indicator of socio-economic status (owner-occupied housing) and liberalism for both north-

13See above, p. 58, fn. 1.
14See above, 27–30.

ern Democrats and Republicans, but again it must be noted that the correlation is low and that the statistical procedure employed is questionable.[15]

Again, the present study yields anything but clear results on this matter. Neither indicator of socio-economic status employed here (percentage of blue collar workers and median family income) is impressively related to higher Party Opposition Scores for northern Democrats. On the other hand, both of these factors are somewhat related to party opposition for Republicans in the Eighty-sixth, but not the Eighty-seventh Congress. Preliminary analysis, the results of which are not discussed above, indicated no relationship of these factors to conservatism or liberalism in the case of southern Democrats. In the latter case, it was supposed that the percentage of Negroes in the various constituencies might be a more powerful influence. Analysis of this factor, however, revealed some relationship with intra-southern Democratic differences in the case of the Eighty-sixth but not the Eighty-seventh Congress. Analysis of extreme deviants on each of the scales presented in Chapter IV, additionally suggested little relationship between either blue collar labor or median family income and intra-party voting differences. For the southern Democrats the percentage of Negroes in the constituencies appears clearly and consistently related to voting behavior only on the Minimum Wage, Housing, and Foreign Aid scales.

Despite the persistent feeling of observers of congressional voting behavior that aggregate socio-economic status differences in the constituencies reflect themselves in intra-party voting differences at least for northern members of the two parties, the evidence from the three studies considered suggests that they do not do so to any great extent. That is to say that both Democrats and Republicans from very atypical constituencies are little if any less loyal (or less typical in terms of policy choice) than other members of their party. While both parties are characterized by considerable internal cleavages, the evidence suggests these cleavages cannot be accounted for to any great extent by socio-economic or class factors. Nor is the Negro factor as closely related to southern voting behavior as might be expected on the basis of traditional generalizations about black belt conservatism. Again, it would seem that this aggregate social characteristic will not adequately account for a major portion of intra-southern Democratic differences.

With respect to sectional influences on intra-party voting behavior one finding emerges from this study and those conducted by Turner,

---

[15]Froman, *Congressmen and Their Constituencies*, 92–93.

MacRae, and Truman: southern Democrats since 1937 have been much more disloyal than party members from other sections of the nation. MacRae found that southern Democrats were more conservative on the average than other members of the party on domestic economic matters, matters involving race relations, of course, and foreign policy.[16] This study fully confirms his finding. Southern Democrats were markedly more conservative in all policy areas examined than other members of the party.

The evidence from these studies is less clear for the Republicans, but certain suggestions do emerge. In the case of the 1944 session Turner found that coastal Republicans were somewhat more disloyal to party majorities than those from the interior.[17] Truman in *The Congressional Party* has noted that some of the Republican blocs in the House appeared to be sectionally based, though the sectional factor by no means served to account for the bloc structures that emerged in his analysis of the Eighty-first Congress.[18] The present study of the Eighty-sixth and Eighty-seventh Congresses suggests that Republicans from the northeastern portion of the nation were far more likely than those from other sections to join Democratic majorities on roll calls where majorities of the two parties opposed one another, and to fall into the extreme deviant category on all of the policy scales examined. Something (and what that something may be is by no means obvious) in the constituency characteristics of Republicans from the Northeast or perhaps something about the representatives themselves, apparently has disposed them to considerable defection from party positions in recent years.

Therefore, although it would serve the purpose of neatness and theoretical nicety to be able to argue that constituency differences account for intra-party voting differences, evidence from the studies by Turner, MacRae, Truman, Froman, and the present author indicate only *some relationship at some times* between constituency characteristics and intra-party differences. Though the findings of these studies are complex, it is clear that they suggest very few straightforward relationships between intra-party differences and constituency characteristics. Obviously, many members of both congressional parties who represent quite atypical districts are highly loyal to majorities of their colleagues, and yet some from what would appear to be far more typical districts are more disloyal. While there is at times a relationship apparent between atypical constituency characteristics and deviation from party voting, it would be far

[16]*Ibid.*
[17]Turner, *Party and Constituency*, 152.
[18]Truman, *The Congressional Party*, 179, 191.

too simple to argue that these characteristics will satisfactorily account for all, or even a major portion, of such deviation. Perhaps, of course, the methodology of the attempts to investigate relationships between aggregate characteristics and voting behavior is too crude to capture many constituency influences that in fact exist. The fact that aggregate constituency factors will not account for intra-party differences is not sufficient reason to foreclose the possibility that other constituency factors may operate on the congressman.

While constituency differences undoubtedly account for a sizable amount of inter-party voting differences and for some other intra-party differences, the evidence of several studies on this matter would indicate that the congressional parties are far more than simple reflections of constituency differences. The actions of most party members are more than simple products of constituency pressures. Clarence N. Stone, in a short, astute analysis, has shown that party differences constitute much more than the results of aggregate constituency differences. He documents his finding by the examining the differences in the voting behavior of representatives of *different parties* who represented the *same constituencies*.[19] Working with data for congressmen who represented those districts which shifted from one party to the other from the Eighty-sixth to the Eighty-seventh Congress, Stone has argued persuasively that congressmen of different party affiliation evidence sharply divergent voting behavior despite representing districts with identical aggregate characteristics. In such districts "Democrats scored on the average 68.4 percentage points higher than Republicans" [on the *Congressional Quarterly's* "Larger Federal Role Scores" for the two Congresses]. In more than half of these districts the Larger Federal Role Score of the Democrat exceeded that of the Republican by 70 percent or more.[20] The point is well taken. The party differences noted in Chapters III and IV of this study cannot be adequately accounted for by aggregate constituency characteristics. Whether they can be accounted for by *other* constituency characteristics, such as the congressman's electoral majority, is another question that can only be answered through more sophisticated studies based on other strategies of inquiry.

[19]Clarence N. Stone, "Inter-Party Constituency Differences and Congressional Voting Behavior: A Partial Dissent," *American Political Science Review*, LVII (September, 1963), 665–66.
   [20]*Ibid.*

Chapter VIII

ELECTORAL MARGINS AND
VOTING BEHAVIOR

SEVERAL STUDIES of roll call voting behavior in the House of Representatives have focused on relationships between electoral margins and party voting and/or policy choice. Lewis A. Froman, in a study of the first session of the Eighty-seventh Congress, investigated the hypothesis that congressmen of both parties from marginal constituencies (those in which competition between the two parties is very close) are more likely to oppose party majorities than those whose electoral status is more safe.[1] Froman also explored the possibility that congressmen of both parties from marginal constituencies are more moderate in their policy stands in House roll call voting than those from constituencies with a stronger preference for one party over the other.[2] Duncan MacRae has similarly concerned himself with the proposition that congressmen from marginal constituencies reflect constituency characteristics in their voting behavior to a greater extent than those from other constituencies.[3] Warren Miller and Donald Stokes have inquired into the possibility that electoral margins may be related to tendencies of congressmen to vote either on the basis of their own attitudes or on their perceptions of constituents' attitudes.[4] Finally, Samuel P. Huntington has suggested that policy moderation in roll call voting is inversely related to the intensity of partisan competition in congressional districts—that, in effect, marginal constituencies produce more extreme partisans than those which are relatively safe for one of the two parties.[5]

[1]Froman, *Congressmen and Their Constituencies*, 111–21.
[2]*Ibid.*
[3]MacRae, *Dimensions*, 284–89.
[4]See the presentation of Miller and Stokes' unpublished data on this question in Jewell and Patterson, *The Legislative Process*, 441–44.
[5]Huntington, "A Revised Theory of American Party Politics," *passim.*

The findings of these several studies, unfortunately, are such that the influence of electoral margins on voting behavior in the House remains today a matter of some doubt. Froman's findings indicate little or no relationship between marginal election and party disloyalty for either Democrats or Republicans during the first session of the Eighty-seventh Congress.[6] Although Froman thought otherwise, evidence of any relationship between electoral margins and policy choice is also very slim for both parties.[7] MacRae's attempt to investigate the possibility of marginality leading to closer reflection of socio-economic constituency characteristics in roll call voting yielded the cryptic finding that such a relationship was apparent in the Eighty-first Congress for Republicans but not for Democrats.[8] Miller and Stokes' data would suggest that congressmen from marginal constituencies are more likely than those from safer districts to vote in accord with their *own* attitudes on policy questions than with their perception of what constituents want.[9] Obviously, this finding directly contradicts the hypothesis that marginal electoral status inclines the congressman to vote as a "bound delegate" of his district. Finally, Froman's data (though he does not treat the matter) may be employed to cast considerable doubt on Huntington's suggestion that the two parties are most distinguishable in the voting behavior of congressmen elected from marginal—not relatively safe—districts.[10]

In this chapter, three hypotheses on electoral margins and voting behavior are explored for the Eighty-sixth and Eighty-seventh Congresses. First, it will be determined whether marginality, per se, was related to party loyalty from 1959 through 1962. Second, the possibility that marginality may have sensitized congressmen to socio-economic constituency factors is treated. Finally, Huntington's generalization that Republicans and Democrats from marginal constituencies are the most extreme in their roll call policy stands is tested for the period between 1959 and 1962.[11]

A convenient measurement of party voting for present purposes is the *Congressional Quarterly's* Party Opposition Score.[12] As has been stated,

[6]Froman, *Congressmen and Their Constituencies*, 114.

[7]*Ibid.* The data presented by Froman in tabular forms will not support the conclusion he draws that policy choice in roll call voting follows marginality. Compare the data on page 114 with their interpretation on page 120.

[8]MacRae, *Dimensions*, 286.

[9]This interpretation is placed on Miller and Stokes' data by Jewell and Patterson, *The Legislative Process*, 441.

[10]See Froman, *Congressmen and Their Constituencies*, 114.

[11]The data on which this study is based (roll call votes, electoral statistics, and aggregate socio-economic data for congressional districts) will not facilitate analysis of the questions raised by Miller and Stokes, whose analysis is based partially on survey data of congressmen's and constituent's attitudes.

[12]These data are taken from the *CQ Almanac*, 1959, 1960, 1961 and 1962.

this device represents the percentage of times a congressman voted *against* his party when majorities of the two parties opposed one another on roll calls. Although many methods might be employed to separate congressional districts into classes on the basis of party competition, the approach used here relies on the average Republican vote for five elections from 1952 through 1960. [13] In the case of the Eighty-sixth Congress, members of each party were classed with regard to electoral competition on the basis of four elections from 1952 to 1958. Members of the Eighty-seventh Congress were likewise divided into classes on the basis of five elections from 1952 to 1960. In the case of both Congresses the districts were classed as follows:

Republican average vote over 60 percent—Safe Republican
Republican average vote 55 to 60 percent—Predominantly Republican
Republican average vote 45 to 55 percent—Marginal
Republican average vote 40 to 45 percent—Predominantly Democratic
Republican average vote below 40 percent—Safe Democratic.

Since the South (defined as the former Confederate states) during these years remained with very few exceptions a one-party area, the congressmen from this entire region were excluded from the analysis. Where the decision to exclude the South has some effect on comparisons with the studies mentioned, this matter will be discussed below.

Tables 78 through 81 present frequency distributions of Party Opposition Scores for northern Democrats from each district type, ranging from Safe Democratic to Safe Republican, for each session of these two Congresses. If marginality (or some other factor closely related to it) had a great effect on northern Democratic behavior, the most disloyal members of the group should be found at the bottom of these tables in those constituencies classed as Marginal or Republican. In fact, those Democrats whose hold on their districts was extremely doubtful tended, in each of these tables, to oppose their party's majorities more often than did other party members. This tendency, however, is very slight in each session and results mainly from the behavior of a handful of northern Democrats from constituencies classed as Republican, not Marginal. It will be seen that in each table the behavior of Marginal Democrats differs little from that of those members classed as Predominantly Democratic or Safe. In the Eighty-seventh Congress (Tables 80 and 81) there is some difference apparent in the percentage of northern Democrats in the 0–10 percent opposition category, but in each case there is little difference between the

[13] Electoral information is from Scammon, *America Votes.*

percentage of Marginal Democrats and those from safer constituencies falling into the ranges below 20. In none of the sessions can it be said that a sharp tendency is apparent for the Marginal Democrats to be more disloyal than those from safer districts. In each session, however, those northern Democrats who represented constituencies classed as Republican were less loyal than other members of the party. A significantly larger proportion of these men, who represented but a handful of the Democratic total in the House and who came overwhelmingly from rural areas, apparently were more conservative than their brethren from Safe or Marginal Districts, or else they were convinced that they must deviate toward

TABLE 78

FREQUENCY DISTRIBUTION OF PARTY OPPOSITION SCORES
FOR NORTHERN DEMOCRATS WHOSE CONSTITUENCIES FALL INTO VARIOUS CLASSES
BASED ON PARTY COMPETITION; HOUSE OF REPRESENTATIVES, 1959

Status of Constituency	Party Opposition Score							
	0–10		10–20		20–30		30–40	
	No.	Percent	No.	Percent	No.	Percent	No.	Percent
Safe Democrats	38	66.7	14	24.6	4	7.0	1	1.8
Predominantly Democratic	34	60.7	20	35.7	2	3.6	0	0.0
Marginal	33	64.7	15	29.4	3	5.9	0	0.0
Predominantly Republican	6	31.6	7	36.9	6	31.6	0	0.0
Safe Republicans	0	0.0	0	0.0	1	100.0	0	0.0

TABLE 79

FREQUENCY DISTRIBUTION OF PARTY OPPOSITION SCORES
FOR NORTHERN DEMOCRATS WHOSE CONSTITUENCIES FALL INTO VARIOUS CLASSES
BASED ON PARTY COMPETITION; HOUSE OF REPRESENTATIVES, 1960

Status of Constituency	Party Opposition Score									
	0–10		10–20		20–30		30–40		40–50	
	No.	Percent	No.	Percent	No.	Percent	No.	Percent	No.	Percent
Safe Democrats	11	19.6	34	60.7	9	16.1	2	3.6	0	0.0
Predominantly Democratic	11	19.6	27	48.2	16	28.6	2	3.6	0	0.0
Marginal	8	17.4	32	69.6	6	13.0	0	0.0	0	0.0
Predominantly Republican	3	15.8	7	36.8	7	36.8	1	5.3	1	5.3
Safe Republicans	0	0.0	0	0.0	0	0.0	1	100.0	0	0.0

TABLE 80

FREQUENCY DISTRIBUTION OF PARTY OPPOSITION SCORES
FOR NORTHERN DEMOCRATS WHOSE CONSTITUENCIES FALL INTO VARIOUS CLASSES
BASED ON PARTY COMPETITION; HOUSE OF REPRESENTATIVES, 1961

Status of Constituency	Party Opposition Score									
	0–10		10–20		20–30		30–40		40–50	
	No.	Percent	No.	Percent	No.	Percent	No.	Percent	No.	Percent
Safe Democrats	41	74.5	8	14.5	5	9.1	1	1.8	0	0.0
Predominantly Democratic	34	65.4	16	30.8	2	3.8	0	0.0	0	0.0
Marginal	22	61.1	11	30.6	3	8.3	0	0.0	0	0.0
Predominantly Republican	4	40.0	3	30.0	2	20.0	1	10.0	0	0.0

TABLE 81

FREQUENCY DISTRIBUTION OF PARTY OPPOSITION SCORES
FOR NORTHERN DEMOCRATS WHOSE CONSTITUENCIES FALL INTO VARIOUS CLASSES
BASED ON PARTY COMPETITION; HOUSE OF REPRESENTATIVES, 1962

Status of Constituency	Party Opposition Score									
	0–10		10–20		20–30		30–40		40–50	
	No.	Percent	No.	Percent	No.	Percent	No.	Percent	No.	Percent
Safe Democrats	45	81.8	5	9.1	3	5.5	2	3.6	0	0.0
Predominantly Democratic	38	73.1	11	21.2	3	5.8	0	0.0	0	0.0
Marginal	21	58.3	11	30.6	3	8.3	1	2.8	0	0.0
Predominantly Republican	4	40.0	4	40.0	1	10.0	1	10.0	0	0.0

the opposition to gain reelection. At any rate, the voting behavior of these men *is* noticeably different.

Frequency distributions of Party Opposition Scores for northern Republicans in districts falling into the various classes of party competition are presented in Tables 82 through 85. These data would indicate that the tendency for congressmen from relatively insecure districts to defect from their party majorities is much stronger for Republicans than Democrats throughout the period of this study. In each session there is a clear tendency—by no means limited to those members of the party from districts classed as Democratic—for those Republicans from less than safe districts to defect from party majorities. Although there are some variations apparent from session to session, there is a clear tendency in all four tables for Safe Republicans to cluster in the two lowest ranges of Party Opposition and for Marginal Republicans to be spread throughout the various ranges of Opposition or clustered in the higher ranges. Again, as in the case of the Democrats, it can be said that those members of the Republican congressional party whose electoral hold was relatively weak were more liberal than their colleagues from safe districts, or else they felt compelled to moderate their voting behavior in order to gain favor with their constituents.

It should be noted here that in the case of both House Democrats and Republicans there is a substantial reflection of other factors in these data

TABLE 82

FREQUENCY DISTRIBUTION OF PARTY OPPOSITION SCORES
FOR NORTHERN REPUBLICANS WHOSE CONSTITUENCIES FALL INTO VARIOUS CLASSES
BASED ON PARTY COMPETITION; HOUSE OF REPRESENTATIVES, 1959

Status of Constituency	Party Opposition Score									
	0–10		10–20		20–30		30–40		Over 40	
	No.	Percent	No.	Percent	No.	Percent	No.	Percent	No.	Percent
Predominantly Democratic	0	0.0	1	50.0	1	50.0	0	0.0	0	0.0
Marginal	4	21.1	6	31.6	4	21.1	1	5.3	4	21.1
Predominantly Republican	43	45.3	30	31.6	12	12.6	5	5.3	5	5.3
Safe Republicans	17	77.3	5	22.7	0	0.0	0	0.0	0	0.0

TABLE 83

FREQUENCY DISTRIBUTION OF PARTY OPPOSITION SCORES
FOR NORTHERN REPUBLICANS WHOSE CONSTITUENCIES FALL INTO VARIOUS CLASSES
BASED ON PARTY COMPETITION; HOUSE OF REPRESENTATIVES, 1960

Status of Constituency	Party Opposition Score									
	0–10		10–20		20–30		30–40		Over 40	
	No.	Percent	No.	Percent	No.	Percent	No.	Percent	No.	Percent
Predominantly Democratic	0	0.0	1	50.0	0	0.0	1	50.0	0	0.0
Marginal	1	5.3	5	26.3	3	15.8	2	10.5	8	42.1
Predominantly Republican	15	15.8	40	42.1	20	21.1	8	8.4	12	12.6
Safe Republicans	7	31.9	12	54.5	2	9.1	1	4.5	0	0.0

TABLE 84

FREQUENCY DISTRIBUTION OF PARTY OPPOSITION SCORES
FOR NORTHERN REPUBLICANS WHOSE CONSTITUENCIES FALL INTO VARIOUS CLASSES
BASED ON PARTY COMPETITION; HOUSE OF REPRESENTATIVES, 1961

Status of Constituency	Party Opposition Score									
	0–10		10–20		20–30		30–40		Over 40	
	No.	Percent	No.	Percent	No.	Percent	No.	Percent	No.	Percent
Marginal	8	23.5	10	29.4	9	26.5	3	8.8	4	11.8
Predominantly Republican	37	34.9	38	35.8	19	17.9	9	8.5	3	2.8
Safe Republicans	12	54.5	7	31.8	2	9.1	1	4.5	0	0.0

TABLE 85

FREQUENCY DISTRIBUTION OF PARTY OPPOSION SCORES
FOR NORTHERN REPUBLICANS WHOSE CONSTITUENCIES FALL INTO VARIOUS CLASSES
BASED ON PARTY COMPETITION; HOUSE OF REPRESENTATIVES, 1962

Status of Constituency	Party Opposition Score									
	0–10		10–20		20–30		30–40		40–50	
	No.	Percent	No.	Percent	No.	Percent	No.	Percent	No.	Percent
Marginal	13	38.2	9	26.5	5	14.7	1	2.9	6	17.6
Predominantly Republican	41	38.7	28	26.4	16	15.1	10	9.4	11	10.4
Safe Republicans	11	50.0	4	18.2	3	13.6	4	18.2	0	0.0

on electoral margins. The overwhelming number of Safe Democrats, of course, represented urban areas. Safe Republicans on the other hand, spoke mainly for rural districts. Most Marginal Democrats as well as those whose districts were classed as Republican represented rural areas. Whether marginality itself was the cause of defection from party majorities or whether defection resulted from other underlying factors, it can be easily said that there is some relationship apparent between marginality and deviation from party voting for both Democrats and Republicans during the Eighty-sixth and Eighty-seventh Congresses. For Democrats, this relationship results, it seems, from the behavior of a few members from districts which normally prefer Republican representation. The relationship for Republicans results from a fairly uniform tendency for each gradation in electoral safeness to be accompanied by additional party loyalty.

The second hypothesis, cited at the beginning of this chapter, posits the possibility that electoral marginality may heighten the sensitivity of the congressman to atypical elements in his constituency. In other words, it is possible that marginality itself may not be as important as is marginality in connection with a constituency that is atypical from a socio-economic point of view. It might be supposed that the representative of a typical constituency in terms of socio-economic composition might behave loyally whether his district is marginal or not, while the representative from an atypical constituency might be more likely to modify his voting behavior in order to increase his appeal with his constituents from a less than Safe district. This possibility may be investigated in part by controlling both an indicator of socio-economic status and the electoral marginality of the various districts in order to observe any sensitizing influence which marginality might have for members of each party in atypical districts during the Eighty-sixth and Eighty-seventh Congresses.

In Tables 86 and 87 both the percentage of blue collar labor and electoral marginality are controlled for northern Democrats who were relatively loyal and disloyal to party majorities during the two sessions (1960 and 1962) under investigation.[14] If marginality has the effect of sensitizing the congressman to atypical elements in his constituency, the greatest differences between Democrats from Marginal and Republican constituencies and those representing Safe constituencies should occur in the lowest ranges of blue collar labor. In fact, there is some evidence in Table

TABLE 86

ELECTORAL MARGINALITY, ATYPICAL CONSTITUENCY AND PARTY OPPOSITION
FOR NORTHERN DEMOCRATS FROM TWO TYPES OF BLUE COLLAR LABOR DISTRICTS,
HOUSE OF REPRESENTATIVES, 1960

	Party Opposition Score			
	District Classed Republican or Marginal		District Classed Democratic	
Percentage of Blue Collar	Below 25	Above 25	Below 25	Above 25
	No. Percent	No. Percent	No. Percent	No. Percent
Under 40	3 60.0	2 40.0	3 75.0	1 25.0
40–50	17 100.0	0 0.0	23 92.0	2 8.0
50–60	33 91.7	3 8.3	37 90.2	4 9.8
Over 60	8 100.0	0 0.0	40 93.0	3 7.0

[14]"Blue collar" labor is defined as the percentage of the labor force falling into the combined categories of craftsmen, foremen, operatives, private household workers, and laborers, *U.S. Census of Population and Housing: 1960.* These data were assembled by the author and Professor James Farganis, now of Brooklyn College, for the districts of the Eighty-sixth and Eighty-seventh Congresses.

86 to support this hypothesis, though the number of Democrats in the lowest range of blue collar labor is very small. In Table 87, however, the data for the 1962 session of the Eighty-seventh Congress are directly contradictory, since the greatest difference between the marginal and non-marginal northern Democrats occurs in the higher ranges of blue collar labor. The data for northern Republicans in the same two sessions yield equally inconsistent results, as Tables 88 and 89 make clear. In the first of the two sessions the differences between the marginal and non-marginal Republicans are greater in the 40–50 percent ranges than in the range below 40 percent, but the least difference of all occurs in the most atypical Republican group made up of Republicans from over 60 percent blue

TABLE 87

ELECTORAL MARGINALITY, ATYPICAL CONSTITUENCY AND PARTY OPPOSITION
FOR NORTHERN DEMOCRATS FROM TWO TYPES OF DISTRICTS,
BASED ON PARTY COMPETITION; HOUSE OF REPRESENTATIVES, 1962

	Party Opposition Score						
	District Classed Republican or Marginal				District Classed Democratic		
Percentage of	Below 25		Above 25		Below 25		Above 25	
Blue Collar	No.	Percent	No.	Percent	No.	Percent	No.	Percent
Under 40	3	100.0	0	0.0	2	100.0	0	0.0
40–50	14	93.3	1	6.7	21	91.3	2	8.7
50–60	20	83.3	4	16.7	37	94.9	2	5.1
Over 60	5	83.3	1	16.7	41	97.6	1	2.4

TABLE 88

ELECTORAL MARGINALITY, ATYPICAL CONSTITUENCY AND PARTY OPPOSITION
FOR NORTHERN REPUBLICANS FROM TWO TYPES OF BLUE COLLAR LABOR DISTRICTS,
HOUSE OF REPRESENTATIVES, 1960

	Party Opposition Score						
	District Classed Democratic or Marginal				District Classed Republican		
Percentage of	Below 25		Above 25		Below 25		Above 25	
Blue Collar	No.	Percent	No.	Percent	No.	Percent	No.	Percent
Under 40	2	66.7	1	33.3	11	84.6	2	15.4
40–50	2	33.3	4	66.7	29	78.4	8	21.6
50–60	3	37.5	5	62.5	46	80.7	11	19.3
Over 60	1	25.0	3	75.0	3	25.0	9	75.0

TABLE 89

ELECTORAL MARGINALITY, ATYPICAL CONSTITUENCY AND PARTY OPPOSITION
FOR NORTHERN REPUBLICANS FROM TWO TYPES OF DISTRICTS,
BASED ON PARTY COMPETITION; HOUSE OF REPRESENTATIVES, 1962

	Party Opposition Score			
	District Classed Democratic or Marginal		District Classed Republican	
Percentage of	Below 25	Above 25	Below 25	Above 25
Blue Collar	No. Percent	No. Percent	No. Percent	No. Percent
Under 40	4 80.0	1 20.0	12 80.0	3 20.0
40–50	9 69.2	4 30.8	25 75.8	8 24.2
50–60	8 66.7	4 33.3	45 72.6	17 27.4
Over 60	5 71.4	2 28.6	11 84.6	2 15.4

collar districts. In the 1962 session there is no apparent difference between the marginal and non-marginal groups in the lower three ranges of blue collar labor, but there are some in the higher ranges. The greatest difference, though not striking, occurs in the case of the atypical high working class Republican districts. These data are inconclusive regarding the hypothesis that *marginality and atypical constituency characteristics* may dispose the congressman to be disloyal, whereas marginality alone might not. The present test of this hypothesis has been rather crude, but the data presented here would not provide a great deal of evidence in its favor. On the whole the weight of the evidence would seem to support the supposition that marginality itself is related to defection from party voting whether or not it is coupled with other atypical constituency characteristics.

The final concern of this chapter is with Huntington's suggestion that partisan competition and moderation in the congressman's policy stance are inversely related—that voting behavior diverges most often in the case of congressmen from districts in which competition is keenest. There can be no doubt that this idea contradicts the hypothesis that party opposition is greatest in relatively marginal constituencies—in other words, liberalism for Democrats and conservatism for Republicans, given what is known about the policy stance of the two parties in recent years. Some support has been found for this hypothesis in data presented for both parties in the Eighty-sixth and Eighty-seventh Congresses. A convenient measurement of liberalism-conservatism that is reasonably comparable to those employed by Huntington is available in the *Congressional Quarter-*

ly's "Larger Federal Role Support Score." [15] By averaging the scores for members of each party whose constituencies fall into each of the categories of electoral competition, it can be determined if differences between the parties are greatest where competition is most keen. Table 90 reveals that Huntington's generalization will not hold true for either the Eighty-sixth or the Eighty-seventh Congress.

In the case of the Eighty-sixth Congress the difference on Larger Federal Role Support is far sharper between Safe Democrats and Safe Republicans than between Marginal Democrats and Marginal Republicans. While Huntington's suggestion would imply that Democrats from relatively marginal areas should be sharply more liberal than those from safe constituencies, the data of this study indicate no such pattern. Though those Democrats classed as Marginal do have the highest average Federal Role score, they differ very little from those in the safest constituencies. While Huntington's hypothesis would suggest that Republicans from marginal constituencies should be more conservative than those from safe constituencies, the data indicate precisely the reverse—that Republicans from safe constituencies were by far the most conservative members of the par-

TABLE 90

PARTY COMPETITION AND POLICY CHOICE:
AVERAGE "LARGER FEDERAL ROLE SUPPORT SCORE" FOR HOUSE DEMOCRATS AND REPUBLICANS,
RANKED BY RELATIVE SAFENESS-MARGINALITY OF DISTRICTS; 86TH AND 87TH CONGRESSES

Party, Status of District	Eighty-Sixth		Eighty-Seventh	
	Number	Average "Larger Federal Role" Score	Number	Average "Larger Federal Role" Score
Democratic				
Safe	56	87.2	55	93.7
Predominantly Democratic	57	88.9	52	93.0
Marginal	45	91.2	36	92.5
Predominantly Republican	20	83.4	10	91.1
Republican				
Predominantly Democratic	1	58	....	......
Marginal	19	31.1	34	26.6
Predominantly Republican	99	16.5	103	22.6
Safe	21	5.9	21	20.0

[15]Again, the source of this information is the *CQ Almanac,* 1959–62.

ty. In the case of the Eighty-seventh Congress, the difference in Federal
Role scores is greater between Safe Democrats and Republicans than between the Marginal members of the two parties, though the difference is
by no means as striking as in the Eighty-sixth Congress. Again, there are
no differences of note among Democrats in the various classes of partisan
competition, and while differences between Republicans in the various
classes are less than striking, they vary in the opposite direction from that
suggested by the Huntington hypothesis. Marginal Republicans have a
somewhat higher Federal Role score than those from Predominantly Republican and Safe Republican districts.

What appears at first glance to be a rather sharp contrast between
Huntington's findings and those of the present study can be eliminated
to a great extent by a closer look at the data supporting his argument for
a "revised theory of American party politics." When the South is not considered in the analysis, it will be clear that the data presented by Huntington offer little persuasive evidence to support the conclusion that party
competition and policy differences between the two parties are positively
related. Huntington's indices of liberalism for congressmen whose districts
fall into various classes of party competition (Table 91) suggest no impressive variation in policy stance for members of either party in the
Seventy-ninth and Eightieth Congresses. A cursory glance at the table re-

TABLE 91

DATA PRESENTED BY SAMUEL P. HUNTINGTON TO SUPPORT
"A REVISED THEORY OF AMERICAN PARTY POLITICS"†

Status of District	Average Liberal Index, Northern Democrats	Average Liberal Index, Republicans
Marginal	89.9	20.3
Close	84.5	20.4
Close Intermediate	85.0	17.7
Solid Intermediate	76.4	13.8
Solid	86.3	22.2

†Source: Samuel P. Huntington, "A Revised Theory of American Party Politics,"
American Political Science Review, XLIV (September, 1950), 671.

veals the variation between the most marginal and the safest constituencies amounts to only 3.6 for northern Democrats and 1.9 for Republicans.
Such small differences hardly support Huntington's generalization that a
strong inverse relationship exists between party competition and policy

moderation.[16] Little remains of the "revised theory," therefore, when the South is removed from the analysis (and it should surprise no observer of Congress since 1937 that southern Democrats have been more conservative than their northern counterparts). Huntington's data serve only to support the conclusion that there is little or no apparent relationship between party competition and policy choice for members of either party in the Seventy-ninth and Eightieth Congresses. The comparable data for the Eighty-sixth and Eighty-seventh Congresses presented in Table 90 support the same conclusion for northern Democrats in both cases, but such data indicate that the more marginal Republicans in the Eighty-sixth Congress tended to be clearly more liberal than those from safer constituencies and only somewhat more liberal in the Eighty-seventh. In both Congresses the policy differences between the parties are most pronounced for congressmen representing safest constituencies and less so for those from more marginal constituencies. Although these data—for the two Congresses studied by Huntington and the two included in this study—indicate that the relationship between party competition and policy choice varies considerably over time, they offer little or no support for the revised theory. In fact, when marginality is related to policy differences in roll call voting, the evidence compiled for the Eighty-sixth and Eighty-seventh Congresses indicates that close competition is a factor disposing members of both parties to deviate toward the modal policy position of the opposition party.

In conclusion, it must be said that further testing in this study of three traditional hypotheses on electoral marginality and/or party competition and roll call voting leaves each in some doubt. Whereas data presented in Froman's examination of the first session of the Eighty-seventh Congress indicate that electoral marginality had relatively little if any effect on either party loyalty or policy choice, this study suggests that marginality had some effect on party loyalty for members of both parties in all sessions and some effect on choice of relatively liberal or conservative policy stands for Republicans during the Eighty-sixth but not the Eighty-seventh Congress. The cause of such striking changes in voting behavior as those shown in the relationship of marginality to average Republican Federal Role scores in the two Congresses examined here is by no means apparent. Certainly, the "on again-off again" quality of constituency influences on congressional voting behavior should warn students of Congress that findings must be limited to specific time periods.

At any rate, generalizations on marginality and voting behavior must

16Huntington, "A Revised Theory of American Party Politics," 671.

be made with extreme caution until further research throws additional light on the matter. Now it can only be said that there is *some evidence at some times* that close electoral margins are associated with atypical party behavior. Whether this association results from the selection of atypical individuals or from conscious efforts of these men to please constituents is a matter that can only be settled by other approaches. Such approaches could be based on close observation of individual congressmen or interviews with congressmen representing constituencies characterized by differing amounts of party competition. The second hypothesis discussed above—that marginality may sensitize the congressman to atypical elements in his constituency—has been explored only very roughly here, but the findings provide no clear support for the generalization that marginal congressmen from socio-economically atypical constituences behave differently from those who represent relatively safe constituencies. On the contrary, there is some indication in the case of the Eighty-sixth and Eighty-seventh Congresses that both marginality and atypical socio-economic constituency characteristics are *independently* related to deviant voting behavior.

Finally, the status of Huntington's revised theory would seem to be badly shaken by data presented by Froman and in the present study. Most of the difficulty with the "theory" lies in the inconclusive nature of the original supporting material, which upon close examination appears to be insufficient to support Huntington's sweeping conclusions. At any rate, no existing study presents data strongly supporting the idea that party competition and policy differences between the two parties are positively related. Beyond this negative generalization, the findings of these studies conflict with the theory. While Huntington and Froman offer no evidence that differences between the parties are greatest where competition is least, such a conclusion *is* suggested by the present study. Again, clarification must await further investigation aimed at eliminating these conflicting findings.

Chapter IX

CONCLUSIONS

DESCRIPTION of the congressional parties, and especially of the differences between the parties has concerned students of Congress since Lowell's *Influence of Party Upon Legislation.* Considerable confusion has been created, however, by the failure of some investigators to divorce descriptive concerns from those that are partially normative. After all, "party reform" has been a presistent theme of American political science since the latter part of the nineteenth century; it is not surprising that attempts of various investigators to describe American congressional parties have become enmeshed in this controversy. The resulting confusion, however, has suggested the desirability of divorcing efforts at description from those involving advocacy of either the "reform" or "anti-reform" position.

The purpose of this study is to *describe* the House parties through their roll call votes during the period from 1959 through 1962. It need not be inferred from the distinction drawn between description of the parties and assessment of their behavior either that these concerns are unrelated or that assessment or evaluation is somehow less important than description. The argument here is only that these two concerns must be distinguished analytically, lest the investigator's normative position on "party reform" influence what would seem to be a purely empirical matter—description of the behavior of the parties. It should also be understood that "the facts" about the parties will not by themselves establish that the parties should or should not behave differently than they do. Though this would appear to be a simple point, it has often been ignored. Quite often, it seems, the advocates of party responsibility, as well as those who have defended the American parties, have attempted to make their case objective by refusing to state their values explicitly. The result has been confusion. Even if "the facts" about the parties establish that they fail to satisfy the model of party responsibility, the question re-

171

mains—why should they? The answer offered here is that this question can be answered only by a statement of the observer's values or goals and a logical demonstration that these values will be served by "reform" or continuation of the status quo. Description, then, constitutes the necessary empirical base for evaluation of the parties' performance. It is not, however, the purpose of this study to advocate party responsibility or to oppose it.

Several studies have dealt with the differences between our parties. The approach here has been eclectic. Those methods have been chosen which recommend themselves as efficient means to examine several questions involving the cohesion of the House parties, their opposition to one another, and, finally, their differences on matters of public policy during the period of the Eighty-sixth and Eighty-seventh Congresses.

On the average, during this period House Democrats were slightly more cohesive than Republicans. Approximately 80 percent of Democrats and slightly more than 75 percent of Republicans voted together on the average roll call. Comparison with material presented by Julius Turner in *Party and Constituency* indicates that both parties were somewhat less cohesive in the period from 1959 to 1962 than they were during the selected sessions he studied during the period from 1921 to 1944. As separate calculation of the index of cohesion for northern and southern Democratic groups reveals, however, Democratic cohesion during the period from 1959 through 1962 would have been very high indeed if the southerners had not defected on a wide array of measures. During this period nearly 90 percent of northern Democrats voted together on the average roll call vote. Only the northern Democrats during the Eighty-sixth and Eighty-seventh Congresses came close to satisfying the model of party cohesion advocated by proponents of responsible parties.

Several means have been employed here to gauge party opposition. Lowell's traditional "party vote" standard, when applied to the Eighty-sixth and Eighty-seventh Congresses, makes clear at least that extremely cohesive party opposition was much more infrequent during this period than almost any other period for which comparable information is available. On only 5 percent of the roll calls analyzed for the two Congresses did party votes occur. By comparison, in only one other session of the House for which information is available—1928—was the level of party voting nearly as low. Even as recently as the sessions of the 1940's studied by Turner, the parties "party voted" on about 15 percent of the roll calls. If this demanding standard employed by Lowell were to be the sole indicator of cohesive opposition, it would be necessary to conclude that such opposition was practically absent from these sessions of the House.

Other standards, however, reveal the existence of substantial party opposition during this period. The parties opposed one another by simple majorities, for example, on nearly two-thirds of all roll calls analyzed for the four sessions. If the "modified party vote" (a roll call on which 75 percent of one party opposes 75 percent of the other) is accepted as a reasonable approximation of responsible party behavior, however, it is clear that the two House parties failed to produce this behavior on a large majority of the roll calls analyzed. On only 31.8 percent of the votes analyzed during the Eighty-sixth and Eighty-seventh Congresses did the two parties satisfy the requirements of the modified party vote. While this evidence would seem to call into question the sweeping generalization that "our parties seldom differ," it is also sufficient to establish clearly that the House parties failed in these four sessions to come close to the responsible parties model of voting behavior.

The question of differences between the parties is only partially answered, however, by these data on cohesion and opposition. More important, perhaps, to most observers is the distinctiveness of the parties' behavior on various questions of public policy. Several studies cited above have indicated that the congressional parties have never been opposed to one another "across the board"; rather they have differed on some questions of policy and more or less agreed on others. It is apparent, too, that the issue content of party opposition has altered drastically from era to era, seemingly following party realignments. In the period examined by this study, differences between the two parties were sharpest on domestic social and economic issues. On civil liberties and foreign policy issues, the parties' positions were much less clearly distinguishable. Differences between the parties on matters of public policy are especially apparent in the policy scales presented in Chapter IV. During the Eighty-sixth and Eighty-seventh Congresses the major questions of domestic economic and social policy, particularly on the regulatory and welfare role of the national government, divided the two House parties quite sharply. Despite the defection of a considerable portion of the southern Democrats on many specific policy questions in this area, differences between the parties are clearly apparent. The modal Democratic position was much more liberal than that of the Republicans. In the area of foreign policy, on the other hand, both parties were severely divided (Democrats, sectionally, Republicans more generally) between their pro-internationalist and anti-internationalist contingents. While the Democrats maintained a considerably more internationalist position on the average, the differences between the House parties were much less clearly apparent than in the domestic economic area. On questions of civil liberties, again the Democrats were badly divided, mainly on sectional lines. While Republicans were over-whelmingly anti-civil libertarian on the issues of procedural rights and federal preemption of subversive activities matters, Democratic divisions make it rather difficult to perceive "party positions" in this area. Finally, at least in roll call voting, the behavior of the two parties during this period on the matter of civil rights was very similar. Roll calls on the Civil Rights Act of 1960 reveal sectional, not party divisions in the House of Representatives.

Southern Democratic dissidence during the Eighty-sixth and Eighty-seventh Congresses was much greater than it was during four earlier sessions analyzed by Key in *Southern Politics*. On all four policy areas examined—domestic economic, foreign policy, civil liberties, and civil rights—sharp cleavages often separated southern Democrats from their northern colleagues. Whereas Key concluded in 1944 that the "conservative coalition" was a somewhat overrated phenomenon in the House, this study suggests that coalitional voting assumed major proportions during the period from 1959 through 1962. During both the Eisenhower and Kennedy presidencies, the most controversial matters of social and economic policy and civil liberties often produced alignments of southern Democrats and northern Republicans against northern Democrats and a handful of lib-eral Republicans, mainly those from the Northeast. In the four sessions examined here majorities of southern Democrats and northern Republi-cans opposed majorities of northern Democrats on more than a fifth of the roll calls examined. Under these circumstances, it must be inferred, even the most attentive of electors would have had some difficulty deter-mining party responsibility for actions taken in the House. Clearly, the "conservative coalition" was a phenomenon of major importance in the period covered by this study.

These, then, are "the facts" of House party behavior during the Eighty-sixth and Eighty-seventh Congresses. What one makes of these facts in evaluating the behavior of the parties during this period would seem to depend almost entirely on the values of the particular observer. To the liberal reformist-minded advocate of "responsible parties" they must cer-tainly lead logically to the conclusion that the House parties failed to ful-fill their appointed role in the democratic process. Both parties must, to such observers, share the blame for what James MacGregor Burns has called the "deadlock of democracy" which characterized the Eisenhower and Kennedy presidencies.[1] The internal divisions of both parties and the coalitional nature of voting in the House during the period studied

---

[1]Burns, *The Deadlock of Democracy, passim.*

would appear to have had a decided conservative effect on the political system as a whole. Such behavior on the part of the congressional parties is neither conducive to the focusing of majority opinion or to the fixing of "responsibility" that the advocates of "party government" desire in the legislative process. On the other hand, it seems equally clear that to the conservative who properly appreciates the effects of party disunity and coalitional voting, such behavior on the part of the congressional parties will also logically be considered a key element of what Burns has called "the Madisonian system." To such an observer (James Burnham is a prominent example) the behavior of the House parties during this period recommends Congress as the last and best hope of those who would defend the "American tradition" of opposition to national plebiscitary democracy.[2]

No matter what one's evaluation is of the kind of party behavior prevailing during the Eighty-sixth and Eighty-seventh Congresses, it seems apparent from the descriptive information on the parties culled from studies spanning the greater portion of our political history that this behavior is a deeply ingrained facet of the American political process. Although great fluctuations have been apparent in party cohesion and opposition in the sessions for which we have statistical information, it is apparent that the behavior of the congressional parties in the period from 1959 through 1962 was more typical than atypical. Only in the late 1890's were the House parties capable of maintaining extremely cohesive opposition on a majority of roll calls. In most sessions for which information is available, the parties seem to have been cohesively opposed to one another only on a small minority of roll calls taken.

There is, however, some evidence of cyclical uniformity in the "ups and downs" of cohesive opposition. It would seem a reasonable tentative hypothesis that the parties are ordinarily most cohesive in opposition to one another immediately following national electoral realignments. It would seem that as these alignments are subject to attrition over a period of time, the congressional parties are likely to become more and more disunified until a new realignment occurs. As has been indicated, the sessions characterized by the least amounts of party voting have immediately preceded party realignments. There is some evidence in the present study that such a pattern has characterized congressional voting since 1932. As the "Roosevelt coalition" has been eroded (most noticeably by the defection of the South), party cohesion and opposition have declined. If there is a pattern to the electoral cycle of American politics and if the

[2]James Burnham, *Congress and the American Tradition, passim.*

behavior of the congressional parties follows that pattern, there may be some basis for speculation that a new realignment may soon occur. If current realigning tendencies in the South continue to the extent that the region becomes competitive in congressional as well as in presidential elections, it would not seem improbable that the cohesion of both congressional parties would turn sharply upward in the next few years. If at the same time the electoral fortunes of the Republicans should decline in the Northeast, the sectional sources of disunity in both parties would be largely eliminated. Under these conditions both congressional parties might again be characterized by something like the cohesion that followed the realignments of 1896 and 1932.

The second strand of continuity manifest in the literature of congressional voting concerns party and constituency as factors influencing voting behavior. In light of difficulties inherent in the attempt of one observer—Julius Turner—to compare the influence of party and constituency on voting behavior, this study has taken a somewhat different approach. First, it is asked to what extent will constituency factors account for interparty differences? Are the parties different because the bases of their congressmen's constituencies are different? Second, to what extent can intra-party voting differences be explained by aggregate constituency factors? Third, what is the possibility that the voting behavior of members of both parties varies with the strength of their electoral margins?

As has been clearly shown, the aggregate constituency characteristics of districts which elected Democrats and those which elected Republicans to the Eighty-sixth and Eighty-seventh Congresses vary considerably. The evidence suggests that socio-economic constituency factors were strongly related to the election of Democrats and Republicans to the House. The more urban, non-white and the more blue collar the constituency, the more likely were Democrats to have been elected. The higher the percentage of owner-occupied housing and the median income of families, the more likely were Republicans to have been elected. It would seem reasonable to infer that a good deal of the House Democratic liberalism and Republican conservatism noted in this study may be accounted for by the nature of the constituencies represented by the members of the two parties during this period. Since 1932, it seems, the electoral bases of the two congressional parties have remained fairly stable. The bedrock of Democratic constituency has been the urban, relatively low-status areas, while the most durable basis of congressional Republicanism has been the rural and more affluent suburban areas. The major policy struggles of the post-New Deal period have been not simply party struggles, but also struggles between these elements of our population. At such times

southern congressmen have often cast their lot with Republican spokes-
men for the northern rural and suburban areas, despite the one-party
Democratic status of the South. Constituency factors would again seem to
offer some explanation of southern behavior. The one-partyism of the
former Confederate states (and to some extent the border states) has
forced into the national Democratic coalition those regional social elements that would, in the North, undoubtedly prefer Republican representation. Throughout this period the South remained overwhelmingly
rural and "old stock" in social composition. It is not surprising that the
region has rested uneasily in a party dominated by the northern urban
areas and the social elements of which they are composed—the Negro, the
other ethnic minorities, and the industrial labor force of the nation. In
sum, the observed differences between the two congressional parties would
seem to be accounted for, to a great extent, by the characteristics of the
constituencies their members represented during the Eighty-sixth and
Eighty-seventh Congresses. In roll call analysis, consequently, party and
constituency influences cannot be completely separated. Even if there
were no organizational party pressures of any kind during these years, the
differing constituency bases of the two congressional parties would, it is
reasonable to assume, have led to substantial differences in voting behavior, especially in the domestic economic and civil liberties areas.

The relationship of intra-party voting differences and socio-economic
and sectional differences was explored in Chapter VII for the Eighty-sixth
and Eighty-seventh Congresses with somewhat unclear results. Several previous investigators have attempted to demonstrate that intra-party voting
differences may be accounted for by constituency characteristics. Unfortunately, the difficulties inherent in the existing literature of party and constituency have not been eliminated by the present attempt to summarize
the hypotheses of several other investigators and test them in the case of
two recent Congresses.

Although Julius Turner and Lewis A. Froman found that urban-rural
differences were apparent in the voting behavior of both congressional
parties during the sessions they studied, the present analysis suggests no
straightforward relationship of this factor to voting behavior. Despite
the fact that there is some tendency for northern Republicans from the
most urban districts to rate higher Party Opposition Scores, no such pattern is apparent for Democrats from the more rural areas. For southern
Democrats, there is apparently some relationship between urban-rural differences and Party Opposition Scores, but it exists only for those in the
most rural and most urban categories. On all of the policy scales examined, rural northern Democrats fall disproportionately into the extreme

deviant group. By contrast, on only three of the scales examined—on minimum wages, housing, and civil liberties—were the most urban Republicans more inclined to the extreme deviant position than were other members of the party. In the case of southern Democrats, urbanism and
liberalism were related on some policy scales, but they were not on others. Only on matters involving minimum wages, housing and foreign aid
would there appear to be a clear relationship between these two factors.
In general, investigation of urban-rural constituency composition and
intra-party voting differences with respect to party opposition would not
suggest that this factor accounts for a major portion of the observed tendency of some congressmen to vote with the opposition.

The effects of atypical socio-economic constituency makeup on voting
behavior also remain unclear after considerable investigation. The present study again yields mixed results on this question. Neither indicator of
socio-economic status employed (the percentage of blue collar laborers in
the population and the median family income) seems to be closely related
to Party Opposition Scores for northern Democrats. Rather mysteriously,
on the other hand, both of these factors are related to Republican Party
Opposition in the case of the Eighty-sixth, but not the Eighty-seventh Congress. Since these two socio-economic factors appeared to be unrelated to
Party Opposition for southern Democrats, another factor—the percentage
of Negroes in the population—was introduced. Analysis, however, revealed some relationship of the new factor to party opposition in only
the Eighty-sixth, not the Eighty-seventh Congress. Analysis of extreme
deviants on the scales presented in Chapter IV, in addition, revealed little
relationship between socio-economic factors and extreme deviant voting
for either northern Democrats or Republicans, and only some relationship
on some scales for southern Democrats. The evidence of this study, therefore, suggests that northern Democrats and Republicans from atypical constituencies were only somewhat less loyal to respective party majorities
in the Eighty-sixth and Eighty-seventh Congresses than were other members from more typical districts. Though southern Democrats varied considerably in their voting behavior, there is likewise very little evidence in
this study that socio-economic constituency factors will account for these
variations.

Every investigation of congressional voting has found sectionalism to
be an influence on the voting behavior of members of both congressional
parties. Though the precise direction of sectional influence obviously
changes from period to period, the influence of this factor is nearly always apparent in congressional voting. The present study has shown that
southern Democrats were, on the average, much more conservative in all

policy areas examined than were their colleagues from other areas of the nation. While not all southerners in the Eighty-sixth and Eighty-seventh Congresses were conservative, southerners as a group were noticeably pulled again and again toward the modal position of the Republicans in domestic economic policy, civil liberties, and foreign affairs, and they were isolated from majorities of both of the northern parties on civil rights. This accounts for far more Democratic deviation than any other factor examined in this study. It would also indicate that sectional tendencies in the Republican congressional party were responsible for a greater amount of deviation from party voting than any other influence considered. While it is not at all obvious why this should be the case, northeastern Republicans were considerably more liberal than other members of the party during the Eighty-sixth and Eighty-seventh Congresses. Moreover, it seems that this sectional tendency is more than a reflection of some other factor such as urbanism or electoral marginality— that Republicans from the Northeast were *as such* more liberal than those from other geographical areas. Here, as in many other cases, there would seem to be no impressive clues to the precise causal mechanisms at work.

In summary, it must be said that the several examinations of urban-rural, socio-economic, and sectional constituency differences and intra-party voting differences suggest few straightforward relationships. While there are at times relationships apparent between atypical party behavior and constituency characteristics, it would be far too simple to suggest at this point that constituency factors account for observed variations in party voting. Although no claim is made here that the complex relationship between the congressman and his constituents has been fathomed, the several studies in this area would suggest that constituency factors will not account entirely for observed differences between the parties or for the defection of many congressmen from party majorities. The differences between the congressional parties are far more, it seems, than simple reflections of constituency pressures. The behavior of the congressman is also much more complex than a simple reaction to constituency characteristics.

Finally, investigation of three hypotheses on electoral margins and voting behavior leaves this matter in considerable doubt. Whereas data presented in earlier studies suggest relatively little or no effect of electoral margins on either party loyalty or policy choice, this study indicates that electoral marginality affected the loyalty of members of both parties during both Congresses investigated. Moreover, the evidence presented here suggests it is electoral marginality *as such*, not marginality coupled with atypical socio-economic characteristics, that disposes the congressman to deviate from majorities of his party on roll call votes. The status of Huntington's "revised theory" interpretation of electoral competition and congressional policy choice would appear to be badly shaken by data now presented. In fact, there is considerable doubt that Huntington's original data support his sweeping conclusions. Close examination of existing studies indicates no impressive evidence in favor of the idea that party competition and policy differences between the parties are positively related. The evidence for the Eighty-sixth and Eighty-seventh Congresses, in fact, suggests just the opposite—that the differences between the two parties are greatest in the case of congressmen elected from safe constituencies.

Although a sizable amount of information on various sessions of Congress has now been gathered, it would seem clear that no very satisfying picture of the historical dimensions of party in the legislative process has emerged. While the sessions chosen for investigation by various observers have been selected with no particular theoretical purpose in mind, the resulting variety of information reveals some rather fascinating historical differences in congressional party behavior. Even if the large data-gaps in this literature are ignored, the "ups and downs" of party cohesion and opposition over time are much too great to be encompassed in a single generalization to the effect that "our parties seldom differ." In fact, it seems, while the parties have never differed to the extent that advocates of the doctrine of "responsible parties" would approve of their behavior, they *have* differed very considerably at times. At other times, however, the parties have been much more similar. Surely, these historical dimensions of congressional party behavior deserve more attention from political scientists than they have received.

How are these marked differences in cohesion and opposition to be explained? Why are the parties quite different in their voting behavior in one period, but similar in another? While answers to these questions may prove very elusive, they are surely important enough to merit inquiry. One promising lead, it would seem, lies in the apparent correspondence of fluctuations in congressional party voting to national electoral "party realignments." Although historical case studies of congressional party behavior pose many problems, these would seem by no means to be insurmountable. The methods employed in this study as well as the many others summarized above are readily applicable to historical studies.[3] Un-

---

[3]It should again be noted that this type of study has very recently begun to catch on among both historians and political scientists. Several books have appeared since

less contemporary Congresses are to be studied in the absence of any larger theoretical framework, it would seem necessary to examine congressional behavior in past periods with the purpose of accounting for the ups and downs of cohesive party opposition. Such a broadening of our concerns would seemingly correspond to developments in the field of electoral behavior, where students who began to treat electoral phenomena in a "timeless" framework discovered by experience that historically-oriented concepts were necessary. It seems quite likely at present that further inquiry into fluctuations in the behavior of the congressional parties will reveal these phenomena as being, at least in part, tied to realignments in the national party system as a whole. If this is in fact the case, a more satisfactory view of congressional party behavior will depend on the availability of new, historically-oriented studies.

The several studies that have sought to illuminate factors influencing congressional voting behavior, while they have clarified some questions, have left many others in doubt. Obviously, there is much in this area that is only imperfectly understood. It now seems all too clear, for example, that a major portion of the intra-party variance in voting behavior is left unexplained by the manipulation of aggregate constituency characteristics. Although the easy availability of roll call and aggregate congressional district data will continue to recommend their use in the kinds of studies examined here, there would seem to be little doubt today that some of the most important questions dealing with the congressman, his party, and his constituency can only be settled by other modes of inquiry.

Certainly, a great difficulty with all of the major roll call studies (and the present study is, unfortunately, no exception) lies in their reliance on aggregate census data, which are now clearly incapable of indicating more than the merest shadow of the many complex variables that are often casually subsumed in the concept "constituency." Anyone who has worked with such data must sooner or later conclude that inferences from them to pressures which congressmen feel from their districts are altogether too indirect for comfort. There can be little doubt that aggregate data provide only the roughest indications of the sorts of opinions, contacts, communications, group activities, etc., which make up the "real world" constituency of the congressman. Here, perhaps, some hope for the future of this kind of research may be found in survey methods. There can be no question at all that interviews with congressmen and their constituents provide a much higher order of information than do aggregate data. Not only do

_____

the completion of this manuscript. The most important are those I have cited in footnote 39, Chap. 2.

survey data represent a vast improvement over the investigators inferences on what electoral opinion "ought to be," given certain social and economic indicators, but the extension of the survey approach to Congress refocuses attention on *the representative, his own perception of the constituency, and his concept of his role in the represntative process.* It is, after all, the flesh and blood congressman who must interpret what are usually called "constituency factors," and there is every reason to believe that he deserves to be treated as a crucially important political actor—not as an inanimate black box between the stimuli of party and constituency pressures and the response of voting behavior. It is interesting, therefore, that Warren Miller and Donald Stokes, working with survey data and roll call votes, have given promise of establishing much stronger relationships between *constituency opinion as the congressman sees it* and voting behavior than those uncovered in the aggregate data studies examined here.[4] Their forthcoming book *Representation in the American Congress*[5] may well go far to resolve many of the perplexing problems that the aggregate data studies have left unanswered. Even so, some formidable difficulties will no doubt have to be overcome if durable generalizations in this area are to be formulated.

For most students the financial support required for the survey-interview approach will be a staggering, and perhaps a flatly prohibitive, factor. As a result, while aggregate data studies will probably hold less interest for future generations of scholars, few will be able to muster the financial backing needed to apply the Miller-Stokes approach to future Congresses. Obviously, such a situation is problematical as generalizations based on one survey-interview case study—however technically sophisticated that study may be—will of necessity raise the question of their durability. Whether this can be eliminated is an enigma that can only be answered by those who will examine this area in the future.

A different, if not unrelated, source of difficulty with the studies of congressional voting behavior is to be found in the generally oversimplified models of the representative process on which they are implicity based. On the whole, it seems, American political scientists until very recently have tended to view the representative's role either in terms of the socalled "Burkean dilemma" or as a more or less mechanistic "group basis" or "pressure politics" model.[6] Either, it is assumed, the representative

---

[4]See Warren E. Miller and Donald E. Stokes, "Constituency Influence in Congress," *American Political Science Review,* LVII (March, 1963), *passim.*

[5]The volume, which has been expected to appear for some time, is to be published by Prentice-Hall.

[6]See especially the interesting remarks on this point in Raymond A. Bauer, Ithiel

must choose between the dictates of something called his "conscience" and the opinions of his constituents, or alternatively, his behavior is supposed to be some kind of vector that results from the various pressures exerted upon him. That these two models correspond to two distinct stages in the development of American political science is very clear. The first is an obvious nonempirically-derived product of a moralistically-oriented discipline. The second, in its thoroughgoing reaction to the assumptions of the first, clearly characterizes an early stage of what has been called "the behavioral revolution" in American political science—a time when it was supposed that the empirically-observable regularities of the political world were a good deal more simple than they have turned out to be. The important point to establish here is that neither of these models begins to capture adequately the main components of the legislative system in which flesh and blood congressmen act out their roles. The "Burkean Dilemma" assumes, for example, that constituents are generally attentive to the activities of the representative and are well informed about them. Survey research, however, has clearly established that this is almost never the case.[7] However attentive the electors of Bristol may have been, the mass American electorate knows precious little about the congressman beyond his name, many voters know even that. Nor does it seem to be the case that the congressman often finds himself squeezed, as it were, between constituent demands and "conscience".[8] Following these findings, it seems most important to investigate how the congressman *perceives* his constituency. The evidence is that while he considers it very important,[9] he is often totally mystified about district opinion.[10] What he must represent, it seems, is his *image* of the district, and that image is to a very large extent a product of his own thought processes. One observer has recently stressed that the congressman's limited contacts, his selective perception and retention allow him to see what he wants to see when he considers district opinion. At any rate, there can be little doubt

de Sola Pool, and Lewis A. Dexter, *American Business and Public Policy* (New York: Atherton Press, 1963), 404–405 and Chap. 29, *passim*.

[7]See especially Donald E. Stokes and Warren E. Miller, "Party Government and the Saliency of Congress," *Public Opinion Quarterly*, XXVI (Winter, 1962), 531–46, *passim*.

[8]On this point see Bauer, Pool, and Dexter, *American Business and Public Policy*, Chaps. 29–34, *passim*.

[9]See especially Lewis A. Dexter, "What Do Congressmen Hear?" in Nelson W. Polsby, Robert A. Dentler, and Paul A. Smith, *Politics and Social Life* (Boston: Houghton Mifflin, 1963), 485–95, and "The Representative and His District," *ibid.*, 495–12.

[10]See the articles by Dexter cited above in Bauer, Pool, and Dexter, *American Business and Public Policy*, Chaps. 29–35, and also Dexter, *Congressmen and the People They Listen To* (Cambridge: Center for International Studies, M.I.T., 1955). The latter is a dittoed manuscript constituting an earlier statement of the findings in the Congress chapters of Bauer, Pool, and Dexter, *American Business and Public Policy*.

that the concept of firm and insistent district sentiment that is implicit in the "Burkean Dilemma" model is usually inapplicable to the conditions of modern democratic politics. Put somewhat differently, it is clear that the difficulty the representative has in "reading" the constituency's mind has been grossly underestimated. It has also become apparent that the "group basis" or "pressure politics" model is woefully inadequate. Recent research focusing on the representative's activities has strongly suggested that group, constituency, and party "pressures" are seldom as clear as much of our professional literature portrays them.[11] Rather, it seems, the congressman, in the absence of clear forces that play on him, must gropingly define his own role. In so doing, he appears to be very much an active agent who creates, in part, which "pressures" he chooses to feel.[12]

A third deficiency of the existing studies is that they have generally omitted certain variables which a large portion of the professional literature of Congress emphasizes heavily. Log-rolling and other forms of bargaining behavior inside the legislature are consciously or unconsciously treated as uncontrolled variables. The same may be said for such other factors as the influence of colleagues, the actions of formal party leaders in the legislature, and the activities of the executive. The obvious reason for the ommission of such commonly acknowledged elements of the legislative process is that they are difficult to quantify, or even to control at all, within the confines of a rigorous research scheme. Yet, it should be clear that these factors are ignored only at the cost of our failure to develop anything like an adequate model of the representative process in Congress.

That the literature of congressional voting behavior is so unsatisfying is no doubt largely a result of these perplexing problems. Yet, it is far too early to conclude, as some readers of this study are likely to do, that the seemingly infinite subtleties of the political world will permanently outstrip the imagination of political scientists. It might more convincingly be argued that, despite the complexities of our subject matter, close empirical study of Congress, and of the American political system generally, has recently produced a number of promising leads that may lay the groundwork for a new generation of more sophisticated research on these questions that remain so unsatisfactorily resolved in our present literature. Following these leads, further inquiry may well explain much that remains mysterious in the aggregate data—roll call studies.

---

[11]See especially Bauer, Pool, and Dexter, *American Business and Public Policy, passim.*
[12]*Ibid.*

APPENDIX

SCALING ROLL CALL VOTES

SCALE ANALYSIS has become rather common in studies of legislative voting in recent years.[1] Some readers, however, may be unfamiliar with its logic and application in this area, and therefore a short explanatory discussion may serve as an introduction to scale analysis and its use in the study of roll call voting. Since my own scaling procedure differs somewhat from that employed in a number of other studies, it is necessary to spell out the exact specifics of the procedure I followed. Rather than clutter the text with the technical terms necessary to this sort of discussion, they have been relegated to this appendix, where they might be perused without detracting from discussions of substantive findings.

Cumulative (Guttman) scaling was first employed during World War II in applied attitude research by sociologists and social psychologists attempting to study factors affecting morale and performance in the armed services.[2] Since that time it has been widely used in studies of attitude measurement and public opinion. Once literature on attitude scaling had appeared in the professional journals, students of legislative politics were quick to realize the potential application of the technique to studies of roll call voting. In the late 1940's scaling was employed in an analysis of voting behavior in the United States Senate,[3] and since that time it has seen continued use in a number of well-known studies of legislative behavior.

[1] In addition to MacRae's *Dimensions of Congressional Voting*, discussed at length in Chapter I, see especially Belknap, "A Study of Senatorial Voting by Scale Analysis"; Farris, "A Scale Analysis of Ideological Factors in Congressional Voting," 308–38; and H. Douglas Price, "Are Southern Democrats Different?" in Nelson W. Polsby, Robert A. Dentler and Paul A. Smith (eds.), *Politics and Social Life* (Boston: Houghton Mifflin, 1963). The discussion in Price's article is especially informative on the logic of scaling in roll call analysis.

[2] See Stouffer, *Measurement and Prediction, passim.*

[3] N. L. Gage and Ben Shimberg, "Measuring Senatorial Progressivism," 112–17.

The reader who is interested in scaling will find an extensive literature at his disposal.[4] There will be no attempt here to summarize this literature, as it is characterized by numerous subtleties and nuances. The purpose of this brief appendix is quite limited. First, the logic of scaling will be discussed on an elementary level for those who are totally unfamiliar with the technique. Second, the exact procedure followed in the construction of the scales presented in Chapter IV will be described. Anyone who wishes to familiarize himself further with scaling and its applications in the study of legislative voting should refer to the general and applied literature previously cited.

The logic of Guttman scaling is actually quite simple. A scale is "a test of whether a series of criteria can be so arranged as to result in cumulative divisions of the population under study." [5] Such a device can be applied to a great variety of matters. Scales might be arranged to classify trees cumulatively in terms of their height, for example. Or cars by their weight. Or men by their intelligence quotients. In the latter case, for example, a number of men are arranged in terms of descending orders of intelligence—A, B, C, D, E, F, etc.—and it is demonstrated that it is logically impossible for Jones to be less intelligent than F without also being less intelligent than A, B, C, D, or E. A simple cumulative scale has thus been created. In the social sciences, such cumulative scales are usually employed to array a population cumulatively in terms of some "universe of attributes"—similar characteristics they may possess. In the measurement of attitudes, for example, it is often desirable to be able to say that A is more prejudiced against Negroes than B, B more than C, C more than D, etc. In such a case, as in the example of intelligence ranks above, it can be shown that if A is more prejudiced than B, he is also more prejudiced than C, etc. Such a cumulative scale provides a means of placing a population ordinally along a continuum conceptualized as a universe of attributes. Insofar as the scale is *truly* cumulative, it provides a means of placing *each individual* ordinally in relation to every other individual without ambiguity. The major virtue of cumulative as against other types of scaling, in the eyes of Louis Guttman and other pioneers in its use, lies in its ability to select items related to a single universe of attributes— and to place the members of a population ordinally in terms of that uni-

---

[4]See especially Louis A. Guttman, "A Basis for Scaling Qualitative Data," *American Sociological Review*, IX (April, 1944), 139–50; Chapters I and III of Stouffer, *Measurement and Prediction.*; and Bert F. Green, "Attitude Measurement," in Gardner Lindzey (ed.), *Handbook of Social Psychology* (Reading, Mass.: Addison-Wesley, 1954), I, 335–69.

[5]Price, "Southern Democrats," 743.

verse.[6] In simpler language, it is thought that scaling gives the researcher some guarantee that the attitudes are about similar things and that a fairly exact description of these attitudes can be put symbolically in the form of a single scale score.

Perhaps all of this will be more clear if it is stated in the form of a simple example. Suppose a group of men are to be separated into ordinal ranks on "prejudice against Negroes." Attitudes on this subject might be scaled by asking a number of questions thought to indicate various degrees of prejudice. These questions might take the following form:

(a) Would you mind working with Negroes?
(b) Would you eat at the same table with a Negro?
(c) Would you mind a Negro's moving into your neighborhood?
(d) Would you object to a racially mixed marriage in your family?

If these questions succeeded in separating the population into cumulative groups, the results of such an attitude study might be as follows:

Scale Type 1	+ + + +
Scale Type 2	− + + +
Scale Type 3	− − + +
Scale Type 4	− − − +
Scale Type 5	− − − −

Those members of the population falling into Type 1 would have given an "unprejudiced" response on each question. Those in Type 2 would have answered all questions in an "unprejudiced" manner save the last. Those in Type 3, all but the last two, etc. If a population can be represented in this manner, a "perfect scale" may be said to have resulted. Though we would not be entitled to speak of the degree of prejudice prevailing in each group in terms of true interval measurements, all members of the population would have been arranged ordinally into cumulative groups. If we know, then, that a man objects to eating with Negroes, we know that he also objects to racial intermarriage. A "perfect scale" permits representation of the pattern of responses prevailing in all cases by a simple assignment of a scale score—1, 2, etc. The application of cumulative scaling techniques to legislative voting may readily be seen at this point. Suppose that roll call votes are taken on the following matters in the area of labor relations:

(a) To ban unions.

[6]See Guttman, "Scaling Qualitative Data," *passim.*

(b) To abolish industry-wide bargaining.
(c) To abolish the union shop.
(d) To make mandatory a strict reporting of union finances.

It is not at all difficult to imagine that these roll calls might be scaled cumulatively in a manner very similar to the scaling of attitudes on prejudice. Again, if a "perfect scale" could be constructed, every congressman's response on these roll calls could be represented by a single scale score. A score of 1 in this case might represent the most pro-labor congressmen—those who voted to oppose all of the above measures. Any congressman who voted to ban unions would also have voted for all of the less harsh measures. And, too, any who voted against strict reporting of financial information would also have voted against the ban on unions. Such a scale would rank congressmen ordinally in terms of labor voting. It is not difficult to see that such a system of ranking is to be preferred over a simple percentagizing of pro or con votes on these four questions. The cumulative aspect of the scaling technique makes certain that a score of 1, for example, always means the same thing—a single response pattern on all four items. A score of 75 percent on the other hand, obtained by simple calculation of percentages, might mean that the congressman voted against any one of the four questions.

Of course, in the empirical world, as in contrast to the realm of logic, perfect scales of the sort just discussed are almost never obtained. Consequently, in the literature of scaling, various criteria have been established for judging the "scalability" of a set of items (in legislative voting studies, roll call votes). "In practice," Louis Guttman wrote, "90 percent perfect scales or better have been used as efficient approximations of perfect scales." [7] The original criteria for construction of an attitude scale have been listed by Guttman as:

(a) A "coefficient of reproducibility" of .90 or above. The coefficient is defined as the number of responses that would have been predicted wrongly for each individual on the basis of his scale score—"errors"—divided by the total number of responses, and subtracted from 1.
(b) ". . . attempts should be made to include in the sample as wide a range of marginal distributions as possible." Marginals in this context refer to the proportions replying positively and negatively on each item (or voting "yea" or "nay" on each roll call).
(c) "Errors should occur at random throughout the scale."
(d) ". . . it is probably desirable that more than ten items be used, with

_____

[7] Stouffer, *Measurement and Prediction,* 64.

perhaps a lesser number being satisfactory if the marginal frequencies of several items are in the range of 30 percent to 70 percent." [8]

A close survey of the literature of scale analysis in roll call voting will indicate that all but the last two criteria have been largely ignored by the various researchers who have employed the technique. The last criterion is obviously impossible to meet, since quite often fewer than ten roll calls are taken in a particular policy area in an entire session. This is almost always the case with the House of Representatives, where roll call votes are less frequent than in the Senate. If scales are to be constructed for the House, one must almost always resort to scaling fewer than ten roll calls. In my study, following the practice initiated by Charles Farris in his study of voting in the House,[9] as few as two votes have been scaled on occasion. The justification for this practice, which is admittedly far from ideal, is that a loose scale of this sort still preserves the cumulative element of more rigorous scales. Such a scale, consequently, is a better device for classifying voting positions than is simple percentagizing. The criterion that "errors" occur at random would seem to have much less applicability to scaling of legislators' voting positions than to scaling of attitudes. It seems quite apparent today that scales constructed of roll call votes are not unidimensional in the original sense. They are not to be strictly compared with attitude scales. The legislative situation is highly structured, and there is reason to believe that many factors such as cooperation among state delegations, regional solidarity, or personal friendships might cause "errors" in scales. At any rate, though this criterion is seldom mentioned by those who have employed scale analysis to study voting behavior, it would seem reasonable to assume that it has not been followed. In roll call studies, then, the first two criteria above would seem to be the most important. It has been generally understood that a scale should have an "index of reproducibility" above .90 and that the scale should include items with as wide a spread of marginals as possible. The failure of roll call analysts to heed the fourth criterion is fortunately rendered much less important than it might at first seem by the fact that items with very extreme marginals are usually excluded from analysis for one reason or another. Most roll call items included in scales, it seems, were taken on highly controversial matters, and, especially where members of both parties are placed on a single scale, the marginals are almost never extreme.[10]

---

[8]*Ibid.*, 77–78.

[9]See Farris, "A Scale Analysis of Ideological Factors," *passim*.

[10]It should be understood that Guttman's reason for including the fourth criter-

Having discussed briefly the logic of scale analysis and its application to the study of legislative voting, we turn now to a brief account of the scaling procedure employed in this study. First, it will be apparent to anyone at all familiar with existing work in this area that this effort is quite different from that employed by Duncan MacRae in *Dimensions of Congressional Voting*. And, since the major purpose in selecting scale analysis from the alternative approaches available was to compare the policy stands of the two parties during the period from 1959 through 1962, the decision was made to place members of both parties on common scales. Second, the procedure employed here is much less technically sophisticated than that executed by MacRae and his assistants. No attempt was made here, as in *Dimensions*, to examine all possible roll calls of common content before selecting those actually to be used in the construction of the scales. But since the aim was to highlight differences in party behavior on specific policy questions such as housing and civil rights, only roll calls overtly falling into these categories were considered. The policy dimensions, then, identified by the scaling procedure employed here are narrower than those identified by MacRae. Rather than a Fair Deal Scale, for example, we have constructed several scales out of the roll calls that might have gone into the making of such a scale. Rather than a Foreign Policy Scale, we have constructed somewhat narrower "Foreign Aid Scales" and a "Trade Expansion Scale." And though our scales are much simpler than MacRae's, they do serve our major purpose—to present an accurate record of the parties' behavior on a number of specific major policy questions.

The exact procedures followed in constructing the scales presented in Chapter IV may now be recounted. First, all roll calls falling into a given policy area, such as labor relations, were selected for preliminary analysis. The vote of each congressman was then recorded and punched on Hollerith cards. Not only actual "yea" and "nay" votes, but also pairs for and against and "announced for and against" were recorded as legitimate responses for each item on the grounds that in each case, the congressman was willing to take a public stand on the issue in question.[11] When the various roll calls in these preliminary sets were arranged in order of descending marginal frequencies, each vote in the set was cross tabulated

---

ion was largely based on fear that scales containing several items with rather extreme marginals would necessarily be characterized by "spuriously high reproducibility." If, for example, the marginals of an item are 90–10, "error" cannot exceed 10 percent. The inclusion of many such items would "build-in" the reproducibility of a scale. See Stouffer, *Measurement and Prediction*, 77–78.

11All roll call data were taken from *CQ Almanac*, 1959–62. The "announced for and against" categories are presented here.

against every other on an IBM 101 Statistical Machine to note the percentage of error on each roll call. When it became apparent that a set of roll calls satisfied the criteria of "reproducibility" established by Louis Guttman, the congressmen's votes on each of these roll calls were printed, and final assignments to scale scores were made.

When "errors" occurred in the scales, assignment to scale categories was made on the basis of the criterion for "minimum change." [12] When more than one assignment was possible on the basis of this criterion, the congressman was assigned to the scale score nearest to the one occurring with the greatest frequency.[13] Where more than two errors were registered by a congressman, no attempt was made to place him on the scale. However, these errors were included in calculations of the "index of reproducibility." On several of the scales "combined items" were constructed by combining two roll calls.[14] These items are simply synthetic roll calls made up of two nearly identical voting patterns. Their inclusion seemed wise at points where marginals were practically identical, and the only alternative seemed to be the discarding of certain roll calls as useless and lowering the reproducibility of the scale. By this rather simple procedure seventeen scales were constructed. The reproducibility of each exceeded the minimum requirement of .90.

The roll calls employed in constructing the scales are listed below. In each case citation is made to the official House designation of the measure being considered and to the *Congressional Quarterly* number of the roll call in question. In each case, the date is also given to indicate the session of the roll call and the appropriate volume of the *Congressional Quarterly Almanac* in which the vote may be found.

"Labor Scale"—Eighty-sixth Congress
    S 1555. Labor-Management Reporting and Disclosure Act of 1959. Adoption of the conference report. *CQ* 78 (1959).
    HR 8342. Labor-Management Reporting and Disclosure Act of 1959. Passage. *CQ* 60 (1959).
    HR 8342. Motion to recommit the bill. *CQ* 59 (1959).
    HR 8342. Landrum-Griffin substitute amendment. *CQ* 58 (1959).
"Area Redevelopment Scale"—Eighty-sixth Congress
    S 722. Area Redevelopment Act. Passage. *CQ* 36 (1960).

12See Andrew F. Henry, "A Method of Classifying Non-Scale Response Patterns in a Guttman Scale," *Public Opinion Quarterly*, XVI (Spring, 1952), 94.
    13*Ibid.*
14For a further explanation see Samuel A. Stouffer and others, "A Technique for Improving Cumulative Scales," *Public Opinion Quarterly*, XVI (Summer, 1952), 273–91.

S 722. Question whether House would consider the bill. *CQ* 34 (1960).

S 722. Motion to recommit the bill. *CQ* 35 (1960).

S 722. Motion to dispense with further proceedings. *CQ* 28 (1960).

"Area Redevelopment Scale"—Eighty-seventh Congress

S 1. Area Redevelopment Act. Adoption of the conference report. *CQ* 22 (1961).

S 1. Passage. *CQ* 18 (1961).

S 1. Motion to recommit the bill and cut the expenditures authorized. *CQ* 17 (1961).

"Aid to Education Scale"—Eighty-sixth Congress

HR 10128. School Construction Assistance Act of 1960. Passage. *CQ* 53 (1960).

HR 10128. Substitute amendment to return each year to the states for school construction 25 percent of federal tax on cigarettes sold in the state. *CQ* 50 (1960).

HR 10128. Motion to recommit and substitute a much more conservative measure. *CQ* 52 (1960).

"Aid to Education Scale"—Eighty-seventh Congress

HR 8900. College Academic Facilities and Student Assistance Act. Motion to recommit eliminating a provision for loans and grants to students. *CQ* 94 (1962).

H Res 625. Resolution to send HR 8900 to conference. *CQ* number 35, 1962.

HR 8900. Passage. *CQ* 2 (1962).

"Minimum Wage Scale"—Eighty-sixth Congress

HR 12677. Increase minimum wage provisions of the Fair Labor Standards Act of 1939. Conservative substitute amendment. *CQ* 7 (1960).

HR 12677. Passage as amended by a conservative substitute. *CQ* 76 (1960).

"Minimum Wage Scale"—Eighty-seventh Congress

HR 3935. Fair Labor Standards Amendments, 1961. Motion to recommit the bill *CQ* 15 (1961).

HR 3935. Substitution of a more conservative measure. *CQ* 14 (1961).

HR 3935. Conference report accepted. *CQ* 23 (1961).

HR 3935. Passage of the bill as amended by a more conservative substitute. *CQ* 16 (1961).

"Housing Scale"—Eighty-sixth Congress

S 57. Housing Act of 1959. Amendment to make all funds authorized available only through enactment of specific appropriation legislation. *CQ* 21 (1959).

S 57. Recommit and substitute a much more conservative measure. *CQ* 22 (1959).

S 57. Adoption of the conference report. *CQ* 45 (1959).

S 2539. Revised Housing Act of 1959. A motion to recommit and substitute a much more conservative measure. *CQ* 68 (1959).

"Housing Scale"—Eighty-seventh Congress

HR 6028. Housing Act of 1961. A motion to recommit and substitute a more conservative measure. *CQ* 46 (1961).

S. 1922. Housing Act of 1961. Conference report accepted. *CQ* 51 (1961).

HR 6028. Passage. *CQ* 47 (1961).

"Welfare Scale"—Eighty-seventh Congress

HR 10606. Public Welfare Amendments of 1962. Recommit and reduce grants for payments to old age and blind persons. *CQ* 14 (1962).

HR 10606. Passage. *CQ* 15 (1962).

"Foreign Aid Scale"—1959

HR 7500. Mutual Security Act of 1959. Adoption of conference report. *CQ* 53 (1959).

HR 7500. Passage. *CQ* 42 (1959).

HR 8385. Mutual Security Appropriations bill. Passage. *CQ* 56 (1959).

"Foreign Aid Scale"—1960

HR 11510. Mutual Security Act of 1950. Passage of authorization. *CQ* 20 (1960).

HR 11510. Adoption of conference report. *CQ* 40 (1960).

HR 12619. Mutual Security Appropriations for fiscal 1961. Passage. *CQ* 62 (1960).

"Foreign Aid Scale"—1961

HR 9033. Foreign Assistance Appropriation Act of 1961. Amendment increasing military aid appropriation. *CQ* 88 (1961).

S 1983. Foreign Assistance Act of 1961. Acceptance of conference report on authorizations. *CQ* 87 (1961).

HR 8400. 1961 Foreign Aid Authorization. Passage. *CQ* 75 (1961).

HR 7500. Peace Corps Act. Conference report accepted. *CQ* 108 (1961).

HR 7500. Peace Corps Act. Passage. *CQ* 99 (1961).

"Foreign Aid Scale"—1962

HR 13175. Foreign Aid Appropriation Act for fiscal 1963. Motion to recommit and reduce economic aid. *CQ* 95 (1962).

S 2996. Foreign Assistance Act of 1962. Conference report accepted *CQ* 65 (1962).

HR 13175. Adoption of conference report. *CQ* 96 (1962).

"Trade Expansion Scale"—Eighty-seventh Congress

HR 11970. Trade Expansion Act of 1962. Motion to recommit and extend for one year the expiring act. *CQ* 49 (1962).

HR 11970. Passage. *CQ* 50 (1962).

HR 11970. Adoption of the conference report. *CQ* 109 (1962).

"Civil Liberties Scale"—Eighty-sixth Congress

H Res 288. An open rule for debate on HR 3 (a bill to limit federal preemption of subversive activities matters). *CQ* 44 (1959).

HR 3. A motion to recommit the bill. *CQ* 46 (1959).

HR 3. Passage. *CQ* 47 (1959).

"Civil Rights Scale"—Eighty-sixth Congress

HR 8601. Civil Rights Act of 1960. Amendment adopting provision for court-appointed voting referees. *CQ* 13 (1960).

HR 8601. Motion to recommit the bill after deleting a section making it a crime to obstruct court orders for school desegration by "threatening letter or communication." *CQ* 14 (1960).

HR 8601. Approval of Senate Amendments. *CQ* 19 (1960).

HR 8601. Passage. *CQ* 15 (1960).

BIBLIOGRAPHY

BOOKS

Agar, Herbert. *The Price of Union*. Boston: Houghton Mifflin, 1950.

Bauer, Raymond A., Ithiel de Sola Pool, and Lewis Anthony Dexter. *American Business and Public Policy*. New York: Atherton Press, 1963.

Burnham, James. *Congress and the American Tradition*. Chicago: Henry Regnery, 1959.

Burns, James MacGregor. *Congress on Trial*. New York: Harper, 1949.

————. *The Deadlock of Democracy*. Englewood Cliffs, N. J.: Prentice-Hall, 1963.

Committee on Political Parties, American Political Science Association. "Toward a More Responsible Two-Party System," *American Political Science Review*, XLIV, Supplement (September, 1950). New York: Rinehart, 1950.

Dahl, Robert A. *Congress and Foreign Policy*. New York: W. W. Norton, 1964.

Dexter, Lewis A. *Congressmen and the People They Listen To*. Cambridge: Center for International Studies, M.I.T., 1955.

Froman, Lewis A. *Congressmen and Their Constituencies*. Chicago: Rand McNally, 1963.

Grassmuck, George. *Sectional Biases in Congress on Foreign Policy*. Baltimore: Johns Hopkins University Press, 1951.

Griffith, Ernest S. *Congress: Its Contemporary Role*. New York: New York University Press, 1951.

Jewell, Malcolm E., and Samuel C. Patterson. *The Legislative Process in the United States*. New York: Random House, 1966.

Keefe, William J., and Morris S. Ogul. *The American Legislative Process.* Englewood Cliffs, N.J.: Prentice-Hall, 1964.

Key, V. O., Jr. *Southern Politics.* New York: Vintage Books, n.d.

———. *Public Opinion and American Democracy.* New York: Alfred A. Knopf, 1961.

———. *Politics, Parties, and Pressure Groups.* 5th ed. New York: Thomas Y. Crowell, 1964.

Lowell, A. Lawrence. *The Government of England.* 2 vols. New York: Macmillan, 1908. Vol. II.

MacRae, Duncan, Jr. *Dimensions of Congressional Voting.* Berkeley: University of California Press, 1958.

Ranney, Austin. *The Doctrine of Responsible Party Government.* Urbana: University of Illinois Press, 1962.

Rice, Stuart A. *Quantitative Methods in Politics.* New York: Alfred A. Knopf, 1928.

Rossiter, Clinton. *Parties and Politics in America.* New York: New American Library, 1964.

Scammon, Richard (ed.) . *American Votes: A Handbook of Contemporary American Election Statistics,* Vol. IV: 1960. Pittsburgh: University of Pittsburgh Press, 1962.

Schattschneider, E. E. *Party Government.* New York: Farrar and Rinehart, 1942.

Selltiz, Claire; Marie Jahoda, Morton Deutsch and Stuart W. Cook. *Research Methods in Social Relations.* New York: Henry Holt, 1959.

Sindler, Allan P. (ed.) . *Change in the Contemporary South.* Durham, N.C.: Duke University Press, 1963.

Smith, Frank E. *Congressman From Mississippi.* New York: Pantheon Books, 1964.

———. *Look Away From Dixie.* Baton Rouge: Louisiana State University Press, 1965.

Stouffer, Samuel A. (ed.) . *Measurement and Prediction,* Vol. IV: *Studies in Social Psychology in World War II.* Princeton: Princeton University Press, 1950.

———. *Communism; Conformity and Civil Liberties.* New York: John Wiley and Sons, Science Editions, 1966.

Truman, David B. *The Congressional Party.* New York: John Wiley and Sons, 1959.

Turner, Julius. *Party and Constituency: Pressures on Congress.* Baltimore: Johns Hopkins Press, 1951.

Westerfield, H. Bradford. *Foreign Policy and Party Politics.* New Haven, Conn.: Yale University Press, 1955.

ARTICLES AND PERIODICALS

Burnham, W. Dean. "The Changing Shape of the American Political Universe," *American Political Science Review*, LIX (1965), 7-28.

Converse, Philip E. "Stability and Change in 1960: A Reinstating Election," *American Political Science Review*, LV (June, 1961), 269-80.

Crane, Wilder. "A Caveat on Roll-Call Studies of Party Voting," *Midwest Journal of Political Science*, IV (August, 1960), 237-49.

Cummings, Milton C., and Robert L. Peabody. "The Decision to Enlarge the Committee on Rules," *New Perspectives on the House of Representatives*. Edited by Robert L. Peabody and Nelson W. Polsby. Chicago: Rand McNally, 1963, pp. 167-94.

Farris, Charles D. "A Scale Analysis of Ideological Factors in Congressional Voting," *Journal of Politics*, XX (May, 1958), 308-38.

Gage, N. L., and Ben Shimberg. "Measuring Senatorial Progressivism," *Journal of Abnormal and Social Psychology*, XLIV (January, 1949), 112-17.

Green, Bert F. "Attitude Measurement," *Handbook of Social Psychology*. Edited by Gardner Lindzey. Reading, Mass.: Addison-Wesley, 1954, I, pp. 335-69.

Guttman, Louis. "A Basis for Scaling Qualitative Data," *American Sociological Review*, IX (April, 1944), 135-50.

Henry, Andrew F. "A Method of Classifying Non-Scale Response Patterns in a Guttman Scale," *Public Opinion Quarterly*, XVI (Spring, 1952), 94-95.

Huntington, Samuel P. "A Revised Theory of American Party Politics," *American Political Science Review*, LXIV (September, 1950), 669-77.

Key, V. O., Jr. "A Theory of Critical Elections," *Journal of Politics*, XVII (February, 1955), 3-18.

MacRae, Duncan, Jr. "The Relation Between Roll Call Votes and Constituencies in the Massachusetts House of Representatives," *American Political Science Review*, XLVI (December, 1952), 1046-1055.

Miller, Warren E., and Donald E. Stokes. "Constituency Influence in Congress," *American Political Science Review* LVII (March, 1963), 45-56.

Phillips, William. "Congress: A Study in Political Realities," *American Federationist*, February, 1961, pp. 12-17.

Price, H. Douglas. "Are Southern Democrats Different?" *Politics and Social Life*. Edited by Nelson W. Polsby, Robert A. Dentler, and Paul A. Smith. Boston: Houghton Mifflin, 1963, pp. 740-56.

Schnitzler, William. "Usurpers of Power—The Conservative Coalition," *American Federationist*, December, 1961, pp. 10–11.

Stokes, Donald E. and Warren E. Miller. "Party Government and the Saliency of Congress," *Public Opinion Quarterly*, XXVI (Winter) 1962.

Stone, Clarence N. "Inter-Party Constituency Differences and Congressional Voting Behavior: A Partial Dissent," *American Political Science Review*, LVII (September, 1963), 665–66.

Stouffer, Samuel A., and others. "A Technique for Improving Cumulative Scales," *Public Opinion Quarterly*, XVI (Summer, 1952), 273–91.

Turner, Julius. "Responsible Parties: A Dissent from the Floor," *American Political Science Review*, XLV (March, 1951), 143–52.

REPORTS

Lowell, A. Lawrence. "The Influence of Party Upon Legislation in England and America" in *Annual Report of the American Historical Association for 1901* (2 vols., Washington, 1902), I, 321–44.

PUBLIC DOCUMENTS

The Congressional District Data Book, Districts of the 87th Congress. Washington, D.C.: Government Printing Office, 1961.

Congressional District Data Book, Districts of the 88th Congress. Washington, D.C.: Government Printing Office, 1963.

U.S. Bureau of the Census. *U.S. Censuses of Population and Housing: 1960.* Census Tracts.

U.S. *Congressional Record.* Vol. CVI.

UNPUBLISHED MATERIAL

Belknap, George M. "A Study of Senatorial Voting by Scale Analysis." Unpublished Ph.D. dissertation, University of Chicago, 1951.

OTHER SOURCES

Congressional Quarterly Almanac, XV (1959).

Congressional Quarterly Almanac, XVI (1960).

Congressional Quarterly Almanac, XVII (1961).

Congressional Quarterly Almanac, XVIII (1962).

Congressional Quarterly Weekly Report, XVIX (1961).

Congressional Quarterly Weekly Report, XX (1962).

INDEX

Administration support index, 48

AFL–CIO Committee on Political Education: its voting classification scheme, 23–24, 24n

Agar, Herbert, 7n

Aid to education bills: and the conservative coalition, 85–86; and northern Democrats, 85–86; defined, 192

Alexander, Thomas B., 54n

American Federationist, 96, 96n

Area redevelopment bills: and conservative coalition, 84–85; and northern Democrats, 84–85; defined, 191–92

Bauer, Raymond A., 182n, 183n, 184n

Belknap, George M., 26, 26n, 185n

Beyle, Herman C., 30–34 passim, 48

Blue collar labor: see Constituency Characteristics

Burnham, W. Dean, 34n, 175, 175n

Burns, James MacGregor, 7n, 174–75

Celler, Emmanuel, 97

Chi square test of significance: utility of, 13–14, 55–56

Civil liberties bills: and party agreement, 78; defined, 92, 194; and northern Democrats, 93; and conservative coalition, 93, 112

Civil rights bills: and party agreement, 77–78; and liberal coalition, 93–94; and southern Democrats, 93–94; defined, 194

Cluster-bloc analysis: explanation of, 31–32

Congress:
—Eighty-seventh (1961-62) : characteristics of, xvi, 64–65
—Eighty-sixth, (1959-60) : characteristics of, xvi, 63–64
—in nineteenth century: party voting in, 3–6

Congressional Quarterly scores: defined, 52

Conservative coalition: and aid to education bills, 85–86; and area redevelopment bills, 84–85; and civil liberties bills, 93, 112; and domestic economic issues, 111–12; and foreign policy bills, 112; and labor reform issues, 83; and minimum wage and "responsible party" controversy, 96–98, 174–75; criticized by liberals, 96–98; its increased potency over time, 106–107; voting frequency of, 103–107. See also Southern Democrats; Sectionalism; Republicans

Constituency characteristics:
—and intraparty voting differences: characteristics employed, 133; failings of the approach, 133; among northern Democrats, 133–40; summary of findings, 138, 146, 151; by issue, 138–40, 144–46, 148–51; among Republicans, 140–46; among Democrats, 146–51; conclusions, 151–56, 177–79
—and party: assessment of the approach, 116; constituency characteristics employed, 117, 117n; in South,

199

117; summary of findings, 126, 128–31, 176–77
—blue collar labor percentage in constituency: and party, 124–25; and loyalty among Democrats, 135–36; and electoral margins and voting behavior, 164–66
—family income (median) in constituency: and party, 125–29; and loyalty among Democrats, 136–38; and loyalty among Republicans, 141–44
—foreign-native composition of constituency: and within party voting differences, 19–21
—nonwhite percentage in constituency: and party, 121–24; and loyalty among southern Democrats, 148
—owner-occupied housing percentage in constituency: and party, 119–21
—social-class composition of constituency: and intraparty voting differences, 28
—urbanism in constituency: and intraparty voting differences, 19, 21, 27–28; and party, 117–19; and loyalty among Democrats, 133–35; and loyalty among Republicans, 140–41; and loyalty among southern Democrats, 146–47
Constituency voting: in nineteenth century Congresses, 5–6; characteristics employed, 17–18, 35; measuring the significance of, 18–19; and party voting, 22, 35; and electoral margins, 28–29; amount of, 56–61
Converse, Philip E., 43n
Cook, Stuart W., 13n
Crane, Wilder, xvin
Cummings, Milton C., 65n
Cumulative (Guttmann) scaling: utility explained, 23–26; and liberal-conservative rankings, 81–82; early uses, 185; procedure involved, 186–89; applications here, 190–94
Curtis, Thomas B., 114

Dahl, Robert A., 51, 51n, 80
Democrats: and public welfare bills, 89; and trade expansion bills, 92.
—northern Democrats: extent of internal cohesion, 66–67; and labor reform bills, 83; and area redevelopment bills, 83–85; and aid to education bills, 85–86; and minimum wage bills,

86–87; and housing bills, 88–89; and foreign aid bills, 90–92; and civil liberties bills, 93; loyalty to party majorities, 107–11; and electoral margins and voting behavior, 159–61
—southern Democrats: need for study of, 63; extent of internal cohesion, 66–67; and domestic economic bills, 74–75; and housing bills, 88–89; and foreign aid bills, 90–92; and civil rights bills, 93–94; voting likeness to Republicans, 99–101; voting opposition to Republicans, 102–03; loyalty to party majorities, 107–11; causes of alienation from party, 112–14; and "responsible parties" controversy. See also Conservative coalition; Sectionalism
Dentler, Robert A., 183n, 185n
Deutsch, Morton, 13n
Dexter, Lewis A., 182n, 183n, 184n
Domestic economic issues: and party voting, 72–74; stability of party divisions on, 79; and conservative coalition, 111–12

Eighty-seventh Congress. See Congress
Eighty-sixth Congress. See Congress
Electoral margins and congressman's policy stances, 58–59, 60; and voting behavior: in earlier research, 28–29, 59–60, 157–58; measurement of, 159; for northern Democrats, 159–61; for Republicans, 161–63; and constituency characteristics, 163–66; and liberalism-conservatism, 166–69; conclusions, 169–70, 179–80
Electoral realignments: and party voting, 43, 181; and "responsible parties" controversy, 175–76

Fair Deal bills, 26–29
Family income (median). See Constituency characteristics
Farris, Charles D., 81, 81n, 185n, 189, 189n
Federal aid to education bills. See Aid to education bills
Foreign affairs bills: and party voting, 49–52; and party agreement, 77; and conservative coalition, 112. See also Foreign aid bills; Trade expansion bills

Foreign aid bills: and Republicans, 89–92; and northern Democrats, 90–92; and southern Democrats, 190–92; defined, 193–94

Foreign-native composition of constituency. *See* Constituency characteristics

Froman, Lewis A., 52, 52n, 57–58, 80, 132, 152–58 *passim*, 169, 170, 177

Gage, N. L., 26, 26n, 185n

Grassmuck, George, 51, 51n

Green, Bert F., 186n

Griffith, Ernest S., 7n

Guttmann, Louis A., 185–88

Henry, Andrew F., 191n

House of Commons: party voting in, 3–6

Housing: owner-occupied, percentages of. *See* Constituency characteristics

—bills: and Republicans, 88–89; and southern Democrats, 88–89; and northern Democrats, 88–89; defined, 192–93

Huntington, Samuel P., 58–59, 157, 158, 158n, 166–70, 180

Index of cohesion: defined, 11, 41; discussion of its utility, 66

Index of likeness: defined, 17

Index of party loyalty: defined, 18n

Jahoda, Marie, 13n

Jewell, Malcolm E., 157n

Key, V. O., Jr., xvi, xvin, 23, 34n, 43, 43n, 63, 63n, 65, 95, 95n, 99–106 *passim*, 130, 174

Labor reform bills: and the conservative coalition, 82–83; and northern Democrats, 83; defined, 191

Liberal coalition: and civil rights, 93–94

"Liberalism-conservatism": its limited utility here, 45, 45n; and cumulative (Guttmann) scaling, 81–82; and electoral margins and voting behavior, 166–69

Lindzey, Gardner, 186n

Lowell, A. Lawrence, 3–6, 10, 14, 17, 38–39, 43n, 45, 46, 53, 54, 68, 69, 171, 172

MacRae, Duncan, Jr., 23–30, 47, 56–57, 72, 81, 82, 132, 152–58 *passim*, 185n, 190

Mayhew, David E., 54n

Measurement, techniques of: compared, 12–14, 23–24, 31–32, 172–73; and researcher's bias, 15–16, 171–73

Miller, Warren E., 58, 58n, 157, 157n, 158, 182, 182n, 183n

Minimum wage bills: and conservative coalition, 86–87; and northern Democrats, 86–87; defined, 192

Modified party vote: defined, 71; and "responsible parties" controversy, 71–72, 80; and policy dimensions of party voting, 72

New Republic: its voting classification scheme, 23–34, 24n

Nineteenth century congresses. *See* Congress

Nonwhite, percentages of. *See* Constituency characteristics

Northern Democrats. *See* Democrats

Owner-occupied housing. *See* Constituency characteristics

Party agreement: and policy dimensions of party voting, 72, 77–78

Party cohesion: extent of, 66–68; and party opposition, 70–72

Party opposition voting: extent of, 68–72; and party cohesion, 70–72; and policy dimensions of party voting, 72, 75–77; defined 158–59

Party voting: in nineteenth century congresses, 3–6; and "responsible parties" controversy, 7; in early twentieth century congresses, 10–11; cross-national comparisons, 10–11; extent of, 12, 38–45, 172; measurement of, 12–16; policy dimensions of, 17–18, 27, 43–54, 72–75; and constituency voting, 22; and electoral realignments, 43, 181; and control of White House, 49

Patterson, Samuel C., 157n

Peabody, Robert L., 65n

Phi coefficient: defined, 58n

Phillips, William, 96, 96n

Polsby, Nelson W., 183n, 185n

Pool, Ithiel de Sola, 182n, 183n, 184n

Pressure, concept of: defined, 8

Price, H. Douglas, 185n, 186n

Public housing bills. *See* Housing bills

Public welfare bills. *See* Welfare bills

Ranney, Austin, 7n
Republicans: and housing bills, 88–89; and welfare bills, 89; and foreign aid bills, 90–92; and trade expansion bills, 92; voting likeness to southern Democrats, 99–101; voting opposition to southern Democrats, 102–103; and electoral margins and voting behavior, 161–63. *See also* Conservative coalition; Sectionalism
Research methods of author: by roll call vote, 63, 63n; by aggregate census data, 116, 133, 181–82; alternatives, 182–84
"Responsible parties" controversy: and techniques of measurement, 7, 14, 55, 71–72, 80, 171–72; and party voting, 10; and particular issues, 173–74; and the conservative coalition, 96–98, 174–75; and southern Democrats, 174–75; and electoral realignments, 175–76; and the historical factor, 180–81
Rice, Stuart A., 6, 11, 17, 18, 30–34 *passim*, 48
Rossiter, Clinton, 7n, 49–50, 54, 80

Scammon, Richard, 159n
Schattschneider, E. E., 7n
Schnitzler, William, 96, 96n
Sectionalism: and intraparty voting differences, 20–22, 29, 33, 178–79; defined, 29, 133n; decline of in American politics, 34; among Republicans, 144–46. *See also* Democrats: southern

Selltiz, Claire, 13n
Shimberg, Ben, 26, 26n, 185n
Silbey, Joel H., 54n
Sindler, Allan P., 114n
Smith, Frank E., 113, 113n
Smith, Paul A., 183n, 185n
Social classes: composition of, *See* Constituency characteristics
Southern Democrats: *See* Democrats; Conservative coalition; Sectionalism
Stokes, Donald, 58, 58n, 157, 157n, 158, 182, 182n, 183n
Stone, Clarence N., 156, 156n
Stouffer, Samuel A., 131n, 185–91 *passim*

Thompson, Frank, 97–98
Trade expansion bills: and Democrats, 92; and Republicans, 92; defined, 194
Truman, David B., xv, 30–36, 48, 57, 57n, 80, 132, 152, 155, 155n
Turner, Julius, 6–25, 38, 40–41, 46–47, 53, 55, 56, 56n, 65–69 *passim*, 79, 80, 106–108, 115, 132, 152–55, 172, 176, 177

Urbanism. *See* Constituency characteristics

Walfare bills: and Democrats, 88–89; and Republicans, 89; defined, 193
Westerfield, H. Bradford, 51–52
Wilson, Woodrow, 5

Young, James S., 54n

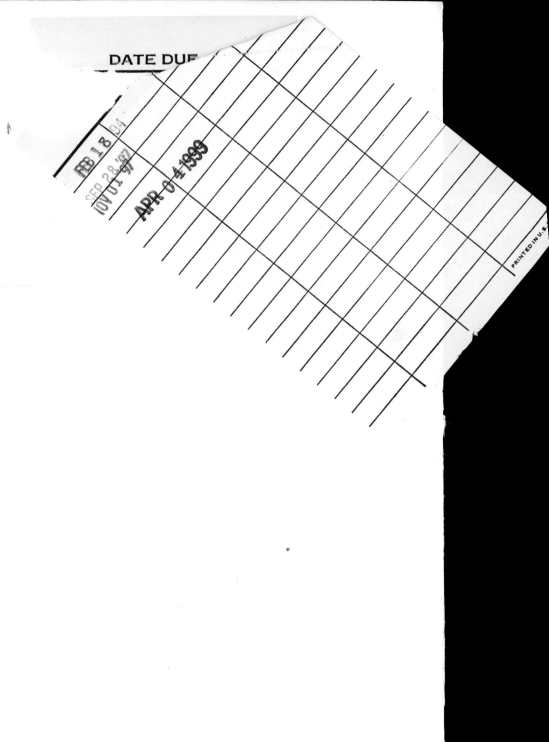